VERSION 6.1
MW01618369
Cram
for the
Exam
our Guide to Passing the
lew York Real Estate
alesperson and Broker Exams
larcia Darvin Spada

Cram for the Exam
Your Guide to Passing the New York Real Estate Salesperson and Broker Exams
Marcia Darvin Spada

Executive Editor: Sara Glassmeyer

Project Manager: Elizabeth King, KnowledgeWorks Global Ltd.

Product Specialist: Deborah Miller

Manager, Creative Services: Brian Brogaard

Cover Image: UberImages/iStock/Getty Images

For product information and technology assistance, contact us at
Mbition Customer Support, 800-532-7649

For permission to use material from this text or product, please contact **publishingsupport@mbitiontolearn.com.**

Library of Congress Control Number: 2018945941
ISBN-13: 978-1-62980-221-3
ISBN-10: 1-62980-221-2

Mbition, LLC
18500 W Corporate Drive, Suite 250
Brookfield, WI 53045
USA

Visit us at **www.mbitiontolearn.com**

Printed in the United States of America
1 2 3 4 5 6 22 21 20 19 18

Contents

Preface

Congratulations on your decision to invest extra effort to prepare for your qualifying courses and state exams. This guide will help you face the exams with greater confidence, which should enhance your test performance.

Cram for the Exam is exactly what it says—a quick way to prepare. Why spend more time than needed? Here you have a directed review in an easy-to-study format. With *Cram for the Exam*, allowing for your individual needs, you can spend about ten hours accomplishing a comprehensive review.

Before you begin your review, take a few minutes to read the first section, *Your Questions Answered.* It gives you details concerning test preparation, time, place, and question types. Also, review the *Quick Tips to Help You Pass* and read the instructions on *How to Cram for the Exam* for optimal results.

About the Author

Marcia Darvin Spada was the owner of the Albany Center for Real Estate Education, a New York–licensed proprietary school.

A professional educator and nationally known real estate author, Marcia teaches real estate and has developed content for numerous real estate courses. Her textbooks and courses are widely used by colleges, real estate–related organizations, and proprietary schools throughout the country. In addition to *Cram for the Exam: Your Guide to Passing the New York Real Estate Salesperson and Broker Exams*, she is the author of:

- New York Real Estate for Salespersons
- New York Real Estate for Brokers
- New Jersey Real Estate for Salespersons and Brokers
- Real Estate National Licensing Exam Prep: The Smart Guide to Passing
- Cram for the Exam! Your Guide to Passing the New Jersey Real Estate Salespersons and Brokers Exam
- The Home Inspection Book: A Guide for Professionals
- Environmental Issues and the Real Estate Professional

Marcia holds a BA and an MA in English from the University at Albany and a BS in Real Estate Studies from Empire State College and is a member of the Author's Guild. Her website, marciadarvinspada.com, includes links for her textbooks, Mbition LLC courses, and other information. Marcia welcomes all comments and questions about the content in this exam guide. Contact her at msdarvin7@gmail.com or call/text to the phone number listed on her website: marciadarvinspada.com.

Acknowledgments

Sincere appreciation goes to my husband, Eugene R. Spada, Esq., for his ongoing help and support of my writing efforts for this and other textbooks throughout the years.

A very deep note of gratitude to Sara Glassmeyer, Executive Editor, Real Estate, of Mbition LLC, whose encouragement, guidance, and expertise has been invaluable in completing all of the New York textbooks and others over many years. Thank you always, Sara, for your belief in me and showing me the way. I also thank Erin Shepard, Senior Director of Sales, Real Estate, and Ivey Turner, Regional Sales Manager, Real Estate.

I am also very thankful for the expertise, hard work, and support of Elizabeth King, Project Manager, Books, KnowledgeWorks Global Ltd; copyeditor Sheila Zwiebel; and the entire production team at KGL for their excellent work with the revision including the new look and clarity of this edition 6.1.

The Cram that Will Help You Pass!

Everything you need to succeed on your NYS real estate licensure exam for salesperson or broker is in this *Cram* review

- ✓ Your Questions Answered, which contains important information you need to know about licensing requirements and taking your exam.
- ✓ Quick Tips to help you succeed on exam day.
- ✓ Comprehensive review of all key terms and important points for each subject. Note that this *Cram* covers the new content of Licensee Safety, added to the salesperson course in March 2017, as well as the new broker curriculum revised in 2018.
  - Links to websites that contain more information or forms for study or use.
  - Quick View tables that summarize important information for each topic in the NYS curriculum.
- ✓ *Marcia's List,* which summarizes the most important key terms or concepts that you must know.
- ✓ A total of 730 questions, including 380 review questions and two salesperson and two broker practice exams with explanations and references to both *New York Real Estate for Salespersons, 6th edition* Revised and *New York Real Estate for Brokers, 6th edition.*

Your Questions Answered

1. How do I obtain a salesperson license in New York?

Essentially, you need to complete three steps in addition to being at least 18 years old:

- ✓ Complete a New York State (NYS)-approved 75-hour qualifying course including the course exam
- ✓ Pass the NYS licensure exam
- ✓ Obtain broker sponsorship

2. How can I obtain a real estate broker license in New York?

In addition to being at least 20 years of age, one must:

- ✓ Complete 120 hours of NYS-approved qualifying course education or its equivalent
- ✓ Meet NYS-mandated experience requirements, which include the following:
  - Two years of active experience as a NYS-licensed salesperson under the supervision of a NYS-licensed broker, or
  - Three or more years of equivalent experience in the general real estate business, or
  - Proof that an equivalent license was issued by a state with which New York has a reciprocal agreement

3. What exams must I pass to obtain salesperson or broker licensure in New York?

All applicants for New York licensure must pass a final exam *in person* whether the course was taken in the classroom or online at the completion of the qualifying course. Applicants must also pass an exam given by the NYS Department of State (NYSDOS), the New York regulatory agency that oversees the licensure process.

4. When and where are these exams given?

The qualifying courses may be completed either in a classroom setting or online. For the classroom format, the final qualifying course classroom exams are scheduled at course completion by the entity offering the course. The NYS exams are given at DOS test centers throughout New York. See the Useful Links below that lists the DOS website for exam sites.

Note that if you take your course online for salesperson or broker licensure, you must still take your final course exam in person at the entity where you signed up for the course. Sometimes arrangements may be made by your course provider to allow you to take your exam at another state-approved school or other approved and proctored location.

5. Must I take the state exam at the test site closest to where I live?

You may take your state exam at any test center in New York State. Arrive at least 15 minutes before the starting time.

6. Do I need to schedule an appointment to take the NYS licensure exam?

Applicants are required to schedule their real estate salesperson exam on the DOS secure password-protected Occupational Licensing Management System, *eAccessNY*. In addition to applying for the exam on *eAccessNY*, applicants can view their scheduled exam details or exam results and, in most cases, apply for their salesperson license online.

The initial broker license, however, must be applied for by sending the application and other application documents and payment to the NYSDOS. The mailing address for the NYSDOS is:

NYS Department of State
Division of Licensing Services
P.O. Box 22001
Albany, NY 12201-2001

If you use mailing services such as UPS, FedEx, or DHL, you must use the DOS physical address:

NYS Department of State
Division of Licensing Services
1 Commerce Plaza
99 Washington Avenue, 6th Floor
Albany, NY 12231

The *eAccessNY* system requires that applicants create a personal ID and password when they register online. Registration should take place on or about the time an applicant enrolls for a qualifying course, needs to take the licensure exam, and/or plans to apply for a real estate license. Persons with disabilities who require accessibility information for the exam should call 518-473-2731. Applicants who require testing modifications should not schedule an exam but should instead call that phone number as well.

Useful Links

NYS Salesperson Real Estate Exam Procedures

dos.ny.gov/licensing/realestate/re_salesexams.html

NYS Salesperson and Broker Real Estate Licensing Exam Sites

dos.ny.gov/licensing/realestate/re_examsites.html

NYS Broker Real Estate Exam Procedures

dos.ny.gov/licensing/re_broker/re_broker_exams.html

eAccessNY

dos.ny.gov/licensing/eaccessny.html

7. When do I receive my exam results?

Exam results are reported as passed or failed; applicants will not receive a numerical score. Results are not given over the phone. Exam results are available online through your account in *eAccessNY*. The exam results are available as soon as possible after the NYSDOS Exam Unit receives the exams and scores them.

8. Should I first complete my salesperson or broker-qualifying course before taking the NYS exam?

You can take the NYS exam at any time during the licensure process. Since the qualifying courses prepare you for the questions on the NYS exam, it is to your advantage, in most cases, that you first complete the course.

9. For the salesperson license, do I require broker sponsorship to take the NYS exam?

No. You may take the NYS exam and the 75-hour qualifying course without having a broker sponsor. However, before taking the course or during the course, it would benefit you to seek a broker who would be your sponsor. This broker will sign and attest to sponsorship on your online licensure application.

10. For the broker license, if I have equivalent real estate experience and plan to obtain a broker license, do I need to take the salesperson exam?

No. If you have prior real estate experience, you may choose to obtain broker licensure without first becoming a salesperson. You are still required to complete 120 hours of qualifying education; that is, the 75-hour salesperson course and the 45-hour broker qualifying course. If you have taken the old 45-hour salesperson-qualifying course (before July 2008) and not the current 75-hour salesperson-qualifying course, you will need to make up 30 hours. In this case, to obtain a broker license, you will need to complete a 30-hour remedial course given both online and in the classroom in addition to the 45-hour broker-qualifying course. This rule applies to all applicants for the broker license.

Although you must pass the final exam given with your qualifying (and/or remedial) courses, you need only take and pass the broker NYS licensing broker exam if you do not plan to obtain a salesperson license. There is no "remedial course" NYS exam. The same rules apply, however, for taking the final classroom remedial course exam in person as for the other qualifying courses (see Question 4). In addition to the required courses and passage of the exams, you must also demonstrate three years' equivalent real estate experience.

11. How often can I take the salesperson or broker exams?

Depending on the policy of the entity conducting the qualifying courses, you can generally take one makeup exam if you do not pass the first time. Inquire about this policy when you begin the course. You may take the NYS exam as often as you want until you pass. If you pass the exam, salesperson applicants, in most cases, should apply for licensure online utilizing their accounts in *eAccessNY*. Broker applicants cannot apply for their initial license online but must send it in to the DOS. Those who do not pass the exam can schedule another exam by utilizing their accounts in *eAccessNY*.

12. If I do not want to be licensed immediately, how long is my passing grade valid for the salesperson or broker exams?

Passed exam results for both exams are valid for two years.

13. Is there a fee for the NYS exam?

The fee is $15 for each time you take the exam. You must schedule a new online appointment to retake the exam.

14. What should I bring to the state exam?

1. Bring two #2 pencils. Calculators are permitted if they are battery- or solar-powered, silent, nonprinting, and do not contain an alphabetic keyboard. PDAs are not allowed. You should bring a government-issued, signed photo ID. Identification must be current and from the following list:

- ✓ Driver's license
- ✓ IDNYC Card (NYC Identification Card)
- ✓ State-issued identification (for example, non-driver ID)
- ✓ Military ID
- ✓ U.S. passport
- ✓ USCIS-issued ID (U.S. Citizenship and Immigration Services)
- ✓ Certificate of U.S. citizenship
- ✓ Foreign passport
- ✓ Brazilian, Mexican, and Ecuadorian Consular ID

2. You should also bring the page you were requested to print when you scheduled your exam on *eAccessNY.* This page is called the "Summary of Your Submission" and includes your examination information, including your candidate number.

15. What question types are on the NYS exam?

All questions on the NYS exam are multiple-choice.

16. How many questions are there for each subject on the exams and what is the passing grade?

The numbers of questions on the classroom and NYS exams are weighted according to the number of hours allotted for each subject in the course. For example, for the salesperson exam, the subject *Law of Agency* requires 11 classroom hours, so that topic will contain more exam questions than the subject *Mortgage Brokerage* that requires only one classroom hour. The same weightage for classroom hours applies to the broker exam.

The final salesperson classroom or online qualifying course exam consists of 75 or 100 questions. The NYS salesperson state exam has 75 questions. Each question on the NYS exam is worth 1.33 points. The passing grade is 70%. The DOS "rounds down" the grade, which means that you need a minimum of 52 correct questions to pass (which also means that 23 wrong would give you a passing grade). You are given 1.5 hours to complete the classroom or state exam.

The final broker classroom or online qualifying course exam and the NYS exam consists of 100 questions, each worth one point. Note that the broker classroom exam has about four or five questions on local concerns, a topic chosen by the entity that offers your course. These local concerns questions are not on the NYS exam. The passing grade for the broker exam is 70%, so you can miss up to 30 questions and still pass. You are given 2.5 hours to complete the broker classroom or state exam.

17. Are all NYS exams the same?

Several different exams are developed from a large question bank. If you repeat the NYS exam, you probably will have a different set of questions.

18. Can I review my NYS licensure exam?

Yes, if you fail an exam, you may request an exam review. An exam review will help to evaluate your performance and the areas that require further study. You must request a review within 60 days of the examination date. You can ask for an *Examination Review Request* form at the exam and give the completed form to the proctor. You can also call DOS to obtain one and then mail it back. You will have up to one hour for the review using your exam and your answer sheet.

19. How should I prepare for the exam?

Completing the 75-hour qualifying course, as well as studying all of the topics covered on your class and state exams, is your primary preparation for the exam. After completing the course, review your textbook and notes. You should be familiar with the key terms, important points, laws, and general theory for each subject. These items are summarized for you in *Cram for the Exam*.

Your completion of *Cram for the Exam* is an excellent final step in exam prep.

Other Preparation Sources

Here are some other resources for exam preparation:

- ***New York Real Estate for Salespersons, 6th edition***, Revised. This textbook completely covers the required New York curriculum for the 75-hour course. If you have not used this textbook in your course, have missed some classroom hours, or want to spend more time studying, you may want to review this textbook. The book provides additional information on the licensure process in the Introductory Chapter and Chapter 1, "License Law and Regulations."
- ***New York Real Estate for Brokers, 6th edition***. This textbook, geared to those who are preparing for New York broker licensure, completely covers the curriculum for the required 45-hour broker course. More information regarding licensure and the duties of a real estate broker are included in the Introduction and Chapter 1 Parts 2 and 3 of this textbook. This edition 6.1 of *Cram* has been revised to cover the new NYS Department of State added content for the salesperson topic of Licensee Safety added March 2017 and the new broker curriculum added in 2018.
- ***30-Hour Remedial Course Supplement***. This companion text for the salesperson or broker course is for students who have completed the old salesperson 45-hour course (completed before July 1, 2008) and need to complete the entire 75 hours for the salesperson course or the 120 hours for the broker course.
- **Author website: marciadarvinspada.com**. Marcia's website contains other textbooks for sale, author contact information, and important information and updates for students and instructors.

Mbition LLC

18500 W Corporate Drive, Suite 250

Brookfield, WI 53045, USA

Phone: 855-733-7239

Fax: 770-424-3150

E-Mail: publishingsales@mbitiontolearn.com

Retail website to purchase textbooks: http://www.mbitiontolearn.com/

Quick Tips to Help You Pass

Before the Exam

- ✓ Try to get a good night's sleep.
- ✓ Know the exact location of the test, and arrive about a half hour before the test begins.
- ✓ Take the necessary ID, Record of Your Submission, pencils, and calculator.
- ✓ Because fear can be contagious, avoid pre-exam socializing and stay calm.
- ✓ If possible, sit toward the front of the examination room, where there are fewer distractions.
- ✓ Listen to all instructions.
- ✓ If physically challenged, you may call the NYSDOS and make arrangements for assistance.

During the Exam

Selecting an answer

- ✓ Answer every question as you go along. If you do not know an answer, take a guess or mark down the question number on scratch paper to return to it later. (DOS exam proctors collect all scratch paper after the exam.)
- ✓ Read the questions *slowly* and *cautiously.* The question may ask for a negative answer rather than a positive one. Do not read into the question; read it as it actually reads. Do not look for deeper hidden meanings. If you have studied, the first answer that occurs to you is generally the correct one.
- ✓ Read every answer before deciding on your choice.
- ✓ Note that questions usually contain two distracters (incorrect choices) that are obviously wrong. Spot them and you have a 50% chance of selecting the correct answer. There may be a third distracter that is not as obviously wrong as the others are, so if you eliminate all three, all that is left is the correct answer! Sometimes you can find the correct answer through this elimination process without actually knowing the correct answer.
- ✓ Do not always apply the maxim "I cannot change my first answer." You may have initially misread the question. One word you may not have noticed previously can change the meaning of the question upon rereading it.
- ✓ Watch out for "must" and "always." If an answer has any exceptions, these words generally indicate a wrong answer.

Timing yourself

- ✓ Because every question counts the same, do not spend a lot of time on one unknown answer if it means running out of time. Finish the exam; go back to the questions you either guessed at or could not answer.

- ✓ Use your allotted time. You have 1.5 hours to answer 75 multiple-choice questions for the salesperson exam. You have 2.5 hours to answer 100 questions for the broker exam. You might want to leave when you have finished, but use this time to go back to the answers you are unsure of. By rereading a question, you might see it in a different light. *Most people do better on any exam if they just take their time.*
- ✓ Before handing in your exam, review all of your answers. If you spot just one wrong answer, remedying it could make the difference between passing and failing.
- ✓ If you are unsure of an answer, go with your first impression.

Marking your answer sheet

- ✓ The DOS is using the "bubble sheet," which is filled in with a No. 2 pencil, so be sure that your answer sheet is lined up correctly with each of the questions.
- ✓ If you erase, then erase completely. The computerized test reader could pick up a faint mark.
- ✓ When marking the answers for which you are certain (and will not return to later), firmly press down with the pencil on the answer sheet so that the test reader picks up the answer.

How to Cram for the Exam

1. First, review your textbook and any notes you have from your qualifying courses. Focus on areas where you had some difficulty. Then begin this *Cram.*

2. Next, use the "Subject Review" section in this book to review the key terms and key points for the qualifying course subjects. Note that the title of the topic is indicated in the heading for the salesperson course and the broker course. Although the topic headings are different for the salesperson and broker courses, the subject matter is somewhat similar; however, some key terms and key points appear in the broker course only. The practice exams in this *Cram* will give you a good idea of the subject matter that appears in each of the courses. *Remember that broker candidates are expected to know all content from the salesperson course for the broker exam. Also, salesperson and broker candidates who completed the old 45-hour salesperson course (before the new 75-hour course was instituted in July 2008) are required to take the remedial course, which contains 30 hours of the current salesperson course.* The only topics that salesperson applicants do not need to know from this review are "General Business Law" and "Achieving Agreements through Transaction Analysis," both of which appear in the broker course and exam only. Broker applicants must study the entire review.

   The "Key Terms" section includes important words and phrases that you should know. Knowing the meaning of these key terms is essential, as you will see them repeatedly in exam questions.

3. If you have questions regarding key terms or key points, refer to your textbook.

   This *Cram* is best suited for use with *New York Real Estate for Salespersons, 6th Edition* Revised by Marcia Darvin Spada or *New York Real Estate for Brokers, 6th Edition* by Marcia Darvin Spada and Linda J. Fields. These textbooks cover all content required for the NYS exams in an easy-to-understand format. See "Other Preparation Sources" earlier in this book for information on how to obtain a copy of either textbook. Note that the broker curriculum was revised in 2018. Be sure you are taking the revised 45-hour broker course and using any course content from this newer curriculum. You can view the salesperson and broker courses curriculums on the NYSDOS website.

4. Now you are ready to begin your self-test review. "Questions for Your Review" contains questions for each subject in the qualifying courses. When answering the review questions, pay attention to all choices. Even the wrong choices may be terms that will be on the NYS exam. If you do not know their meaning, look them up in the "Subject Review" or your textbook. Do not time yourself for this review, but complete it under exam conditions.

5. Use the Answer Key in the back of the book to grade your work. Then review the subject areas that are problematic. The Answer Key provides a rationale for each question. Remember that sporadic wrong answers do not reflect weakness. You are doing quite well if you miss no more than 35 of the 380 questions in the review.

6. After you complete the review, complete the Sample Practice Exams. There are two for the salesperson and two for the broker. Broker applicants should complete the salesperson practice exams as well.

These practice tests are similar in content and weightage of questions to the NYS exams. The exams are based on information that you should know according to the NYS curriculum. Take the Practice Exams under exam conditions with no interruptions. Allot yourself a maximum of 1.5 hours for the salesperson practice exams and 2.5 hours for the broker practice exams, as for the NYS exam. The Answer Key provides the correct answers and rationale for the answer. Further explanations can be found in *New York Real Estate for Salespersons,6th Edition* Revised or *New York Real Estate for Brokers, 6th Edition*. If you do not pass these practice exams, further study is needed. The exams are divided into topics so that you can easily see the problem areas. These sample exams are very good predictors of your performance on the NYS exams, so you should not attempt the NYS exam until you are comfortable with the content in this review.

A Word of Encouragement

The best guarantee for success on any exam is preparation. Your willingness to spend time working with *Cram for the Exam* will help you realize your goal. However, some people, no matter how well prepared, may not succeed on the first try. Many factors may come into play—how well you feel on that particular day, your anxiety level, and sometimes plain luck. Take care of the details that you can control. Try to relax. Most importantly, do not give up! If you do not pass on the first attempt, you can take the exam as many times as needed, and you have many resources to help you succeed.

Disclaimer

The situations in the questions are fictional and the names of people and businesses are not related to real people or businesses. Although the *Cram* offers comprehensive exam prep, use of the *Cram* does not guarantee success on your exams.

Subject Review

Review the key terms and key points for each subject before completing the review questions and sample exams. Instead of memorizing, strive for understanding. For those preparing for the NYS broker licensing exam, they must understand and be able to apply all of the subject matter and principles included in the 75-hour salesperson qualifying course as well as the broker 45-hour course. So, broker applicants should review all content in this review even though it is not all specifically in the broker curriculum. Additional content is fully explained in the textbook *New York Real Estate for Salespersons, 6th Edition* Revised or *New York Real Estate for Brokers, 6th Edition*. The topic name in the salesperson curriculum appears first in the heading. The topic name for the broker curriculum, if different, appears after the slash in the heading. There are two topics in the broker course that are not in the salesperson course, "General Business Law" and "Achieving Agreements through Transaction Analysis."

License Law and Regulations/Operating a Real Estate Office

Key Terms

Agricultural District Disclosure For the protection and preservation of architectural districts in New York, the agricultural districts law imposes certain limitations including eminent domain and restrictions on public acquisitions and construction; brokers must disclose if a property lies in an agricultural district

Apartment information vendor An individual who, for a fee, furnishes information about the location of residential real property, including apartments, that are available to be rented, shared, or sublet

Apartment sharing agent An individual who, for a fee, arranges and coordinates meetings between the current owners or occupants of real property, including apartments, who wish to share their housing with others

Article 12-A of the Real Property Law Contains most of the law pertaining to salespersons and brokers

Article 78 proceeding The method for judicial review of determinations by regulatory agencies such as DOS

Associate real estate broker A licensed real estate broker who may perform the acts performed by a broker but by choice wants to work under the name and supervision of a licensed broker

Bedbug Disclosure Act (2010) NYC landlords must inform prospective tenants about bedbug infestation within the past year, or a problem in the building within that time

Blind ads Ads placed by a broker that do not indicate that the advertiser is a broker and do not give the broker's name and telephone number

Broker Point System A method through which the NYS Department of State assigns a value or number of points to a broker applicant's real estate experience

Broker price opinion (BPO) Used by lenders and mortgage companies to value properties when they believe that the delay and price of an appraisal is not necessary

Commingling The mixing of others' funds, such as deposit money, with a broker's business or personal funds; brokers are prohibited from commingling funds

eAccessNY The NYSDOS Occupational Licensing Management System that processes salesperson and broker licensure and other real estate licensure functions

Escrow account An account in an insured bank for the purpose of holding deposit money

Felony Any serious crime above a misdemeanor and generally punishable by imprisonment

Kickback An improper payment by a broker or salesperson to someone who is not licensed or is not exempt from the license law; additionally, salespersons may not share a commission with other licensees

Misdemeanor A crime punishable by a fine of not more than $1,000 and/or imprisonment for not more than one year

Multiple Listing Service A system that pools the listings of all member companies

New York State Department of State (NYSDOS), Division of Licensing Services Governs the real estate licensure process and approves all real estate licenses

Photo ID card A state-issued identification card that salespersons and brokers must carry in the course of business

Real estate broker Any person, partnership, association, or corporation that, for another and for compensation of any kind, negotiates any form of real estate transaction; also supervises and accepts responsibility for the activities of sponsored associate brokers and salespersons

Real estate salesperson One who performs any of the acts allowable under law by a real estate broker for compensation of any kind but does so in association with and under the supervision of a licensed broker

Reciprocity An arrangement in which nonresident salespersons and brokers licensed in another state must take the New York exam and maintain an office in New York, unless their home state does not require New York licensees to have an office in their state or pass their exam to practice real estate there

Revocation Permanent removal of a license by NYS

Sponsor A broker that holds the license for the salesperson

Suspension Temporary lifting of a license by NYS for a designated time

Team Two or more people, one of whom must be an associate broker or salesperson, associated with the same brokerage firm, that operate as a group

Truth-in-Heating Disclosure A NYS law that requires sellers and landlords of residential property to furnish prospective buyers and tenants with a complete set of heating/cooling bills, or summary of the bills for the life of the structure or the preceding two years

Uniform Irrevocable Consent and Designation Form Gives the New York courts jurisdiction over unlawful actions of an applicant who does business in New York and allows summonses and other legal documents to be served on the NYS Secretary of State in place of personal service on the applicant

Unlicensed assistant Employees that may legally perform real estate office duties not requiring a real estate license

Key Points

1. License laws are an exercise of the police power of New York. Much of license law pertaining to salespersons and brokers is contained in Article 12-A of the New York Real Property Law.
2. The purpose of license laws is to protect the public and elevate the standards of the real estate industry.
3. A real estate broker is a person or an organization that, for compensation of any kind, performs or offers to perform aspects of real estate transactions for others.
4. Real estate salespersons perform acts that a broker is authorized to perform, but they do so on behalf of a broker with whom they are associated.
5. Associate real estate brokers must fulfill the same requirements as a broker, but their status in the firm is the same as that of salespersons.
6. Attorneys do not need a license to practice real estate brokerage unless they employ licensees to work under their supervision.
7. The NYS Department of State (NYSDOS), Division of Licensing Services, oversees the licensure process. Most applicants can apply for the salesperson license online through the NYSDOS license management system *eAccessNY.*
8. The DOS has the power to deny, revoke, fine, or suspend a license.
9. The licensure term for real estate salespersons and brokers is two years.
10. New York has reciprocal arrangements with other states for the licensure of nonresident licensees.
11. Real estate salespersons and associate brokers may not be officers of real estate brokerage corporations, hold voting stock in such a corporation, or be a partner in a licensed real estate brokerage partnership.
12. Brokers have a responsibility to comply with change in status and address notices, and termination notifications, which must be completed online with a fee to DOS.

13. Other licenses and registrations related to real estate include mortgage bankers, mortgage brokers, mortgage loan originators, and mortgage loan servicers, as well as apartment information vendors and apartment sharing agents, licensed or certified appraisers, and NYS-licensed home inspectors.

14. Net listings, kickbacks, and commingling of funds are illegal. There are many other violations of license law.

15. The DOS has specific guidelines for real estate advertising by licensees and for the employment and duties of unlicensed real estate assistants.

16. Ads made by real estate salespersons and associate brokers must be approved and supervised by the real estate broker. Ads must include the name of the real estate broker or brokerage and the address or phone number of the real estate broker or brokerage. Real estate brokers must be able to educate their licensees about, and enforce compliance with, the NYSDOS advertising regulations.

17. Violation of the license law may be charged as a misdemeanor and is punishable by a $1,000 fine and/or a maximum sentence of one year in jail. Certain penalties for license law violations may be determined by a DOS administrative hearing and further appeal to the NYS Secretary of State.

18. The revocation or suspension of a broker's real estate license suspends the license of the salespersons and associate brokers in the broker's employ.

19. Licensees must inform sellers that a Property Condition Disclosure Statement is to be provided to the buyer or the buyer's agent before the sellers accept the purchase offer.

20. A seller must disclose to the buyer the existence of any known uncapped natural gas wells on the property. The seller must disclose this information before entering into a contract of sale with the buyer. Other important disclosures that may apply to a particular transaction according to New York law include property condition disclosure, truth-in-heating, and agricultural district disclosure. Federal law mandates lead-based paint disclosure for residential property built before 1978. NYC law requires bedbug disclosure.

21. To effectively operate a real estate brokerage office, brokers should carefully screen the sales agents and other employees that work for the company. This screening may include intensive interviews and certain personality profile testing. Initial and ongoing training is also necessary especially for new licensees.

22. A comprehensive policies and procedures manual should be written and distributed to all agents and other employees of the brokerage firms. Regularly scheduled meetings should be held to discuss policies and procedures and address any issues that require definition or amendment. The broker and/or manager of the office should make himself readily available during the course of business.

23. The real estate office should have available other real estate licensees and professionals to which clients may be referred or with which the broker or agent may consult, as needed. This includes NYS-licensed and certified real estate appraisers, NYS-registered mortgage brokers and licensed mortgage bankers, and NYS-licensed home inspectors.

24. Brokers who own the company or are put in the position of managing the finances should know the principles of financial management and how to budget the operations of the brokerage firm and implement the budget.

Useful Links

NYS Department of State

www.dos.ny.gov

eAccessNY

www.dos.ny.gov/licensing/eaccessny.html

Frequently Asked Questions, eAccessNY

www.dos.ny.gov/licensing/eaccessny_faq.htm

Law of Agency (Includes Independent Contractor and Antitrust)

Key Terms

Advance informed consent to dual agency Buyers or sellers can consent to dual agency in advance of it occurring by indicating consent on the NYS Agency Disclosure Form

Advance informed consent to dual agency with designated agents Buyers or sellers can consent to dual agency in advance of it occurring by indicating the name of the agent or agents who will represent them on the NYS Agency Disclosure Form

Agency disclosure form Mandatory written disclosure of representation form used for the sales or rental of residential one- to four-unit properties and residential condominiums and cooperatives in any size building

Agency When one person, the agent, agrees and is authorized to act on behalf of another person, the principal, an agency relationship is created

Brokerage The business of bringing buyers and sellers together and assisting in negotiations for the terms of sale of real estate

Broker's agent One who is engaged by a broker to work for that broker; in this relationship, the principal is not vicariously liable for the acts of any of the broker's agents; the broker who engaged these agents accepts this liability

Buyer's agent One who represents the buyer of real property by entering into an agreement to work in the best interest of the buyer

Clayton Antitrust Act (1914) Supplements the Sherman Act and has the same general purpose; covers restraints on interstate trade or commerce not covered by the Sherman Act

Client The principal is also known as the agent's client

Cooperating agents Licensees from the same or other offices who participate as agents of buyers or sellers in a real estate transaction

Customer The party whom the agent brings to the principal as a seller, buyer, or tenant of a property

Designated agent A salesperson or an associate broker, supervised by a broker, who is assigned to represent a client when the supervising broker also represents a different client in the same transaction

Disclosure and informed consent Explanation by a real estate agent of his position in the agency relationship and the verbal and written consent of the relationship for which the agency is created

Dual agent/dual agency An agent who attempts to represent both the buyer and the seller in the same transaction; must have the written approval of both parties after the agent's informed disclosure that the buyer and seller each will relinquish the agent's duty of undivided loyalty in the fiduciary relationship

Employee Employment status in which the employer must withhold federal, state, and social security (FICA) taxes and use special reporting forms; employee is supervised by employer

Estoppel An agency relationship created when an individual claims incorrectly that someone is his agent and a third party relies on the incorrect representation

Exclusive agency listing A listing with one broker as the only or exclusive agent; the broker is legally entitled to the commission agreed upon if the exclusive broker or another broker effects sale of the property but not if the owner sells the property without the assistance of any broker

Exclusive right to sell A listing with one exclusive broker under which the broker is entitled to the commission no matter who effects the sale, including the owner

Express agency An agency relationship created by an oral or written agreement between the principal and agent

Fiduciary A position of trust; under a fiduciary relationship, the principal is owed faith, trust, and confidentiality by his agent

Fiduciary duties Responsibilities including reasonable care, skill and diligence obedience, accountability, loyalty, and disclosure of information

First substantive meeting The first contact or meeting when some detail and information about the property is shared with parties who express some interest in the real estate transaction

General agent Someone authorized to handle all affairs of the principal concerning a specified matter or property, usually with some limited power to enter contracts

Group boycott A conspiracy in which a person or group is persuaded or coerced into not doing business with another person or group

Implied agency Creating an agency by words or actions of the principal and agent that indicate that they have an agency agreement

Independent contractor A work situation in which the employer does not have the right to control the details of a worker's performance; Form 1099-MISC is filed with the IRS indicating the worker's annual income

Market allocation agreement A conspiracy between competitors dividing or assigning a certain area or territory for sales

Net listing A listing contract that allows the broker to keep as a commission any money obtained from the sale above a sale price specified by the seller

Open listing agreement A listing with one or more brokers; any broker effecting the sale is entitled to the commission unless the owner sells the property

Price fixing A conspiracy by competitors in a group or industry to charge the same or similar price for services rendered

Principal The person who selects the agent to act on his behalf

Ratification The creation of an agency when a person claims to be an agent but has no express agreement and the principal ratifies or accepts the agent's actions

Ready, willing, and able Generally refers to a purchaser who is ready, willing, and able to purchase a property on terms acceptable to the seller

Section 443 of the Real Property Law Requires that licensees present a written disclosure form that details consumer choices as to representation at the first substantive contact with a prospective seller or buyer; applies to the sales and rental of one- to four-unit residential properties and condominiums and cooperatives in any size building

Self-Dealing Occurs when a broker has an undisclosed interest in a property

Seller's agent A listing agent, an agent who cooperates with a listing agent as a seller's subagent, or a broker's agent who represents the owner of real property establishing a principal/client relationship to work in the seller's best interests

Sherman Antitrust Act (1890) Enacted to preserve a system of free economic enterprise and to protect the public against the activities of monopolies, contracts, or other combinations that unreasonably restrain trade

Single agent An agent who works only for the buyer or the seller and who may elect to reject subagency

Special agent An individual with narrow authorization to act on behalf of the principal; an example is a real estate broker who has a real estate listing

Subagents The principal's authorization of an agent to use other people to assist in accomplishing the purpose of the agency; these people are agents of the seller/principal and the broker with whom the property is listed

Tie-in arrangements An illegal agreement between a party selling a product or service with a buyer that, as a condition of the sale, the buyer must buy something else from the seller or must not buy the product or service of another party

Undivided loyalty As part of their fiduciary duties, agents must remain loyal to the principal and work in the best interest of the the principal; the agent may not work for personal gain or for the interest of others adverse to the principal's interest without the principal's informed consent

Undisclosed dual agency A situation in which an agent represents the seller and the buyer in the same transaction but does not disclose his position

Vicarious liability One person is responsible or liable for the actions of the other; according to Section 442-c of the New York Real Property Law, a broker's license may be revoked or suspended for a salesperson's actions if the broker had actual knowledge of such violation or if the broker retains the benefits from the transaction after he knows that the salesperson has engaged in some wrongdoing

Key Points

1. When one person is hired to act on behalf of another, an agency relationship is created. Agency is usually created with an agreement (express agency) between the parties but also can be implied by the parties' conduct. A position of trust, which is a fiduciary relationship, exists between every principal and agent in an agency relationship.
2. Real estate agents are special agents with specific authority.
3. The agent's fiduciary duties and responsibilities include obedience; loyalty; disclosure of information; confidentiality; accountability; and reasonable care, skill, and diligence.
4. A brokerage contract is created when the principal, usually a real estate owner, hires a broker (agent) to perform services relating to the real estate. Every agency relationship is consensual.
5. The principal can authorize the agent to use other people to assist in accomplishing the purpose of the agency. These people are subagents.
6. Neither the nature of the compensation (commission or flat fee), nor the person who pays it, determines the agency relationship.
7. An agent may decide to represent the seller or the buyer in a real estate transaction.
8. A single agent works only for the buyer or seller directly and may elect to reject subagency.
9. A seller's agent represents the owner of real property. The seller's agent and the principal enter into an employment contract that is a listing agreement, establishing a client relationship in the seller's best interest.
10. A buyer agent represents the buyer/purchaser of real property. The buyer agent accepts and enters into an employment agreement establishing a client relationship in the buyer's best interests.

11. A dual agent is an agent who attempts to represent the buyer and the seller in the same transaction. Dual agency occurs in real estate companies when the firm attempts to represent the buyer and the seller in the same transaction.
12. According to New York law, an alternative for handling a dual agency in a brokerage firm is the designated sales associate or agent. With disclosure and informed consent, one sales agent in the firm is designated to represent the buyer. Another agent is designated to represent the seller.
13. Sellers and buyers may provide advance informed consent to dual agency with designated sales agents by indicating consent on the agency disclosure form. Advance consent to dual agency is allowed under an amendment to Section 443 of the NYS Real Property Law.
14. A multiple listing service (MLS) offers cooperation and compensation to participating members. It does not create an automatic subagency.
15. Although there is a fee for services and the possibility of less commission, multiple listing services generally offer a greater exposure for listed property, perhaps rendering a faster sale and a better price.
16. Cooperating agents are seller's agents from another real estate firm acting as subagents of the listing broker and seller. Cooperative agents are also buyer's agents from another real estate firm. These agents work through the usual system of offerings published within an MLS.
17. In the sale or rental of one- to four-unit residential properties and residential condominiums and cooperatives in any size building in New York, a dual agent must have the written approval of both parties after the agent's informed disclosure. The buyer and the seller each agree to relinquish the individual, undivided loyalty in the fiduciary relationship.
18. An undisclosed dual agency can result in a violation of the New York Real Property Law.
19. New York real estate firms can provide consensual dual agency for in-house sales.
20. All agents must disclose the party that they represent in a real estate transaction.
21. In the sale or rental of one- to four-unit residential properties in New York and condominiums and cooperatives in any size building, the agent must present a mandatory disclosure form to all parties signing listing agreements. The form is also presented at other meetings and discussions between prospective buyers and sellers at the first substantive contact or meeting.
22. There are two separate agency disclosure forms: NYS Disclosure Form for Buyer and Seller and NYS Disclosure Form for Landlord and Tenant.
23. The IRS code classifies real estate salespersons and brokers as independent contractors. To qualify, the real estate agent must be licensed, and the broker and the sales associate enter into a written contract.
24. As independent contractors, licensees do not receive sick pay or medical benefits and must file a Form 1099-MISC with the IRS. Independent contractor-licensees pay self-employment taxes.
25. Antitrust violations are business activities in which a monopoly, contract, or conspiracy negatively impacts an individual's or a company's ability to do business. The negative compact is called "restraint of trade."

26. Antitrust laws are important to the real estate profession because it is unlawful for brokerage firms, real estate boards, franchises, and MLS services to conspire to fix commission rates. MLS cannot unreasonably prohibit a licensee from becoming a member and using its services.
27. The Sherman (1890) and Clayton (1914) Antitrust Acts and the creation of the Federal Trade Commission (1914) established legislation to control and regulate antitrust activity.
28. The Antitrust Division of the Department of Justice enforces the Sherman and Clayton Acts. Violators are subject to criminal liability and monetary damages.
29. Antitrust laws prohibit price fixing, group boycotts, market allocation agreements, and tie-in arrangements.
30. A series of lawsuits heard in federal district courts in both New York and out-of-state sets forth activities prohibited under antitrust law and defines those activities allowable under the law.

Useful Links

National Association of REALTORS®

www.realtor.org

NYS Association REALTORS®

www.nysar.com

Legal Issues

Part I Estates and Interests

Key Terms

Act of waste When a life tenant abuses or misuses a property

Air rights The rights to the area above the earth

Beneficiary One who receives benefits or gifts from the acts of others given, for example, by a will or trust

Bundle of rights A visual concept that illustrates interests in and title to real property, including air rights, water rights, mineral rights, easements, leases, and mortgages

Corporation A taxable legal entity recognized by law, with tax rates separate from individual income tax rates

Chattel Another name for personal property

Defeasible fee A title subject to being lost if certain conditions occur

Demand Refers to how much (quantity) of a product or service is desired by buyers

Dower and curtesy An automatic life estate owned by a surviving spouse in inheritable property owned by the deceased spouse alone during the marriage; for practical purposes, not valid in New York

Estate in real property An interest in the property sufficient to give the holder of the estate the right to possession

Fee simple absolute This estate provides the most complete form of ownership and bundle of rights in real property

Fee simple on condition A fee simple defeasible ownership recognized by the words "but if" in the transfer

Fixtures Improvements both on and to the land

Freehold estate Ownership for an undetermined length of time

General partnership The partners are personally liable for partnership debts exceeding partnership assets

Holdover tenant A tenant who does not leave upon expiration of the lease

Illiquidity Investments in which one's assets are not readily convertible to cash

Joint tenancy A form of co-ownership requiring all four unities of time, title, interest, and possession

Leasehold estate An estate of less than a lifetime and therefore of limited duration

Life estate Possession and control for the remainder of someone's life

Littoral rights The rights that apply to property bordering a nonflowing body of water, such as a lake or sea

Limited partnership An organization consisting of one or more general partners and several other or limited partners with lesser roles

Parcel A specific portion of land, such as a lot

Partition A legal proceeding dividing property of co-owners so each will hold title in severalty or directing that the property be sold, and the proceeds be divided

Partnership A form of business organization composed of two or more individuals

Periodic estate An estate that renews itself for another period at the end of each period unless one party gives notice to the other during the prescribed time

Personal property Everything that is not real property

Qualified fee simple A fee simple defeasible estate recognized by the words "as long as" in the deed

Real estate Land and all improvements, whether found in nature or placed there by people

Real property Real estate plus all legal rights, powers, and privileges inherent in ownership

Reversionary interest Upon the death of a life tenant, the reversion of possession to the grantor or the grantor's heirs, if no other specification has been made

Right of survivorship When one (or more) of the co-owners of a property dies, the right of surviving co-owners to the interest of the deceased

Riparian water rights Rights that belong to owners of property bordering a flowing body of water

Scarcity As it applies to the real estate market, scarcity means that there is a lesser availability of real property than the demand for it; this would cause property values or prices of real property in the area where the scarcity exists to increase

Severalty Title to real property held in the name of only one person or entity; the interest is severed from all others

Sole proprietorship A business owned by an individual in his or her own name or doing business as (d/b/a) or trade name

Special purpose property Property that combines both the land and improvements for one highest and best use, such as a public park

Subsurface rights Rights to the area below the earth's surface; also called mineral rights

Supply Represents how much the market can offer

Tenancy in common Tenancy characterized by two or more persons holding title to a property at the same time; the only required unity is that of the right to possession

Tenants by the entirety Form of ownership limited to husband and wife; contains the right of survivorship

Trade fixtures Items installed by a commercial tenant and removable upon termination of the tenancy

Transferability The ability to transfer real property from one party to another

Trust A fiduciary relationship between the trustee and the beneficiary of the trust

Trustee One who holds title to property for the benefit of a beneficiary

Trustor One who conveys title to a trustee

Unity of interest Co-owners who all have the same percentage of ownership in a property

Unity of possession Co-owners who have the right to possess or access any portion of a property that is owned without physical division

Unity of time Co-owners who receive title at the same time in the same conveyance

Unity of title Co-owners who have the same type of ownership, such as a life estate, fee simple, or conditional fee

Utility Refers to the capability of real property to serve a useful purpose

Water rights Includes percolating water rights, riparian water rights, and surface water rights

Key Points

1. Real property consists of land and everything attached to the land and the bundle of rights inherent in ownership.
2. Everything that is not real property is personal property.
3. Ownership in land includes the surface of the earth and the area above and below the surface, although these rights may be assigned.
4. Personal property that attaches permanently to the land or improvements and becomes part of the real property is a fixture.
5. Real property has the physical characteristics of immobility, indestructibility, and uniqueness and economic characteristics are based on scarcity, permanence of investment, location, and improvements.
6. In order to have value, these four essential characteristics of real property are necessary: demand, scarcity, utility, and transferability. Demand refers to how much of a product or service is desired by buyers. Scarcity refers to a property's availability or unavailability. Utility refers to the capability of a property to serve a useful purpose. Transferability is the ability to transfer property from one party to another.
7. The greater the supply of a good in comparison to the demand for that good, the lower its value. Conversely, the smaller the supply and the greater the demand, the higher the value. Price balances the supply and demand for a certain item such as real estate.
8. Estates in land are divided into two groups: freehold estates and estates of less than freehold (nonfreeholds or leaseholds).
9. Freehold estates are fee simple estates that are inheritable. Freehold estates are also life estates that are not inheritable.
10. The most complete form of ownership in real property is fee simple absolute.
11. Life estates may be in reversion or in remainder. The duration of a life estate may be measured by the life tenant or by the life of another *(pur autre vie).* A life tenant has the right of possession and enjoyment of the property and the right to derive income from it.
12. Title held in the name of one person only is ownership in severalty.

13. When two or more people or organizations hold title at the same time, it is called co-ownership or concurrent ownership. The forms of co-ownership include tenancy in common, joint tenancy, tenancy by the entirety, and community property.
14. Forms of property ownership include sole proprietorship, partnership, corporation, limited liability company, limited partnership, syndication, and joint venture.
15. In a general partnership, the partners are personally liable for partnership debts exceeding partnership assets. Partners are jointly (together) and severally (separately) liable for these debts. A limited partnership consists of one or more general partners who are jointly and severally liable, and one or more silent, or limited, partners who contribute money or other assets of value to the extent of their ownership interest.
16. Corporations have the power to receive, hold, and convey title to real property. Shareholders are owners of the corporation to the extent of their shareholdings.
17. A subchapter S corporation is a type of corporate organization that is permitted to function as a corporation but is taxed as a partnership.
18. A C corporation must pay corporate income tax to the IRS and the shareholders are also taxed on their dividends that are profits of the corporation. Therefore, a double tax is paid, both at the corporate and the shareholder levels.
19. Joint tenancy and tenancy by the entirety include the right of survivorship and require the unities of time, title, interest, and possession. Tenancy by the entirety is restricted to married couples and adds the fifth unity of marriage (unity of person).
20. Business organizations may receive, hold, and convey title to real property.

Legal Issues

Part II Liens and Easements

Key Terms

Appurtenances Inherent or automatic ownership rights that are a natural consequence of owning real property

Corporation franchise tax A tax calculated on the net profit of the corporation, which if not paid becomes a lien against the corporation's assets

Dominant tenement The land that benefits from an easement appurtenant or from an easement in gross

Easement A nonpossessory interest in land owned by another; someone who owns an easement right does not own or possess the land where the easement lies, only the right to a specified use

Easement appurtenant All easements that are not easements in gross; two landowners must be involved, one receiving a benefit and the other accepting a burden

Easement by condemnation Created by the exercise of the government's right of eminent domain

Easements by grant or reservation Created by the express written agreement of the landowners, usually in a deed

Easements by implication Arises by implication from the conduct of the parties

Easements by necessity Exists when land has no access to roads and is landlocked

Easements by prescription Obtained by use of the land of another for a legally prescribed length of time

Easement for light and air A type of negative easement generally pertaining to the view of a property

Easements in gross Also called commercial easements in gross; usually owned by a government agency or a public utility

Encroachment A trespass on the land of another created by the intrusion of some structure or object, such as a tree limb or roof overhang, across a boundary line

Encumbrance Interest in a property that secures debt or gives use and/or control to another

General liens Claims against all property of a debtor

In rem legal proceeding A legal action brought against the real property and not against an individual and his personal property

Involuntary lien A lien created by a legal proceeding when a creditor places a claim on real and/or personal property to obtain payment of a debt

Judgment A court decree resulting from a lawsuit

License Permission to do a particular act or series of acts on land of another without possessing any estate or interest in the land

Lien A claim or charge against the property of another

Lis pendens A notice that a lawsuit has been filed and a trial is pending; the judgment will affect title to a specific property

Materialman's lien A specific lien filed by a supplier of products required in construction or improvement of a building

Mechanic's lien A specific lien filed by a person who provides labor or furnishes material for the improvement of real property

Nonpossessory A nonownership interest in a property such as an easement

Party wall A common wall used by two adjoining structures

Possessory Having possession; the state of either actively or constructively occupying the property that gives the possessor certain rights

Profit The right to take products of the soil from the land of another

Restrictive covenant Restrictions placed on a private owner's use of land by a nongovernmental entity or an individual

Servient tenement The land that suffers by allowing an easement use

Specific lien Claims, such as a mortgage, against a specific and readily identifiable property

Voluntary lien A lien in which individuals consent to placing a charge against their property as security for a debt; a mortgage is an example of a voluntary lien

Writ of attachment A court order preventing any transfer of the attached property during the litigation

Key Points

1. An encumbrance is a claim, lien, charge, or liability attached to and binding upon real property.
2. Examples are encroachments, easements, leases, liens, assessments, and restrictive covenants.
3. Specific liens are claims against a specific and readily identifiable property, such as a mortgage or a mechanic's lien.
4. The lien for real property taxes and special assessments are specific liens. In New York, these liens have the highest priority for payment.
5. Mechanics' and materialmen's liens are specific liens that may receive preferential treatment for priority of liens.
6. General liens are claims against a person and all of his property, such as a judgment resulting from a lawsuit. The property of a judgment debtor is subject to execution and forced sale to satisfy an unpaid judgment.
7. Easements are nonpossessory interests in land owned by another. Easements can be in gross (commercial) or appurtenant (all other easements that are not easements in gross). Easements are created by grant (reservation), necessity, prescription, implication, and condemnation.
8. Easements appurtenant can be negative or affirmative. With an affirmative easement, the dominant tenement has the right to physically cross the servient tenement. With a negative easement appurtenant, the dominant tenement does not have the right to enter the land of the servient tenement. Instead, the dominant tenement has the right to restrict some activity or use of the servient tenement.
9. Easements are terminated by release, merger, abandonment, necessity, or expiration of the prescribed time.
10. An encroachment is a trespass on land or an intrusion over the boundary of land. A survey of a boundary provides evidence of an encroachment.

11. A profit in real property is transferable and inheritable. A license in real property is not transferable or inheritable.

Legal Issues
Part III Deeds/Conveyances

Key Terms

Accession Real property owners' right to all that their land produces or all that is added to the land, either intentionally or by mistake

Accretion The gradual building up of land in a watercourse over time by deposits of silt, sand, and gravel

Acknowledgment Public officer or notary's witnessing of signatures that make a deed or other instrument eligible for recording; the signatory must appear before a public officer, such as a notary public, and state that signing the deed was a voluntary act

Administrator (man) or Administratrix (woman) The person appointed by a court to distribute the property of a person dying intestate

Adverse possession A method of acquiring title to real property by conforming to statutory requirements; a form of involuntary alienation of title

Alluvion The land mass added to property over time by accretion; owned by the owner of the land to which it has been added

Avulsion The loss of land when a sudden or violent change results in its washing away

Bargain and sale deed May be with or without covenants of warranty; with covenants, the grantor claims that he is conveying substantial title and possession of the property; without covenants, the legal effect is similar to a quitclaim deed

Beneficiary or legatee The recipient of a gift of personal property by will

Bequest or legacy A gift of personal property by will

Codicil A supplement or appendix to a will either adding or changing some bequest

Conveyance A deed

Dedication A gift of land or an easement for public use; an example of an implied dedication is when the public is allowed access to a private road

Dedication by deed Used when a developer deeds to the municipality a parcel of land for a park; a quitclaim deed may be used

Deed The document used to legally convey title to real property

Deed of correction Used when a deed contains an error that requires correction

Deed of gift Conveys real property without consideration; can be accomplished by any type of deed

Delivery and acceptance To effect transfer of title by transfer of a deed, the grantor must deliver a deed to the grantee and the grantee must accept the deed

Description by monument Used in place of the metes and bounds method when describing multiple-acre tracts of land that would be very expensive to survey; permanent objects such as stone walls, large trees, or boulders are used as markers

Description by reference, plat, or lot and block Legal description that references a plat of subdivision or other legal document

Devise A gift of real property by will

Devisee A recipient of the gift of real property by will

Executor (man) or Executrix (woman) A person appointed in a will to carry out its provisions

Formal or witnessed will One signed by the testator or testatrix in front of two witnesses where he declares the writing to be his last Will and Testament and states that it expresses his wishes for the disposition of his property after death

Full covenant and warranty deed Contains the strongest and broadest form of guarantee of title of any type of deed and therefore the greatest protection to the grantee

Grantee The person receiving title; does not need to have legal capacity; a minor or a mentally incompetent person can receive and hold title to real property

Granting clause The essential clause in a deed, containing words of conveyance stating that it is the grantor's intention to transfer the title to the named grantee

Grantor The one conveying the title; must be legally competent

Guardian's deed A deed executed by an individual who is legally vested with the power to manage the rights and property of another

Habendum clause A clause in a deed beginning with the words "to have and to hold," which describes the estate granted and always must agree with the granting clause

Intestate The condition of death without leaving a valid will

Involuntary alienation Occurs when an individual must relinquish title to real property against his/her will

Judicial deed Results from a court order to the official executing the deed; contains no warranties

Land patent Instrument conveying public land to a private party; can also mean the actual land conveyed

Metes and bounds description Legal description of surveyed land where the metes are the distances from point to point in the description and the bounds are the directions from one point to another

Probate Judicial determination of a will's validity by a court of competent jurisdiction and subsequent supervision over distribution of the estate

Public grant A grant of a power, license, or real property from the state or government to a private individual

Quitclaim deed Simply a deed of release; releases or conveys to the grantee any interest, including title, that the grantor may have; contains no warranties

Referee's deed An instrument executed by an individual empowered by the court to exercise judicial power, as in a court-ordered sale and conveyance of real property

Reference to a plat A valid legal description on a deed referring to a plat (map) and lot number as part of a recorded subdivision

Reliction An increase in land by the permanent withdrawal of a sea, river, lake, stream, or other body of water

Sheriff's deed Gives ownership rights in property to a buyer at a sheriff's sale, which is a legal form of dispostion of property with a court order

Tacking A procedure used to preserve the adverse possession claim when the possession of the property is taken over from one person to another sometimes through inheritance

Testate A person who dies having made a valid will while alive; a person may die testate as to some property and intestate as to other property

Testator A man who makes a will; a woman is a testatrix

Voluntary alienation Willing transfer of title during life; accomplished by the grantor's delivery of a valid deed to the grantee while both are alive

Key Points

1. A deed is the document used to convey title to real property. Transfer of title is termed *alienation.* Alienation may be voluntary or involuntary.
2. Examples of voluntary transfer of title during life are by sale, gift, dedication, or grant. Transfer after death is by will or New York statutes, as interpreted by the court.
3. Involuntary transfer of title occurs during the life of a property owner because of a lien foreclosure, bankruptcy, condemnation, or adverse possession. Involuntary transfer after death is escheat, which means the property goes to the state if no heirs can be found.

4. The requirements for deed validity are (1) deed in writing, (2) competent grantor, (3) competent or incompetent grantee, (4) grantor and grantee named with certainty, (5) adequate property description, (6) recital of consideration, (7) words of conveyance that sometimes contain a *habendum* clause, (8) proper execution by grantor, and (9) delivery and acceptance to convey title.
5. To be eligible for recording on the public record, a deed must be acknowledged. Recording protects the grantee's title against future conveyances by the grantor.
6. Deed descriptions include metes and bounds, lot and block (plat of subdivision), and monuments.
7. A full covenant and warranty deed is the strongest and broadest form of title guarantee.
8. A quitclaim deed is a deed of release and contains no warranties. It conveys any interest the grantor may have. The quitclaim deed is used mainly to remove a "cloud" from a title.
9. A bargain and sale deed may be with or without covenants. When the bargain and sale deed contains covenants, it is acceptable to lenders.
10. Judicial deeds result from a court order to the official executing the deed. Forms of judicial deeds include sheriff's deed, referee's deed, tax deed, guardian's deed, and executor's or administrator's deed.
11. When a person dies and leaves no will, the laws of descent determine the order of distribution of property to the heirs.
12. When a person dies and leaves a will, the gift of real property through the will is a devise. A gift of personal property through a will is a bequest. The recipient is the beneficiary or legatee.
13. Surrogate's Court in the county where the deceased lived is the court of jurisdiction over probate matters.
14. The New York statute that defines distribution of property by the deceased is the New York Estate, Powers, and Trusts Law.
15. A person other than the owner can claim title to real property under adverse possession. In New York, the possession must be continuous and uninterrupted for a period of ten years and a court must award title.
16. Natural processes of nature may give or take away land from property owners. These processes and affected land include accretion, alluvion, avulsion, erosion, and reliction.

Legal Issues
Part IV Title Closing and Costs

Key Terms

Abstract of title A condensed history of the title, summarizing all links in the chain of title plus any other matters of public record affecting the title

Actual notice Requires that the person actually knows about a document or situation

Assessments Referring to condominiums and cooperatives, monies payable to the homeowners association for maintenance of the common elements

Certificate of title opinion An attorney's written opinion as to which person or entity owns a property and the quality of title and exceptions, if any, to clear title

Chain of title The successive conveyances of title, starting with the current deed and going back an appropriate time (typically 40 to 60 years); title must be unbroken to be good and, therefore, marketable

Closing statement Sets forth the distribution of monies involved in the transaction—who is to pay what amount for each expense and who is to receive that amount

Combined Real Estate Transfer Tax Return, Credit Line Mortgage Certificate, and Certification of Exemption from the Payment of Estimated Personal Income Tax Form (Form TP 584) Used to transmit the NYS transfer tax and furnished by the NYS Department of Taxation and Finance; also includes other sections

Constructive notice The theory that all the world is bound by knowledge of the existence of a document if evidence of the document is recorded

Credit In a closing statement, money to be received or credit given for money

Debit In a closing statement, an expense; monies that are owed

Insurable title A title that is acceptable to a title insurance company

Marketable title One that is reasonably free and clear of encumbrances

Mortgage recording tax In certain counties, 0.75% of the mortgage amount; in counties with a public transportation system, the amount is 1%, with 0.25% paid by the lender, if there is one

New York City Real Property Transfer Tax In addition to the NYS transfer tax, New York City imposes an additional transfer tax of 1% of the selling price for residential property; if the selling price is over $500,000, the transfer tax is 1.425%; for other property types, the tax is 1.425% and if the consideration is more than $500,000, the tax is 2.65%

Proration A division of closing costs to ensure fair apportioning of expenses between buyer and seller

Real Estate Settlement Procedures Act (RESPA) Applies to certain residential mortgage closing transactions not covered by the TILA-RESPA Integrated Disclosure Rule (TRID)

Real Property Transfer Report Used to document the information associated with all real property transfers within New York (Form RP-5217)

Real property transfer tax A tax on the conveyance of title to real property paid by the seller and based on the consideration the seller receives for the property

Survey The process by which parcels of land are measured; the final document is a map showing measurements, boundaries, and area

TILA-RESPA Integrated Disclosure Rule (TRID) Replaces older disclosure requirements under TILA and RESPA for most residential real property loans

Title Evidence of the right to possess property

Title closing Settlement of the obligations undertaken in the contract of sale; parties to the title transfer and other interested persons review the closing documents, execute the closing documents, pay and receive money, and receive title

Title insurance policy A contract that insures the policy owner against financial loss if title to real estate is not good

Title search Search of the records affecting real estate titles

Key Points

1. At a title closing, all interested parties meet to review closing documents and to transfer title to real estate. The deed is the document that conveys the title from seller to purchaser (grantor to grantee).
2. Recordation of a deed provides protection for the owner's title against subsequent claimants.
3. Deeds and other closing documents are recorded in the county clerk's office of the county where the property is situated; in NYC, they are recorded in the Office of the City Register through its online system ACRIS. Other counties in New York may have online recording systems.
4. The purpose of a title examination is to determine a title's quality. An attorney or a title company makes the examination. Only an attorney can legally give an opinion about the title's quality.
5. A title insurance policy protects the insured against financial loss caused by a title defect.
6. Various types of tests and inspections of the property take place before closing. A licensed home inspector accompanied by the purchaser generally performs the "structural" inspection before (and sometimes after) a contract is signed. A real estate agent may take a prospective purchaser to a walk-through of the property immediately before closing.
7. The TILA-RESPA Integrated Disclosure Rule (TRID), effective October 1, 2015, replaces older disclosure requirements under TILA and RESPA for most residential real property loans. Lenders originating types of mortgages not covered under the Rule will continue to use the Good Faith Estimate, HUD-1 Form, and Truth-in-Lending disclosures required under current RESPA and TILA laws.
8. The loan estimate form under TRID provides disclosures to help consumers understand the key features of the mortgage loan including the interest rate and monthly payment and risks of the loan for which they are applying.
9. Also under TRID, the closing disclosure form provides information that assists the consumer in understanding all of the transaction costs including all costs to close the loan.

10. The purpose of the Foreign Investment in Real Property Tax Act (FIRPTA) is to impose a tax on capital gains derived by foreign people from the sale of their U.S. real property interest. The income tax is assessed on the sale of a U.S. real property interest (USRPI). The seller must deliver a FIRPTA certificate to a buyer. To ensure payment of the income tax, the buyer must withhold 15% of the purchase price at closing and send it directly to the IRS instead of paying the full amount to the foreign seller.
11. The Commission Escrow Act applies to one- to four-unit residential properties as well as individual condominiums and cooperatives sold by real estate brokers and sales agents. The law protects the broker's real estate commission when a seller does not pay the full commission upon closing.
12. The closing statement computes the distribution of monies involved in the transaction.
13. Seller closing costs may include the New York title transfer taxes, broker commission, attorney fees, costs of document preparation, and satisfaction of existing liens, if any.
14. Purchaser costs may include the structural inspection, title policy, survey fees, mortgage recording tax, lender fees, recording fees, and, if relevant, broker commission.

Useful Links

Loan Estimate Form

files.consumerfinance.gov/f/201403_cfpb_loan-estimate_fixed-rate-loan-sample-H24B.pdf

Closing Disclosure Form

files.consumerfinance.gov/f/201403_cfpb_closing-disclosure_cover-H25B.pdf

Automated City Register Information System ACRIS (New York City)

a836-acris.nyc.gov/CP/

The Contract of Sale and Leases

Part I Leases

Key Terms

Actual eviction Wrongful use of self-help in which the landlord, without the aid or control of the court system, physically removes the tenant and his belongings from the premises or takes action to prevent tenant access to the premises

Assignment Transfer of a lease from the present tenant to the assignee; the assignee then must make lease payments to the landlord

Constructive eviction Occurs when the tenant is denied the quiet enjoyment of the premises

Estate at sufferance Describes an estate of a tenant who is originally in lawful possession of another's property but refuses to leave after his right to possession terminates

Estate at will An estate in which the duration of the term is unknown when the estate is created because either party may terminate the lease simply by giving notice to the other party

Estate for years Exists for a fixed period, which can be as short as one day

Eviction A legal action for removal of a tenant and his belongings and a return of possession of the premises to the landlord

Graduated lease A lease in which the rental agreement changes from period to period over the lease term

Gross lease Provides for the owner (lessor) to pay all expenses, such as real property taxes, owner's insurance, liability insurance, and maintenance

Ground lease A long-term lease of unimproved land, usually for construction purposes

Holdover tenant A tenant who remains in possession of a property after a lease has been terminated

Index lease A method of determining rent on long-term leases where the rent is tied to an economic indicator such as an index

Landlease Allows a lessee the right to use land for any purpose for a specified period

Landlord concessions Inducements by landlords to encourage a property rental such as a reduction in rent for a specified time

Lease A contract in which, for a consideration (usually rent), a property owner transfers to a tenant a property interest or possession, for a prescribed time

Lessee The tenant placed in possession of the leased premises

Lessor The landlord or owner of the leased property

Net lease The tenant (lessee) pays some or all of the expenses

Percentage lease A lease with a base rent plus an additional monthly rent based on a percentage of the lessee's gross sales

Periodic lease Automatically renews itself for another period at the end of each period unless one party gives notice to the other at the prescribed time

Periodic tenancy or estate from year to year The period length can be a week, a month, or any other negotiated time period

Security deposit Money paid by the tenant at the start of a lease that will be refunded at the end of the lease based upon the condition of the premises; often negotiated as one month's rent

Sublease A lease under which a tenant leases a property to a third party, the sublessee; the original tenant is still responsible to the landlord for the lease payments under the original lease contract; the sublessee pays the rent to the tenant (lessee), and the tenant pays the landlord

Triple net lease In addition to the rent, the lessee pays all expenses associated with the property

Key Points

1. Rental of property creates a leasehold estate. Types of leasehold estates include tenancy or estate for years, periodic (year-to-year) estates, month-to-month, and estate at sufferance.
2. A contract between the landlord of property and the tenant creates a lease. The landlord is the lessor. The tenant is the lessee.
3. The landlord and tenant are bound by contractual rights and obligations created by the lease agreement.
4. Leasehold estates (or nonfreeholds) are estates of limited duration, providing possession and control but not title, as in the case of freehold estates.
5. The lessee's transfer of the entire remaining term of a lease is an assignment. A transfer of part of the lease term with a reversion to the lessee or a transfer of part of the leased premises is a subletting.
6. The Emergency Tenants Protection Act of 1974 (revised 1997) and the Rent Law of 2011 and the Rent Code Amendments of 2014 govern rent regulation. Two programs, rent control and rent stabilization, are intended to protect tenants in privately owned buildings from illegal rent increases and allow owners to maintain their buildings and realize a reasonable profit.
7. In a lease of residential property, the landlord's warranty of habitability must provide habitable premises to the tenant.
8. When the lease expires, the tenant must maintain and return the premises to the landlord in the same condition as at the beginning of the lease, ordinary wear and tear excepted.
9. An amendment to the NYS Real Property Law, effective December 2014, requires that every residential lease provide conspicuous notice in boldface type as to the existence or nonexistence of a maintained and operative sprinkler system in the leased premises.
10. The tenant can make a claim of constructive eviction when the premises become uninhabitable because of the landlord's lack of maintenance. A determination of constructive eviction terminates the lease.
11. Leases terminate by (a) expiration of lease term, (b) mutual agreement, (c) breach of condition, (d) actual eviction, (e) court-ordered eviction, or (f) constructive eviction. Actual eviction is illegal in New York.

Useful Links

The Division of Housing and Community Renewal

www.nyshcr.org/

New York City Rent Guidelines Board

www.nycrgb.org

The Contract of Sale and Leases
Part II Contracts

Key Terms

Apportionment The division of expenses between seller and purchaser

Arm's length The relationship between parties to a contract; they are assumed to have equal bargaining power and are not related by business interest or familial relationship

As is Wording on an offer to purchase contract indicating that the premises are sold without warranty as to condition and the purchaser agrees to take title in the present condition subject to reasonable use, wear, and tear between the date of the contract and the closing date

Assignment A new party to a contract agrees to satisfy the former contracting party's obligation

Breach of contract Violation of the terms of a contract

Bilateral contract One in which two parties have made promises of some kind to each other

Binder Used in certain areas of New York; a written document for the purchase and sale of real property used by licensees instead of an offer to purchase contract; does not generally contain all the elements of a valid contract; however, if it does, it may be enforced as a contract

Caveat Latin for a warning or caution; for example, in New York, properties that lie within an agricultural district must have a disclosure attached stating that the property lies within an agricultural district

Caveat emptor Latin for "let the buyer beware"

Contingencies Additions, amendments, or agreements annexed to the contract and incorporated into its terms

Contract An agreement between competent legal parties to do or refrain from doing some legal act in exchange for consideration

Counteroffer An acceptance that differs in any way from the offer

Earnest-money deposit Shows the sincerity of the buyer and expresses a commitment to raise the money called for in the contract

Executed contract A contract that has been fully performed

Executory contract A contract that is not fully performed

Express contract A contract in which the parties have agreed on all terms; can be written or oral

Forbearance The act on the part of a lending institution of refraining from taking legal action for nonpayment of a mortgage despite the fact that it is due

Implied contract One inferred from the conduct and actions of another without express agreement

Liquidated damages The parties to the contract can stipulate in the contract an amount of money to be paid upon certain breaches of the contract

Meeting of the minds When the parties to the contract reach agreement on the terms to be included in the contract

Novation A form of agreement that terminates a previous contract; the substitution of a new contract for a prior contract or the substitution of a new party for an old party

Offer to purchase contract A bilateral, express contract that is the "road map" for the real estate transaction

Option A contract in which an optionor (owner) sells a right to purchase a property to a prospective buyer, called an optionee, at a particular price for a specified time period; if no time limit is set, it may contain a clause allowing the optionee the first choice to either purchase or not purchase the property (right of first refusal) if a third party wishes to purchase the property

Power of attorney The right given by one party to another to perform certain acts on his behalf

Rescission To take back, remove, or annul; contract remedy applied when a contract has not been performed by either party and has been breached by a party

Specific performance An order from the court requiring the contract to be completed as originally agreed

Statute of Frauds In New York, this statute is called the General Obligations Law; requires that real estate contracts be in writing; leases and listing contracts for more than one year must be in writing to be enforceable in court

Statute of Limitations Law stating that if a party to a contract fails to bring a lawsuit against a defaulting party within a time period set by statute, the injured party loses the right of remedy

"Time is of the essence" If written on the contract for purchase and sale, the closing must take place on or before the exact date stipulated in the contract

Unenforceable contract One that appears to meet the requirements for validity but would not be enforceable in court

Uniform Commercial Code Contains rules governing the financing of loans to purchase cooperative apartments; provides for the lender to retain a security interest in the personal property until the lender is paid in full

Unilateral contract When one party makes a promise in order to induce a second party to do something; the party making the promise is not obligated under the contract until the other party does what has been asked

Valid contract One that is binding and enforceable on all parties; contains all the essential elements of a contract

Void contract Has absolutely no legal force or effect

Voidable contract May or may not be enforceable between the parties; results from the failure of the contracting parties to meet some legal requirement in negotiating the agreement

Key Points

1. A contract is an agreement between competent parties, upon legal consideration, to do or refrain from doing some legal act.
2. Bilateral contracts are based on mutual promises. Unilateral contracts are based on a promise by one party and an act by another party.
3. A contract is created by the unconditional acceptance of a valid offer. Acceptance of bilateral offers must be communicated.
4. The requirements for contract validity are (a) competent parties, (b) mutual agreement, (c) lawful objective, (d) consideration, and (e) written format when required to be.
5. The remedies for breach of contract are (a) compensatory damages, (b) liquidated damages, (c) specific performance, and (d) rescission.
6. A sales contract is a road map for the real estate transaction and is a bilateral express contract.
7. A binder and an offer to purchase are written outlines of the scope of a real estate transaction. They may contain all of the essential elements of a valid contract.
8. An installment land contract is a sales contract and a method of financing by the seller for the buyer. Legal title does not pass until the buyer pays all or some specified part of the purchase price.
9. An option is often tied to a lease. In some cases, all or part of the rent applies toward the purchase price of the property.
10. A broker is generally entitled to a commission when he produces a buyer who is ready, willing, and able to purchase the subject property on terms acceptable to the seller.
11. Contract preparation differs between upstate and downstate New York.

The Contract of Sale and Leases
Part III Contract Preparation

Key Terms

Attorney review or approval clause A condition making a contract subject to approval by each party's attorney

Down payment/deposit down payment The portion of a property's purchase price that is paid in cash and is not part of the mortgage loan. In certain upstate areas, the term used is *deposit down payment*; generally, when the buyer defaults, the down payment is the amount of liquidated damages to which the seller is entitled

Lawyers' Fund for Client Protection One of its purposes is to reimburse client money that is misused in the practice of law

Mortgage contingency clause States that the closing is contingent, or dependent upon, the purchaser's receipt of a mortgage commitment

Key Points

1. In many upstate counties, the real estate agent fills out a preprinted contract of sale. In other places, such as the downstate area, the agent prepares a binder or an offer to purchase. An attorney prepares the contract of sale.
2. A binder is also called a receipt, purchase offer, or agreement. The real estate agent may prepare a binder. Downstate, the seller's attorney sometimes prepares the binder.
3. Forms of contracts include the Contract of Sale (residential one- to four-unit property); Condominium Contract of Sale; Cooperative Contract of Sale; Commercial Contract of Sale for residential income property; Commercial Contract of Sale for retail, business property, and large tracts of land; Installment Sales Contract; and Option to Buy.
4. At the listing presentation, the agent can collect from the sellers the prior deed and title insurance policy; survey; Certificate of Occupancy (CO); and property tax, fuel, and water bills. These documents assist the attorneys who are preparing the closing documents.
5. Generally, for a residential or commercial sale of improved property, the property's common address (street address) is used. When tracts of unimproved land or lots are transferred, the deed, tax map, plat map filed, or survey may be attached to the contract.
6. The mortgage contingency clause states that the closing is contingent, or dependent upon, the purchaser's receipt of a mortgage commitment. If the purchaser complies with the terms of the clause but does not obtain a commitment, the contract may be canceled and the deposit returned.
7. To show good faith, a purchaser makes a down payment/deposit that is kept in escrow by the listing broker, selling broker, or seller's attorney until closing. The percentage or amount can be negotiated between the parties.

8. One of the purposes of the Lawyers' Fund for Client Protection is to reimburse client escrow money that is misused by attorneys.
9. Generally, the purchaser signs the contract of sale first because the purchaser is the party making the offer. The purchaser is stating the purchase price he wants to offer and the terms.
10. A real estate agent who prepares a fill-in-the-blanks purchase and sale contract can avoid the unlawful practice of law by including in the contract a condition making it subject to approval by each party's attorney. This condition is contained in an attorney approval clause.
11. The New York Judiciary Law prohibits the practice of law by nonattorneys. A violation is a misdemeanor. The DOS can also take action against the licensee.

Real Estate Finance

Key Terms

Acceleration clause A mortgage clause enabling the lender to declare the entire balance remaining immediately due and payable if the borrower is in default

Adjustable rate mortgage (ARM) A mortgage interest rate that varies, depending on fluctuations of a standard financial index

Alienation (due-on-sale) clause A clause in the note accompanying a mortgage that entitles the lender to declare the principal balance immediately due and payable if the borrower sells the property during the mortgage term; makes the mortgage unassumable without the lender's permission

Amortization Provides for paying a debt by installment payments; each payment covers current interest with the remainder applied to reduction of the principal

Balloon mortgage Provides for installment payments that are not enough to pay off both the principal and interest over the term of the mortgage; the final (balloon) payment to satisfy the remaining principal and interest is larger than any previous payment

Blanket mortgage Two or more parcels of real estate are pledged as security for payment of the mortgage debt

Bridge loan A short-term loan often used to finance projects until a permanent loan is obtained

Buydown The voluntary payment of discount points to reduce mortgage interest rates when the loan is made

Construction mortgage Interim, or temporary, short-term financing for creating improvements on land

Conventional loans Involves no participation by federal government agencies

Deed in lieu of foreclosure Conveyance of a property by a borrower in default to the lender to avoid record of foreclosure

Default Failure to perform an obligation, such as making mortgage payments

Defeasance clause A mortgage clause giving the borrower the right to defeat and release the lien by paying the indebtedness in full

Deficiency judgment A court order stating that the borrower still owes a lender money when the proceeds of a foreclosure sale are not sufficient to satisfy the balance due the lender

Department of Veterans Affairs (VA) Federal agency offering a loan program that guarantees repayment of the top portion of the loan to the lender in the event the borrower defaults

Depression The lowest possible point in the economic cycle—this cycle encompasses all facets of the economy, including real estate and business; during a depression, unemployment is generally high, the demand for goods and services is low, and production levels are down

Direct (retail) lender A lender who loans money to individuals rather than institutions

Discount points Cash paid at the time of loan closing to reduce the interest rate on a loan; each point equals 1% of the loan amount

Disintermediation The loss of funds available to lending institutions for making mortgage loans, caused by depositors' withdrawal of funds to make investments that seek greater yields

Equity of redemption After default and up to the time a foreclosure sale is held, the borrower has the right to redeem his property by paying the mortgage obligation; the foreclosure sale terminates this right

Equity stripping The process of reducing the equity value of a real estate asset; a type of asset protection strategy that encumbers the property with debt to the extent that there is little or no equity for creditors to acquire; used as type of predatory lending where the victims are about to have their homes foreclosed upon and agree to sell the property to an investor who leases it back to them

Federal Home Loan Mortgage Corporation (FHLMC, Freddie Mac) A federal agency that purchases mortgages on the secondary market to increase the availability of mortgage credit and provide greater liquidity for savings associations; a secondary mortgage institution which purchases mortgages and packages them into securities that are sold to investors

Federal Housing Administration (FHA) A federal agency that insures mortgage loans to protect lending institutions; does not make mortgage loans but protects lenders against financial loss; part of HUD

Federal National Mortgage Association (Fannie Mae) The oldest secondary mortgage institution and the single largest holder of home mortgages; taken over by the federal government in September 2008 along with Freddie Mac

Flexible payment mortgage Mortgage plan based on the borrower's ability to pay

Foreclosure The process leading to the sale of real property pledged to secure mortgage debt

Gap mortgage financing Usually a short-term loan, or one that provides funds over and above an already existing loan, until more permanent financing is in place

Government National Mortgage Association (Ginnie Mae) A federal agency that purchases FHA and VA mortgages on the secondary mortgage market

Grace period A specified time during which a mortgage payment may be made before the lender requires a penalty payment

Graduated payment mortgage A mortgage with lower payments in the early years of the term; payments increase at specified intervals until they are sufficient to amortize the loan over the remaining term

Home Affordable Refinance Program (HARP) Allows borrowers whose homes have dropped in value to refinance with better mortgage terms; aimed at underwater and near underwater homeowners

Home equity line of credit (HELOC) A type of loan against an owner's equity in his/her home

Hypothecating Pledging property as security for a loan

Inflation An increase in money and credit relative to available goods, resulting in higher prices

Installment land contract A means of buying land by making payments to the seller; when the property is paid for, title is transferred to the purchaser

Junior (subordinate) mortgage Describes any mortgage that is subordinate (lower in priority) to another mortgage

Loan-to-value ratio Compares the loan amount to the property value; expressed as a percentage

Margin For an adjustable rate mortgage, the amount above the designated index the lender adds to set the rate the borrower pays

Mini-perm A type of interim financing that a developer or other may acquire until the project starts earning income and permanent financing is in place

Mortgage A two-party legal document pledging a property as security for the repayment of a loan under certain terms and conditions

Mortgagee The lender who receives the mortgage

Mortgagor The borrower who gives the mortgage

Negative amortization Occurs when the monthly payment is less than full interest and does not pay any principal; the unpaid interest accrues, and the principal balance owed increases; prohibited by many ARMs

Open-end mortgage The borrower has the right to demand that the lender advance additional funds without rewriting the mortgage or incurring additional closing costs

Payment cap If the interest rate on an adjustable rate loan increases, a lender may allow a payment cap to keep the monthly payment the same, with the money for the higher interest rate being added to the principal

Predatory lending A practice in which a lender loans money to unqualified buyers

Prepayment privilege or penalty clause A clause in a note accompanying a mortgage stating that the borrower may pay off the loan at any time without incurring a financial penalty or that a prepayment penalty will be imposed if the debt is paid off early

Promissory note or bond A note, in writing, required by a lender to provide evidence that a valid debt exists

Purchase money mortgage A mortgage given by a buyer to the seller to cover part of the purchase price or given to a third-party lender to secure a loan, the proceeds of which are used to acquire the property

Rate caps With adjustable rate mortgages, limits on interest rates during the lifetime of the loan

Recession A moderate and temporary decline in economic activity that occurs during a period of otherwise increasing prosperity; often occurs in a recovery period following a depression

Regulation Z The Federal Reserve Board implemented TILA regulations through Regulation Z that protects people when they use consumer credit that includes mortgage loans and reverse mortgages, home equity lines of credit, open-end credit, certain student loans and installment loans; does not apply to commercial loans

Release clause With a blanket mortgage, allows certain parcels of property to be removed from the mortgage lien if the loan balance is reduced by a specified amount

Rural Economic and Community Development (RECD) Operates federal loan programs targeted to rural areas; makes direct loans and guarantees loans

Rural Housing Service An agency of the U.S. Department of Agriculture (USDA); the service operates federal loan programs that strengthen family farms and finance rural housing; the Community Facilities Programs (CFP) is an agency of the USDA and within the mission area of the Rural Housing Service

Sale leaseback A transaction in which a property owner sells a property to an investor who immediately leases back the property to the seller as agreed in the sales contract

Satisfaction of mortgage An instrument drawn by the mortgagee (lender) when the mortgage is paid in full

Secondary mortgage market Buys and sells mortgages created in the primary mortgage market; mortgages must be assignable to qualify

Seller concessions Also known as seller contributions; an arrangement in which the seller pays certain financing or closing costs for the buyer

Stagflation When economic growth is stagnant, but inflation persists

State of New York Mortgage Agency (SONYMA, also known as Sonny Mae) Raises money for mortgage loans from the sale of New York tax-free bonds; generally available through participating lenders at interest rates lower than most conventional loans

Straight term mortgage The borrower pays interest only for a specified term and pays the principal at the end of the term

Subprime mortgage A loan that may charge more points and have a higher interest rate than other loans; made to borrowers with lower-than-average credit ratings

Swing loan An interim or bridge loan usually not secured by a mortgage

Truth-in-Lending Act (TILA) First enacted in 1968, and amended many times through 2015, the act deals with the informed use of consumer credit; addresses open-end loans such as credit cards and closed-end loans such as mortgage loans

Usury Laws that fix a maximum legal interest rate; the maximum rate is subject to fluctuation

Wholesale mortgage lender A lender that works with independent mortgage brokers and loan officers to originate mortgage loans

Wraparound mortgage A subordinate mortgage that "wraps around" the existing first mortgage, which stays in place and is superior to the wraparound

Key Points

1. The purpose of a mortgage is to secure the payment of a debt. A mortgage creates a lien against the property. Without the mortgage, comparatively few transactions would occur.
2. As to mortgages, New York is a lien theory state. The buyer holds the deed to the property during the mortgage term. The buyer promises to make all payments to the lender and the mortgage becomes a lien on the property, but title remains with the buyer. The lender's lien is removed once the payment of all loan payments has been completed.
3. In a title theory state, a mortgage transfers title to a property to the mortgagee (lender), who holds title until the mortgage has been paid off, at which time title passes to the mortgagor (borrower and then owner). Only a few states are title theory states.
4. The security interest of a mortgage lien encourages lenders of all types including thrifts, investment banks, mortgage bankers, and private investors, through the use of direct or retail lending, or wholesale lending, to participate in the U.S. real property market.
5. If a borrower defaults on a loan, a lender may institute foreclosure proceedings. If the sale proceeds available to the lender do not satisfy the debt, the lender may sue for a deficiency judgment.

6. The borrower's rights are (a) possession of the property before default, (b) defeat of lien by paying debt in full before default, and (c) equity of redemption.

7. The lender's rights are (a) possession of the property after foreclosure, (b) foreclosure, and (c) right to assign the mortgage.

8. A buyer assuming a seller's mortgage assumes liability on the mortgage and the note. The seller remains liable on the note unless released by a mortgage clause or by the lender. A buyer taking title subject to an existing mortgage has no liability on the note.

9. Conventional loans need not be insured if the loan amount does not exceed 80% of the property value. Most conventional insured loans are 90% and 95% loans. The insurance is called private mortgage insurance (PMI). The borrower pays the premium.

10. Lending institutions may charge discount points in making mortgage loans. Each point that the lender charges costs someone (either the buyer or the seller, depending upon the situation) 1% of the loan amount, paid at the time of closing.

11. A fully amortized mortgage requires payments of principal and interest that will satisfy the debt over the mortgage term.

12. Types of mortgages and loans include term, adjustable or variable rate, balloon, amortized, pledged account, graduated payment, open-end, blanket, wraparound, swing (or bridge), purchase money, construction, shared equity, home equity, reverse annuity, and package.

13. Qualified lending institutions make FHA, VA, SONYMA, and RHS (Rural Housing Service) loans.

14. The FHA is a government agency that insures loans that may have lower down payments and lower credit rating requirements than conventional loans.

15. The FHA annual mortgage insurance premium (MIP) and the upfront mortgage insurance premium (UFMIP) protect the lender from financial loss because of foreclosure. FHA establishes a maximum loan limit.

16. The Department of Veterans Affairs (VA) guarantees to the lender a maximum of 25% of a home loan amount up to $104,250 in case the borrower defaults. This limits the maximum loan amount with no down payment to $417,000 in most counties of New York and $625,500 in some downstate counties.

17. Mortgage loans that meet Fannie Mae and Freddie Mac criteria such as loan amount limits for a certain area are known as conforming loans. Loans that exceed the loan limit are nonconforming loans called jumbo mortgages.

18. The primary mortgage market is the activity of lending institutions making loans directly to individual borrowers. The secondary market is the activity of lending institutions selling and buying existing mortgages. The secondary mortgage market, which purchases mortgages from lenders, frees up capital so that lenders have money available for mortgages. The secondary market mortgage companies include Fannie Mae (FNMA), Ginnie Mae (GNMA), and Freddie Mac (FHLMC).

19. The Housing and Economic Recovery Act of 2008 established the Federal Housing Finance Agency (FHFA) as the supervisor and regulator of the Federal National Mortgage Association

(Fannie Mae) and the Federal Home Loan Mortgage Corporation (Freddie Mac). These two organizations are called the Enterprises. Over the years, there has been public and Congressional debate about the compensation paid to executives and employees of the Enterprises and various methods of oversight have been put into place.

20. Methods of financing include insured and uninsured conventional mortgage loans, FHA-insured loans, VA-guaranteed loans, State of New York Mortgage Agency (SONYMA) mortgages, RHS loans, and various types of private financing.

21. Lender criteria for granting a loan include investment quality of the property, sales price and appraised value, loan-to-value ratio, type of property, and purchaser's ability to pay.

22. Income, qualifying ratios, employment history, the borrower's business organization (if any), liquid assets, monthly obligations, and credit history are lender considerations for loan qualification.

23. Commercial mortgages are extremely dependent on the borrower's financial strength and may include personal guarantees as well as a substantial down payment. Package mortgages are used in commercial lending.

24. A provision in a convertible mortgage gives the lender the option of converting the outstanding balance into an agreed-upon percentage of property ownership.

25. The real estate market is subject to cyclical changes in the economy and is often the first industry to feel the adverse effects of depressed conditions.

26. Factors such as employment levels, interest rates, the stock market, seller valuation of property, and buyers' ability to afford property effect changes in market activity.

27. The cycles in the economy can be defined by four main economic events: recession, depression, inflation, and stagflation.

28. Lender policies reflect the changing real estate climate. Some of the policies include non-income verification loans, loan-to-value and income ratios, and condominium and cooperative loans.

29. A capital-short market occurs when lenders do not have funds for underwriting. The strength or weakness of the mortgage market is dependent on factors such as U.S. government spending and borrowing, the strength or weakness of foreign investor demand for U.S. Treasury bills, the employment rate, wages, and the debt of U.S. consumers.

30. At certain times, investors may favor stocks, bonds, CDs, and/or foreign business investment. Federal Reserve intervention with the money supply including discount rates, liquidity asset requirements and/or the purchase and sale of US Treasury securities (bonds) also influences mortgage fund availability.

31. The U.S. economic system functions in relationship to the real estate market. This relationship covering a wide cross-section of prospective buyers, includes the level of employment rates and wages, the fluctuations of the stock market, the realistic versus inflated valuation of properties, and the affordability of property.

32. Subprime mortgages are mortgages in which a lender charges a higher interest rate and high closing costs to compensate for potential losses from customers who may later default. While the loans have increased homeownership, they can increase mortgage defaults and foreclosures.

33. The New York Anti-Predatory Lending Law protects borrowers from lenders who charge excessive interest and points to high-risk borrowers.

34. The NYS Mortgage Foreclosure Law gives certain rights and protections to borrowers who face foreclosure.

Useful Links

FHA loan information

https://www.hud.gov/program_offices/housing/fhahistory

VA loan information

www.vahomeloancenters.org

The Rural Housing Service

www.rd.usda.gov/about-rd/agencies/rural-housing-service

SONYMA loan information

www.nyshcr.org/SONYMA/

Land Use Regulations/Development

Key Terms

Absorption rate The rate in which homes are sold in a given area over a certain time frame; it is calculated by dividing the number of available homes by the average number of sales per month

Abutting land Parcels of land with a common boundary

Accessory apartment An apartment not intended for commercial rental; an example is an in-law apartment in a residential home

Accessory uses Use of a property that is incidental or subordinate to the main use

Air rights Ownership right of the air space above the surface of the land; landowners may lease or sell air space to others

Area variance Permission to use land in a manner not normally allowed by the dimensional or physical requirements of the current zoning ordinance

Article 9-A Covers the sale or lease of vacant subdivided lands within and without New York only when sold through an installment land contract; covers a sale made by a salesperson, broker, owner, or any other individual empowered to sell the land

Building codes State and local rules and regulations that govern construction practices; they regulate construction materials and electrical wiring, enforce fire and safety standards, and ensure sanitary equipment facilities

Building permit Local government permission to undertake construction or renovation

Census tracts Small geographical areas established by the local community and the Census Bureau; they have numerical identification numbers

Certificate of occupancy A document permitting occupation of a structure by tenants or the owner after a satisfactory final inspection

Cluster zoning Allows a developer to place single-family houses, townhomes, apartments, and other dwellings closer together in exchange for leaving parts of the development open for community enjoyment

Completion bond Also known as a subdivision bond, it assures the municipality that off-site improvements to the subdivision will be made upon completion of the total project

Condemnation Actual taking of property under the power of eminent domain

Conditions Restrictions that provide for a reversion of title if they are violated

Cul-de-sacs Streets with only one outlet; dead-ends

Cumulative zoning A type of zoning permitting a higher-priority use even though it is different from the use intended for the area

Deed restrictions In the form of covenants or conditions, they run with the land (move with the title in any subsequent conveyance) as private controls placed on real estate

Demography The study of the social and economic characteristics of a community

Density A measure of the number of people inhabiting an area of land

Doctrine of aches If property owners do not act to enforce a restrictive covenant on a timely basis, the court will not apply the restriction against the violator and the covenant will be terminated; if landowners are lax in protecting their rights, they may lose them

Eminent domain The right or power of government and its agencies to take private property for public use; must be for the public good

Environmental impact statement The process that describes and analyzes a proposed action that may have a significant effect on the environment

Escheat The power of the state to take title to a deceased person's property when no one else is qualified to receive the title

Exclusive-use zoning Zoning regulations that state that property may only be used in the ways specified in a specific zone

Family According to New York law, any of the following: a group of up to three people who are not married, blood relatives, or adopted living together as a single housekeeping unit; an individual or two or more persons related by blood or marriage or adoption living together in one dwelling; one or more persons living as a single housekeeping unit, as distinguished from a group occupying a hotel, club fraternity, or sorority house

Group home A residential facility for five or more adults who have been institutionalized for various reasons and then released

Home occupation Use of residential property by an owner or lessee for a small business; may be conducted only by the residents of the dwelling and must be incidental and secondary to the use of the dwelling

Infrastructure Support systems of a community such as water, wastewater treatment, utilities, schools, roadways, medical services, and police and fire departments

Lead agency The agency that oversees the environmental assessment process and makes the final decisions

Moratorium Imposed by a municipality, it is a delay in allowing property development in the municipality

Nonconforming use ("grandfathered in") A preexisting use of property different from that specified by the current zoning code

NYS Office of Parks, Recreation and Historic Preservation Administers federal and state preservation programs authorized by federal law and by the New York Historic Preservation Law

Outlots Land that is outside of the main area of development

Police power Enables government to fulfill its responsibility to provide for the public health, safety, and welfare

Public land use control Regulation of land use by government organizations in the form of zoning laws, building codes, subdivision ordinances, and environmental protection laws

Restrictive covenants Restrictions placed on a private owner's use of land by a nongovernmental entity or individual

Setback Specified distances from the front property line and from the interior property lines to the building line

Special use permit A use not permitted in the zone except with the special permission of the planning board or other legislative body

Spot zoning Rezoning of a specific property to permit a use different from the zoning requirements for that area; illegal in New York

Subdivision Land that is divided into lots for development purposes

Subdivision plat A map of a subdivision dividing or platting the land into lots; recorded on the public record

Subdivision regulations Public control of residential subdivision development

Survey The measurements of the boundaries and the total physical dimensions of the property

Taking The act of a government body obtaining a property under its power of eminent domain

Topography The physical features and contours of the land

Transfer of development rights (TDR) Programs that encourage a shift in growth away from agricultural, environmentally sensitive, or open space regions of a municipality to more appropriate areas; the exchange of zoning privileges from areas with low population needs, such as farmland, to areas of high population needs, such as downtown areas

Use variance Permission to use the land for a purpose prohibited under current zoning restrictions

Variance A permitted deviation from zoning ordinance requirements

Zoning board of appeals Local government body that has the power to review administrative rulings made by the planning board or other legislative body, to grant or deny exceptions and special permits, and to process applications for variances

Zoning ordinance A statement setting forth the type of use permitted under each zoning classification and specific requirements for compliance

Key Points

1. Individual owners have the right to place private controls on their own real estate. The purpose of a deed restriction is to limit the use or appearance of a property.
2. The home rule provision of the NYS Constitution grants local governments lawmaking powers and allows local governments to be free from state interference. However, local governments' powers may be limited in certain cases through two legal doctrines: "preemption" and "state concern." This means that local governments must also follow mandates enacted by the State Legislature.
3. Generally, cities, counties, and other local governing units may impose land use regulations and building codes.
4. A subdivision is a tract of land divided into lots or plots for future building purposes. Local planning boards coordinate the site plan review and approval process.
5. Subdivision regulations protect owners within a subdivision, as well as protecting taxpayers from undue tax burdens resulting from the additional services that a subdivision requires.

6. The home rule provision of the NYS Constitution gives the governing body of a municipality, such as the planning board, rule-making powers that govern subdivision development.
7. The development process includes a feasibility study, application to a municipality and/or other appropriate agencies, an environmental review, financing, construction, and marketing.
8. To obtain financing for a subdivision project, the developer may have to raise funds through a combination of sources.
9. Developers generally place restrictive covenants on their entire subdivision to maintain quality and consistency.
10. In New York, the State Environmental Quality Review Act (SEQRA) controls environmental impacts. An environmental impact statement (EIS) evaluates the effect the property development would have on the environment.
11. Public land use controls include police power, taxation, eminent domain, and escheat.
12. The Interstate Land Sales Full Disclosure Act regulates the sale of unimproved lots in interstate commerce to prevent fraudulent schemes in selling land sight unseen.
13. The NYS Uniform Fire Prevention and Building Code provides minimum standards for all types of buildings. Federal construction standards for certain housing are created and enforced by the Federal Housing Authority (FHA). The complete texts of state and many local building codes can be found online or through local building departments and other local government agencies.
14. The New York building code requires that a property owner obtain a building permit from the appropriate local government authority (usually the building department) before constructing or renovating a commercial building or residential property.
15. If an individual dies without a will and there are no heirs or creditors, his property reverts to the state through the power of escheat.
16. Types of zones include residential, commercial, industrial, vacant land, agricultural, public open space, parklands, recreation areas, and institutional.
17. In New York, local planning boards oversee the type of land use within the municipality and have the authority to review site plans.

Construction and Environmental Issues

Part I Construction

Key Terms

Amperage The amount of electricity flowing through a wire

Balloon framing An alternative to platform framing; uses wall studs that run from the foundation through the first and second floors to the ceiling support; rarely used in residential construction

Bearing walls Walls, including the outside wall frame, that support the ceiling and/or the roof

British Thermal Unit (BTU) A measure of heat energy; the amount of heat required to raise the temperature of one pound of water by one degree Fahrenheit

Building envelope Includes the materials and components that physically separate the interior and exterior of the structure

Building plan A detailed architectural rendering of a structure; blueprint

Building specifications Written narratives that describe the building plan and materials

Circuit breakers Devices that switch off electrical power for a given circuit if the current increases beyond the capacity of the system

Distribution panel Metal box containing electrical circuit breakers or fuses; where outside power enters a structure to be distributed inside

Double top plate Also known as a flitch beam, used to tie walls together and provide support for the ceiling and roof system

Energy Conservation Construction Code of New York State (ECCCNYS) A New York law that sets minimum efficiency requirements for the design of new buildings and renovations and additions to existing buildings

Eave The lowest part of the roof that projects beyond the walls of the structure

Fascia The material facing the outer edge of the soffit; if guttering is installed on a roof, it is fastened to the fascia

Flashing Metallic material used in certain areas of the roof to prevent water from seeping into the structure

Footing The most important foundation building block; the concrete base below the frost line that supports a structure's foundation

Foundation walls Generally composed of poured concrete, masonry block, or sometimes brick; the height of the foundation wall determines whether the structure will have a full basement or a crawl space

Frieze board A component of the roof overhang fastened directly under the soffit against the top of the wall; both decorative and functional

Fuse A device that melts to open a circuit and cut off electrical power when overheating occurs

Girder A main carrying beam, either a steel beam or several wooden members fastened together, that spans the distance from one side of a foundation to the other

Headers Also known as lintels; framing members that reinforce door and window openings

Infrastructure Support systems of a community such as water, sewers, utilities, schools, roadways, medical services, and police and fire departments

Joists Framing members used for floor and ceiling framing

Lally columns Support the main carrying beam of the structure; round steel columns filled with concrete that rest on a base plate, which is the column-footing pad

National Electric Code A national standard for electrical installation and service written to safeguard people and property from hazards arising from the use of electricity

Pitch Slope of the roof

Platform framing Framing in which the structure rests on a subfloor platform; the most common type of framing for residential construction

Post-and-beam framing Framing in which studs are much larger than ordinary studs (they may be four or six inches square); the larger posts are placed several feet apart; seldom used in residential construction

R-factor The degree of a wall's resistance to heat transfer; used to rate insulation: the larger the R-factor, the greater the degree of insulation

Rafters Long wood members fastened to the ends of the ceiling joists to form roof gables

Ridge beam The highest part of the framing; forms the apex, or top line, of the roof

Septic system A household wastewater treatment system consisting of a house sewer, septic tank, distribution box, and absorption field or seepage pit

Sheathing A plywood covering placed over exterior framing members; sheetrock or wallboard may be used

Sill plate The first wooden member of a structure; used as the nailing surface for the floor system

Slab-on-grade construction A concrete slab used instead of a foundation wall; the slab is poured directly on the ground, eliminating the crawl space or basement

Soffit The area under the roof extension; made of wood, aluminum, or vinyl

Sole plate A horizontal base plate that serves as the foundation for the wall system

Studs Wood framing members are lumber with a nominal dimension of 2 inches thickness

Urea Formaldehyde Foam Insulation (UFFI) Widely used in homes from 1970s to the 1980s; a hot, viscous mixture sprayed inside the sheathing where it solidifies

Voltage The electrical pressure that pushes through a wire

Key Points

1. In New York, residential and commercial structures must comply with state and local building codes. The NYS Uniform Fire Prevention and Building Code dictates minimum requirements. The Energy Conservation Construction Code of New York State (ECCCNYS) governs building energy efficiencies.
2. Local building codes may be found online for some localities or available at local building departments, city and town halls, or village offices where these records may be accessed online or in hard copy.
3. Although real estate agents do not have to be adept at recognizing building code violations, they should have other professionals to assist them should a problem be observed. This observation could be made by a seller (verbally or through the property condition disclosure form), posed by a buyer or his or her real estate agent, or discovered through an inspection of the property.
4. Building science has evolved greatly over the years due to advances in technology, building materials, energy efficiency, and consideration for environmental concerns.
5. Sustainable design is not only a design approach but also a philosophy that promotes the environmental quality of the indoor building environment by reducing negative impacts on the building and the natural environment. Sustainable applications greatly affect the materials and design of the building envelope.
6. The effect of new initiatives in building science and home design often sets new construction apart from the traditional already-built residential properties of the past. Buyer preferences vary as to what aspects they want to include in a property and whether or not some of the new and energy-saving environmentally friendly materials can be remodeled into an older structure. Some buyers may want to stay with the older, often less expensive and known entities in their buying choices.
7. Price may also be a factor in a completely modernized structure although many energy and environmental factors can save money going forward.
8. The licensing of NYS home inspectors, under NYS Professional Home Inspection Licensing Law (Article 12-B of the Real Property Law), does not cover a residential building in which the "structure [is] newly constructed or not previously occupied as a dwelling unit." However, this modified role of the licensed home inspector can be a practical means of ensuring and initiating the application of the new home warranty from the builder.
9. The visual acuity of a skilled and well-trained NYS-licensed home inspector can assist buyers of a newly built property to understand the quality of construction and the property owner's role in maintaining that quality.
10. It is not the duty of the broker to verify all representations by the owner, but if the broker uses those representations as a selling point, the broker could incur liability. If the broker knows or has reason to know that the owner has made a false representation or has not disclosed a material defect, the broker must disclose this information or terminate the agency.
11. Brokers must disclose any material defects that they have knowledge of to a prospective purchaser. Liability may be imposed upon the agent for concealing defects or failing to disclose the existence of defects.

12. New York has laws and regulations that govern on-site well regulations and on-site sanitary waste systems. The sanitary waste or drainage system of a structure carries wastewater and used water from the structure and deposits it in the public sewer system or private wastewater treatment system.
13. Other site considerations in the planning stage include drainage, landscaping, shading, and walkways.
14. Framing is the wooden skeleton of a structure. Framing members are lumber with a nominal dimension of 2 inches thick.
15. The floor system starts with the sill plate nailed to the foundation system. Wood joists support the subfloor material.
16. Wall framing is usually 2" × 4" or 2" × 6" studs placed 16" on center. The most common wall-framing system is the platform method. Alternative methods are balloon and post-and-beam framing.
17. The main purpose of insulation is to resist the flow of heat from one area to another. Insulation is rated on an R-factor; the larger the R-factor, the greater the degree of insulation.
18. HVAC stands for heating, ventilation, and air conditioning. Some systems use fuel oil or natural gas for energy, while others use electricity.
19. Heating systems found in the home usually include forced hot water, steam, forced warm air, and the heat pump.
20. Forced-air heating and cooling systems use a blower to distribute the heated or cooled air throughout the structure. Hot water heating systems use circulator pumps to cause the heated water to travel through pipes to the convectors or radiators.
21. A heating system's efficiency is rated by the annual fuel utilization estimate (AFUE). A cooling system's efficiency is rated by seasonal energy efficiency rating (SEER). For these federal standards, in both cases, the higher the number, the more efficient the equipment operates because it utilizes the fuel with less waste.
22. Air conditioning units are placed inside or outside a structure. Components of an air conditioner include the liquid refrigerant, evaporator, compressor, condenser, and air handler.
23. The plumbing system consists of two systems: the water supply system for drinking, cooking, and washing and the drainage system for wastewater.
24. Hot water systems commonly found in residential construction include gas and electric water tanks as well as other systems that are connected to the heat source.
25. Electric power is brought to a structure through outside cables and is delivered through conductors (wires) to the building wiring system.
26. Article 36-B of the New York General Business Law, the housing merchant implied warranty, provides for a one-year builder's warranty against construction defects; a two-year warranty for all plumbing, electrical, heating, cooling, and ventilations systems due to improper installation by the builder; and a six-year warranty covering material defects. However, the statute defines a "new home" to be "any single-family house or one for sale in a multi-unit residential structure of five

stories or less." So, the merchant implied warranty does not cover high-rise buildings such as newly constructed condos and co-ops.

27. Article 36-B also gives condo and co-op sellers in buildings of five stories or less the option of drafting written contracts that modify or exclude the housing merchant implied warranty. However, if a seller modifies or excludes the implied warranty, the seller is obligated to offer the buyer an express limited warranty that must comply with certain minimum requirements documented in the statute. All new construction must also comply with applicable state and local building codes.
28. In New York, every one- and two-family dwelling, as well as apartments with multiple dwellings including residential condominiums and cooperatives, must have an installed operable single-station smoke alarm.
29. A carbon monoxide detector must be installed in one- and two-family homes, residential condominiums or cooperatives, and multiple dwellings, regardless of the date of construction or sale. Because of Amanda's Law, carbon monoxide detectors are required in nearly all residential structures in New York. When a one- or two-family property or a residential condominium or cooperative property is transferred, a smoke alarm and carbon monoxide detector affidavit is required.

Useful Links

NYS Department of Health

www.health.ny.gov

NYC home improvement contractor license information

http://www1.nyc.gov/nyc-resources/service/2952/home-improvement-contractor-license-verification

Construction and Environmental Issues
Part II Environmental Issues

Key Terms

Asbestos A fibrous mineral found in rocks and soil throughout the world; formerly used in construction because it is strong, durable, fire retardant, and an efficient insulator; improper handling of asbestos products results in lung disease

Chlordane A chemical insecticide and termiticide banned in the early 1980s because of its toxicity

Chlorofluorocarbons (CFCs) Manufactured chemical substances formerly used in hundreds of applications, including refrigerators and air conditioners, Styrofoam™ products, aerosol dispensers, and cleaning agents; these substances are being phased out because the release of these chemicals threatens the ozone layer

Clean Air Act (1972) A comprehensive federal law intended to control air pollution and mandate the states implement protective measures; a 1990 amendment bans the release of CFCs and HCFCs during the service, maintenance, and disposal of air conditioners and other equipment that uses these refrigerants

Comprehensive Environmental Response, Compensation, and Liability Act (CERCLA) A federal law enacted to correct environmental problems created by uncontrolled waste disposal

Due diligence Because liability for environmental problems passes to new owners in the sale of large tracts of land or commercial property, lenders, purchasers, and tenants often conduct environmental reviews of the property

Electromagnetic fields Magnetic fields created by electricity flowing through a wire

Friable Flaky or crumbly texture of asbestos when hand pressure is applied

Hydrochlorofluorocarbons (HCFCs) Also known as Freon©, a nontoxic chemical substance formerly used in most home air-conditioning units; when released, poses a danger to the ozone layer; in recent years, Freon© has been replaced with Puron©, which does not threaten the ozone layer

Kilovolt A measure of voltage flowing through a power line

Lead A toxic metallic element found worldwide in rocks and soils; can be present in drinking water, interior and exterior house paint, dust, and soil around a home

Mold A superficial growth caused by a fungus; various molds grow on wood, ceiling tiles, wallpaper, paints, carpet, drywall, and insulation, due to excess moisture from a leaky roof, high humidity, or flooding conditions

PCB A manufactured, odorless, liquid organic compound; PCBs were formerly used to cool and insulate electrical transformers; known to appear in groundwater and soil; a carcinogen; some of New York's soils and waterways may contain PCBs

Radon A colorless, odorless, tasteless, radioactive gas present in soil and well water; a carcinogenic contaminant that affects indoor air quality; enters homes from surrounding soil through openings such as cracks in concrete, floor drains, sump pump openings, wall/floor joints in basements, and the pores in hollow block walls; the only way to detect radon is to test for it

Sick building syndrome Occurs when many people in a commercial building fall ill with a variety of complaints ranging from allergic reactions and flu-like symptoms to more serious complaints; may be blamed on poor air quality inside the building

State Environmental Quality Review Act (SEQRA) Calls for the preparation of an environmental impact statement on any actions that may affect the environment; this action may be proposed by a governmental body, private individuals, or entities whose projects require governmental approval

Superfund Amendments and Reauthorization Act (SARA) An amendment to CERCLA imposing stringent cleanup standards and expanding the definition of persons liable for cleanup costs

Wetlands Marshes, swamps, and bogs that are protected areas as they provide flood and storm water control, surface and groundwater protection, erosion control, pollution treatment, fish and wildlife habitats, and natural beauty

Key Points

1. Long-standing environmental issues relative to real estate include drinking water, wastewater treatment, and pest infestation. Contemporary issues include the use of chemical contaminants such as asbestos, lead, radon, and PCBs. Other present and future concerns include underground storage tanks, electromagnetic fields, mold, and the release of chlorofluorocarbons.
2. Federal and state legislation provides regulations and guidelines for environmental policy.
3. The federal Safe Drinking Water Act is New York's guideline for drinking water regulations. The NYS Department of Health oversees the safety of drinking water in New York.
4. The Residential Lead-based Hazard Reduction Act, a federal law, mandates that in the sale or lease of pre-1978 residential properties, sellers or their agents must distribute a lead hazard pamphlet and disclose any known information to the buyers or their agent concerning lead paint. The parties must agree to a ten-day period for a lead paint assessment before a purchaser becomes obligated under the contract. Sales and lease contracts must include specific disclosure and acknowledgment language.
5. The NYS Department of Environmental Conservation (NYSDEC) oversees and protects wetlands. Construction can take place on or near a wetland. Builders must obtain approval for regulated activities from the state through local and federal governments.
6. One source of air pollution in the home may be urea-formaldehyde foam insulation (UFFI), which contains large amounts of formaldehyde.
7. Another source of home air pollution is insecticides. Chlordane is a chemical insecticide and termiticide that has been banned since the early 1980s.
8. Bacteria is a source of air pollution in homes and buildings. Sometimes large numbers of people in a commercial building fall ill from a chemical illness called sick building syndrome.
9. An environmental impact statement (EIS) describes and analyzes a proposed action that may have a significant effect on the environment.
10. The NYS Department of Environmental Conservation (NYSDEC) oversees many environmental concerns and regulations in New York. The agency regulates the bulk storage of chemicals and petroleum both aboveground and underground. These tanks must be monitored for leakage.
11. Electromagnetic fields are present where there are power lines. New York has adopted a prudent avoidance policy.

Useful Links

EPA radon prevention in construction information

https://www.epa.gov/radon/radon-resistant-new-construction-home-buyers

NYS Department of Environmental Conservation

www.dec.ny.gov

Valuation Process and Pricing Properties

Key Terms

Appraisal An unbiased estimate of the nature, quality, value, or utility of an interest in or aspect of identified real estate and related personality, based on factual data; it is an opinion of the market value of a property, as of a given date, supported in writing with collected data and logical reasoning

Comparative market analysis (CMA) An analysis of the competition that a property offered for sale will face in the marketplace; not an appraisal

Cost The total expenditure for labor, materials, legal services, architectural design, financing, taxes during construction, interest, contractor's overhead and profit, and entrepreneurial overhead and profit

Cost approach Appraisal method for evaluating properties that have few, if any, comparables and are not income producing

Depreciation Loss in value from any cause

Direct costs Also called hard costs, they include the cost of labor and materials

Evaluation The study of the nature, quality, or utility of certain property interests in which a value estimate is not necessarily required; examples are studies of land utilization, highest and best use, marketability, feasibility, and supply and demand

External obsolescence Changes in surrounding land use patterns resulting in increased traffic, air pollution, and other hazards and nuisances

Functional obsolescence Flawed or faulty property rendered inferior because of advances and change in such items as wiring, equipment, or design

Highest and best use The use of land that will preserve its usefulness, provide the greatest income, and result in the highest land value

Income approach Appraisal method used to estimate the present value of properties that produce income

Indirect costs The costs that create and support the project include architectural and engineering fees, professional fees such as surveyors, attorneys, and appraisers, financing costs, administrative costs, filing fees, and other costs

Insured value The cost of replacing or reproducing a structure in the event of a total loss due to an insured hazard

Investment value Value based on the amount of financial return that a property would produce

Market value The most probable price, as of a specific date, in cash (or in terms equivalent to cash or in other precisely revealed terms), at which the specified property rights should sell after reasonable exposure in a competitive market, under all conditions requisite to a fair sale, with the buyer and seller each acting prudently, knowledgeably, and for self-interest, and assuming that neither is under duress

Mortgage value Value based on what a lender believes the property will bring at a foreclosure sale or subsequent resale

Paired sales analysis An appraisal technique that finds the value of one attribute; the appraiser locates two sales where the only difference is the attribute being appraised; the difference in value is the attribute's value

Plottage Small plots of land are combined to form a larger plot

Price The amount a purchaser agrees to pay and a seller agrees to accept under the circumstances surrounding the transaction

Residential market analysis A careful study of the individual property being listed as it stands on its own and in light of current market conditions

Sales comparison approach Primary appraisal method for estimating the value of single-family, owner-occupied dwellings and vacant land

Valuation Establishes an opinion of value utilizing an objective approach; it is the process of estimating the value of an identified interest in a specific property as of a given date

Value in use Property considered more for its value to the owner and not for its value if placed on the market

Key Points

1. An appraisal is an estimate of value based on factual data as of a specific date for a particular purpose on a specified property.
2. Valuation is the process of estimating the value of an identified interest in a specific property as of a given date. Besides market value, other types of value include value in use, insurance value, investment value, assessed value, and mortgage loan value.

3. Market value is the amount of money a typical buyer will give in exchange for a property.
4. Evaluation, as compared with valuation, is a study of the quality or utility of a property without reference to a specific estimate of value.
5. Various evaluation studies include marketability, feasibility, supply and demand, land utilization, and highest and best use. In the context of market value, highest and best use is the most probable use. It may or may not be the present use of the property.
6. Price is the amount a purchaser agrees to pay and a seller agrees to accept under the circumstances surrounding the transaction.
7. Cost is composed of a number of factors that equal the total dollar expenditure to construct the improvements. Included are direct costs, such as labor and materials, and indirect costs, such as professional fees, filing fees, and other items in the construction process.
8. A comparative market analysis (CMA) is an analysis of the competition in the marketplace that a property encounters upon sale attempts.
9. A residential market analysis consists of a study of recently sold properties, currently competing properties, recently expired properties, buyer appeal, market position, assets and drawbacks, area market conditions, recommended terms, and price range.
10. The degree of competence, diligence, documentation, and effective communication skills by the licensee is integral to effective marketing.
11. Highest and best use refers to the use of land aimed at preserving its usefulness, providing the greatest income, and resulting in the highest land value. To achieve the highest and best use, land is improved through the use of capital and labor to make the land productive.
12. A first step in site valuation is to conduct a feasibility study. Factors reviewed are site development costs (including environmental factors), financing costs (including prevailing interest rates), tax considerations, rates of return on similar types of investments, and the benefit to and acceptance by the community.
13. A site is generally valued using the sales comparison approach.
14. Appraisals commonly use three approaches to value: the sales comparison, cost, and income approaches. The sales comparison approach most closely resembles the comparative market analysis.
15. Part of the listing process involves recommending to the owner a market price that will be the listing price.
16. A comparison of the property with similar properties that have sold recently (within the last six months), other currently listed properties, and evaluation of expired listings determines the price.

Human Rights and Fair Housing/Advanced Fair Housing and Fair Lending

Key Terms

Americans with Disabilities Act (1992) Protects the rights of individuals with disabilities with regard to access to commercial facilities, public accommodations, and new housing developments with at least four units

Blockbusting Occurs when real estate salespersons induce owners to list property for sale or rent by telling them that persons of a particular race, color, national origin, sex, religion, disability, or familial status are moving into the area; also when real estate firms sell a home in a neighborhood to a person from one of the protected classes with the sole intent to cause property owners to panic and place their property for sale at reduced prices

Cease and desist zone Established by the NYSDOS after determining that some homeowners within certain geographic areas have been subject to intense and repeated solicitation by real estate agents; upon establishment of a cease and desist zone, homeowners in the zone may be placed on a list indicating that they do not desire to sell, lease, or list their residential property or be solicited by real estate agents

Civil Rights Act of 1866 The first significant statute affecting equal housing opportunity; it is interpreted to prohibit all racial discrimination

Community Reinvestment Act (CRA; 1977, last updated 2005) Called the Fair Lending Law, the law encourages lenders to help meet the credit needs of communities where they are located, including low- and moderate-income neighborhoods

Department of Housing and Urban Development (HUD) A federal regulatory agency through which civil rights violations can be reported

Disability Legally defined as a physical or mental impairment that greatly limits one or more of a person's major life activities

Disparate Impact A legal doctrine under the Fair Housing Act that states that a policy may be considered discriminatory if it has a disproportionate "adverse impact" against any group based on race, national origin, color, religion, sex, familial status, or disability when there is no legitimate, non-discriminatory reason

Equal Credit Opportunity Act (ECOA; 1974) A federal law that prohibits discrimination based on race, color, religion, national origin, sex, marital status, age, source of income, or whether a person exercises rights granted under the Consumer Credit Protection Act for any credit transaction

Fair Housing Amendments Act of 1988 Prohibits discrimination based on mental or physical handicap or familial status

Familial status Legally defined as an adult with children under 18, a person who is pregnant, or one who has legal custody of a child or who is in the process of obtaining custody

Federal Fair Housing Act (Title VIII of the Civil Rights Act of 1968) Prohibits discrimination in housing on the basis of race, color, religion, or national origin

Filtering down Properties in neighborhoods that were once middle or upper income decline in value, allowing people with lower incomes to purchase them

Gentrification A process of renovation and revival of deteriorated urban neighborhoods by the influx of more affluent residents; the result is increased property values but very often displacement of lower-income families and small businesses

Housing and Community Development Act of 1974 Federal law prohibiting discrimination based on gender

HUD Equal Housing Opportunity poster An official poster required by an amendment to the Fair Housing Act of 1968 required to be prominently displayed in real estate brokerage offices

Human Rights Law Known as Article 15 of the NYS Executive Law; prohibits discrimination in the rental and leasing of housing, land, commercial space, and other non-real-estate-related activities

Institutionalized discrimination Refers to the unjust and discriminatory mistreatment of an individual or group of individuals by society and its institutions as a whole, through unequal selection or bias, intentional or unintentional; as opposed to individuals making a conscious choice to discriminate

Jones v. Alfred H. Mayer Co. The U.S. Supreme Court applied the older Civil Rights Act of 1866 to prohibit any racially based discrimination in housing. This court ruling is important because the Federal Fair Housing Act provides exemptions under certain circumstances. Because of the court's determination in *Jones v. Mayer*, exemptions in the Fair Housing Act cannot be used to allow racial discrimination under any circumstances

Marital status Protected class under federal and NYS human rights laws that protects individuals who are either married or single

Multiple dwellings Residences that contain three or more family units

Nonsolicitation order An order from the NYSDOS prohibiting licensees from soliciting listings for the sale or purchase of real property in certain areas of the state

Redlining Term applied to lending institutions refusing to make loans to purchase, construct, or repair dwellings by discriminating on the basis of race, color, religion, sex, national origin, handicap, or familial status

Steering Illegal practice of directing prospective minority purchasers to presently integrated areas to avoid integration of nonintegrated areas

Testers Volunteers or employees of federal and state agencies as well as private civil rights groups who visit real estate offices posing as prospective home seekers to see if race influences the information or services provided

Key Points

1. The Civil Rights Act of 1968, known as the Fair Housing Act, prohibits discrimination in housing because of race, color, religion, sex, national origin, age, handicap, or familial status.
2. Discrimination is prohibited in the (a) sale or rental of housing, (b) advertising of the sale or rental of housing, (c) financing of housing, and (d) provision of real estate brokerage services. The act forbids blockbusting.
3. The Federal Fair Housing Act has certain exemptions, but New York laws that are more restrictive preempt these exemptions.
4. The Civil Rights Act of 1968 prohibited discrimination in any housing program receiving federal money but did not cover privately financed housing.
5. The Civil Rights Act of 1866 prohibits discrimination based only on race. The prohibition is not limited to housing but includes real estate transactions. The act may be enforced only by civil suit in federal court. This law has no exemptions.
6. Supreme Court decisions—such as *Plessy v. Ferguson* (1896), separate but equal; *Buchanan v. Warley* (1917), disallowing block-by-block segregation; and *Brown v. Board of Education* (1954), separate but unequal—shaped much of U.S. policy.
7. Enforcement of Title VIII of the 1968 Civil Rights Act was amended in 1988. Enforcement procedures include (a) administrative procedure through the Office of Equal Opportunity of HUD that attempts voluntary conciliation first and then possible referral to an administrative law judge, who can impose financial penalties; (b) civil suit in federal court; and (c) action by the U.S. attorney general, who may file a suit in federal court.
8. The Americans with Disabilities Act provides that individuals with disabilities cannot be denied access to public transportation or any commercial facility or public accommodation. Barriers in existing buildings must be removed if readily achievable. New buildings must be readily accessible and usable by individuals with disabilities.
9. Article 15 of the Executive Law, called the Human Rights Law, governs human rights law in New York. This law adds other protected classes not included in federal law related to housing discrimination—marital status, age, sexual orientation, gender identity, and military status. Same sex marriage falls under the protected class of sexual orientation. The New York law also covers the lease and sale of commercial space and land as well as residential housing.
10. The human rights agency in New York is the Division of Human Rights (DHR). Complaints must be filed with the DHR within one year of an alleged discriminatory act.
11. The New York City Commission on Human Rights is the enforcement agency for antidiscrimination policy in the five boroughs that comprise NYC. NYC law includes other protected classes related to housing discrimination to those covered by New York law: citizenship or alienage, lawful occupation, partnership status, lawful source of income, and victims of domestic violence, stalking, and sexual offenses.

12. The NYS Secretary of State can establish a cease and desist zone if some homeowners within a certain geographic area are subject to intense and repeated solicitation by real estate agents. Upon establishment of the cease and desist zone, homeowners may file a request with the DOS to be placed on a cease and desist list. To protect consumers from unsolicited calls from service providers and others, consumers may place themselves on a Do-Not-Call list registry maintained by the Federal Trade Commission. Consumers are also protected by the CAN SPAM laws that protect consumers from receiving unwanted commercial emails.

Useful Links

National Association of REALTORS® (NAR)

www.realtor.org

Department of Housing and Urban Development (HUD)

www.hud.gov

HUD New York

https://www.hud.gov/states/new_york

NYS Division of Human Rights

https://dhr.ny.gov

New York City Commission on Human Rights

www.nyc.gov/cchr

Fair Housing Guide

https://dhr.ny.gov/sites/default/files/pdf/nysdhr-fair-housing-guide.pdf

Real Estate Mathematics

Key Terms

Acre 43,560 square feet

Commission A percentage of the sales price

Front foot A linear foot of property frontage on a street or highway

Gross income Income received without subtracting expenses

Income The amount of money one receives

Interest Calculated by multiplying the rate as a percentage times the principal balance

Net operating income Gross income less operating expenses

Point Fee charged by a lender equal to 1% of the loan amount

Rate A percentage

Tax rate Determined by the amount of the tax levy and expressed either in dollars per $100 of assessed value or in mills (one mill is one-tenth of a cent) per $1,000 of assessed value

Value The total amount of worth or cost of the unit

Key Points

1. In the real estate business, many calculations including the broker's commission involve percentages which is a number divided by 100.
2. An increase in property value is called appreciation; a decrease in value is known as depreciation.
3. An acre is 43,560 square feet.
4. A hectare is equal to 2.47 acres.
5. The perimeter is the entire outer boundary of a figure such as a plot of land or the measure around a figure, such as a house or building.
6. Many mortgages are paid through a type of installment plan each month known as amortization.
7. Prorations at closing involve the division between the seller and the buyer of annual real property taxes, rents, homeowners association dues, and other items that may have been paid or must be paid.
8. Profit or loss is always based upon the amount of money invested in the property.
9. The capitalization rate is the percentage of the investment the owner will receive back each year from the net income from the property. The rate is based upon the dollar invested and the annual net income from the property.
10. Real estate agents should know basic math formulas and area calculations: see Table 10 *Formulas* and *Area Calculations* under the section *Quick View Tables* in this *Cram.*

Municipal Agencies

Key Terms

Architectural review board Composed mostly of people with expertise in art, architecture, and planning; oversees building design

Building department Enforces the building code; protects the public by ensuring that code restrictions are followed

Conservation Advisory Council Advises in the development, management, and protection of the municipality's natural resources

County health department Cooperates with the NYS Department of Health; these local agencies may have laws that are more restrictive than state law

Historic preservation/landmark commission Identifies and protects historic landmarks

Planning board On all government levels, makes plans for the region; considers the available natural and supplied resources of the community

Receiver of taxes The collecting officer for each city and town who receives real property taxes and assessments during a specified collection period

Tax assessor An elected or appointed local official or officials who have the legal authority to independently estimate the value of real property in an assessing unit

Village board of trustees The governing body of villages

Key Points

1. Sources of information regarding the agencies within a municipality include the city charter and town or village ordinance; the county, city, town, and village handbooks; information officers; and websites.
2. A legislative body creates an administrative government agency. These agencies are empowered by the state legislature and by the legislative bodies of cities, counties, towns, and villages.
3. The legislative power of a city is vested in its city council or common council. The town council or board is the governing body of towns. The village board of trustees is the governing body of villages. All members of these government bodies are elected.
4. The factors that contribute to the viability of a market area include supply and demand, employment, growth initiatives, municipal services, infrastructure, and property taxes.
5. To assert influence and communicate their views, community residents can have input through various venues including the local planning board, a legislative body such as a town or village board, zoning boards of appeal, school boards, the assessor's office, property tax grievance procedures and appeals, community organizations and committees, and community action groups.
6. Planning boards on all government levels plan for the region's future, considering the communities' available natural and supplied resources. Planning boards work with the master plan of the municipality or region.
7. The zoning board of appeals (ZBA) decides on granting variances for the municipality. The ZBA is an interpreter of the zoning ordinance.
8. The local legislative body of any city, town, or village can appoint a conservation advisory council to advise in the development, management, and protection of its natural resources. The council can conduct research regarding environment projects.

9. All properties are assessed at a uniform percentage of value. The tax assessor maintains tax maps and tax records for the municipality.
10. The city or town engineer estimates the costs of paving, sewers, and sidewalks, as well as other public works projects. The engineer supervises street development and other public works activities.
11. County departments of health oversee drinking water safety, including standards for private and community well construction and well water safety and regulation, septic system approval, and certain wastewater treatment approval.

Property Insurance

Key Terms

Actual cash value (ACV) A type of insurance in which the insured is reimbursed for the replacement cost minus the physical depreciation of the lost or damaged property

Deductible The amount the insured must pay toward a claim before receiving any policy benefits

Liability insurance Insurance coverage to protect against claims alleging that one's negligence or inappropriate action resulted in bodily injury or property damage

Package policy A policy that includes several different types of coverage, such as property insurance and liability insurance

Property insurance Protects a home or income/business property against any physical damage or loss of assets in the case of fire, theft, or vandalism

Replacement cost A type of insurance in which the insured is covered and reimbursed for the actual cost of replacing the damaged property

Umbrella policy An excess liability policy that provides additional coverage above that offered by primary policies

Key Points

1. Property insurance protects a home, a business, or income property against any physical damage or loss of assets in the case of fire, theft, or vandalism. The typical homeowner's policy has two main sections: Section I covers the property of the insured; Section II provides personal liability coverage to the insured.
2. Generally, if the insured purchases coverage on a replacement cost basis and insures the home for at least 80% of its replacement cost, the insurance is automatically issued on a replacement cost basis.

3. The New York Property Insurance Underwriting Association (NYPIUA) is a pool of all insurance companies writing fire insurance in New York. It offers fire and extended coverage as well as coverage for vandalism, malicious mischief, and sprinkler leakage to consumers who are unable to purchase this type of insurance from individual insurance companies.
4. The Federal Emergency Management Association (FEMA) administers the National Flood Insurance Program. Insurance coverage for losses resulting from floods is generally not provided in any homeowner's or tenant's policies.
5. The New York Insurance Law requires that insurers provide proper disclosure to their insureds of any windstorm deductibles attached to their homeowner's policies.
6. Under New York law, an insurance company may cancel a homeowner's or tenant's policy by issuing a cancellation notice during the first 60 days it is in effect, as long as the cancellation notice states the specific reason or reasons for the cancellation.
7. Specific insurance is available for rental/income property. Commercial General Liability (CGL) insurance is a basic business liability policy that covers four forms of injury: bodily injury that results in actual physical damage or loss, property damage that results in actual physical damage or loss, personal injury, and advertising injury.

   Real estate agents should counsel their buyers as to the importance of obtaining property insurance, lender requirements, and the escrow account for property insurance premiums.

Useful Links

NYS Insurance Department

www.dfs.ny.gov/insurance/dfs_insurance.htm

NY Property Insurance Underwriting Association

www.nypiua.com

National Flood Insurance Program

www.fema.gov/national-flood-insurance-program

Taxes and Assessments

Key Terms

Ad valorem Latin for "according to value"; in New York, the real property tax is based on the fair market value of real property

Apportionment Division of property and school tax monies so that school districts, counties, towns, and cities in the different municipalities all pay their fair share of the tax levy

Appropriation Occurs when a government agency sets aside funds for a certain purpose

Approved assessing unit One that has completed a property reevaluation and is certified by the Office of Real Property Tax Services (ORPTS)

Assessed value The value of a property as determined by a tax assessor

Assessing units Counties, cities, towns, villages, school districts, and special districts that raise money through real property taxes

Assessment A percentage of a property's market value; this figure is used for property tax purposes and ultimately determines how the total tax is shared among property owners

Assessment roll Usually in section, block/lot order, it lists all real property in the taxing jurisdiction, with information about each parcel, including its assessed value and exempt status

Board of Assessment Review (BAR) An appointed body consisting of three to five members that hears and decides upon grievances from taxpayers

Equalization rate Represents the average percentage of market value at which a municipality's assessment is set

Exemptions Full exemptions or partial reductions in property taxes available to certain people, institutions, and organizations, such as veterans, seniors, and those with disabilities

Grievance A written complaint filed with the local board of assessment review protesting a property tax assessment

Homestead Properties that are completely or partially used as the owner's residence and are classified as such for tax purposes

Non-homestead All properties not classified as homesteads; includes commercial, industrial, special franchise, utility properties, and some vacant land

Residential assessment ratios (RARs) An indication of the level of assessment for residential real property in a municipality; a measurement of the overall ratio of the total assessed value of residential property in the municipality compared to the full market value of that residential property

Special assessment A tax levied by the taxing unit to collect payment for a share of the cost of improvements made to areas nearby or adjoining the property; constitutes a specific lien against the property until paid

Special assessment districts Localities that raise money through real property taxes

Tax certiorari proceeding A New York Supreme Court review of cases requested by taxpayers who protest their assessment and are still dissatisfied with the decision of the board of assessment review

Tax exemptions Full or partial exclusions from tax obligations granted to certain groups by taxing authorities

Tax levy The amount that a municipality must raise to meet budgetary requirements by taxing real property

Tax lien An encumbrance against a property filed by the taxing jurisdiction for delinquency in paying real property taxes

Tax rate The amount of money needed by a municipality to meet budgetary requirements divided by the taxable assessed and nonexempt value of all the real property within that jurisdiction

Taxable status date The ownership and physical condition of real property are assessed according to price fixed as of the valuation date; all applications must be filed with the assessor by this date

Uniform percentage Each assessing unit sets the percentage of market value to be used as the assessment standard and must apply this percentage uniformly to all properties within its boundaries

Key Points

1. The Office of Real Property Tax Services (ORPTS) is a division within the NYS Department of Taxation and Finance and oversees local property tax administration.
2. In New York, property is taxed on an *ad valorem* basis—that is, according to the market value of the property.
3. A tax bill is determined by a formula that includes two items: the property's assessment and the tax rate of the taxing jurisdiction.
4. A property's assessment is a percentage of its market value; in most areas outside of New York City and Nassau County, the assessment must be a uniform percentage of the property's market value throughout the taxing jurisdiction.
5. All property is subject to assessment; however, not all property is taxed. Property tax exemptions may be full or partial.
6. An approved assessing unit is a taxing jurisdiction that has completed a property reevaluation and is certified by the Office of Real Property Tax Services.
7. The assessment roll that describes all properties and their assessed value is published each year. Taxpayers who disagree with their assessment may file a complaint, which is called a grievance.
8. If taxpayers are still dissatisfied with the decision of the board of assessment review, they may file a complaint with the New York Supreme Court, called a tax certiorari proceeding, or be heard by specially appointed small claims hearing officers.
9. The tax rate must be sufficient to provide the amount of revenue to accomplish the budgetary requirements of the local governmental unit.
10. The equalization rate represents the average percentage of market value at which assessments in a municipality are set at a given point in time.

11. In order to encourage economic development, industrial or commercial properties are sometimes temporarily exempted from property taxes. To take advantage of the tax exemption offered to Industrial Development Agencies (IDAs) by local governments, title to an economic development project such as a building or business location is often transferred from the private owner to the IDA for the duration of the project. In these cases, the exemption may be offset by payments in lieu of taxes (PILOTs) made by the original private owner. At the end of the project, title reverts to the original owner, who then pays taxes in a normal manner on the property.
12. If a property owner is delinquent in paying property taxes, his taxing jurisdiction may impose a lien against the property.

Useful Links

NYS Department of Taxation and Finance–Property Taxes and Assessments

www.tax.ny.gov/pit/property/default.htm

The NYC Tax Commission

http://www1.nyc.gov/site/taxcommission/index.page

Nassau County Department of Assessment

www.nassaucountyny.gov/1501/Assessment

Nassau County Assessment Review Commission

www.nassaucountyny.gov/1510/Assessment-Review-Commission

Condominiums and Cooperatives

Key Terms

Alteration agreement Describes the terms under which the cooperative gives permission to a shareholder before making any changes or improvements to the unit the shareholder occupies

Board package Documents of a proposed purchaser reviewed by a cooperative board

By-laws The shareholder's rights and obligations for a condominium

Common elements Areas and utilities in a condominium or cooperative building shared by owners

Condominium A form of ownership of real property that consists of individual ownership of some aspects and co-ownership in other aspects of the property

Condop A building that includes condominium and cooperative ownership in the same structure; the creation of a condop allows property owners to collect a sizable portion of rent from a nonshareholder building tenant and not violate the IRS 80-20 rule

Conversion A change of the ownership structure of a building to a condominium or cooperative

Cooperative A form of ownership in which stockholders in a corporation occupy property owned by the corporation under a lease

Covenants, conditions, and restrictions (CCRs) In a condominium, the document that sets forth all of the rights, duties, and obligations of the unit owners

Declaration A master deed containing the following: a legal description of the condominium facility; a plat of the property, plans, and specifications for the building and units; a description of the common areas; and the degree of ownership in the common areas available to each owner

Flip tax Sometimes imposed by the board of directors of a cooperative, this is a revenue-producing device for the cooperative corporation; usually paid by the seller at closing

Flipping Investors buying a property at a certain price and then immediately selling the property at a higher price

House rules Rules in a cooperative that cover issues such as garbage disposal, maintenance, noise, and conflict resolution; generally more detailed than items in the proprietary lease, addressing behavior of the tenants and general operations

Letter of intent An agreement to purchase a condominium; may or may not be binding

Maintenance Monthly payment by shareholder to the cooperative corporation

Offering plan or statement The document filed with the New York attorney general detailing the setup and rules for a condominium or cooperative

Proprietary lease A lease for a cooperative apartment

Recognition agreement Describes the relationship between the cooperative and other entities

Share loan A type of loan in which stock is the collateral; used for cooperative purchases

Sponsor The developer of a condominium or cooperative

Key Points

1. The main difference between cooperatives and condominiums is the form of ownership. With a cooperative, a cooperative corporation usually owns the land, buildings, and property rights and all interests in the corporation.
2. The purchaser of a cooperative becomes a shareholder of the corporation and a tenant in the building. The tenant-shareholder has the right of occupancy. A cooperative purchaser does not obtain a deed but instead receives a proprietary lease issued by the cooperative corporation.

3. A financial statement of a condo or co-op development should include a balance sheet describing assets and liabilities, an income and expense statement, and a cash flow statement. For a cooperative, the status of the underlying mortgage is very important.
4. Cooperative ownership documents typically include the articles of incorporation, by-laws, proprietary lease or occupancy agreement, subscription agreement, and house rules.
5. The developer that constructs or converts a building into a cooperative or condominium must file a declaration and disclosure statement with the New York attorney general's office.
6. The co-op members develop house rules for the operation of the cooperative.
7. Two processes can be used by a cooperative to approve a purchaser: (1) acceptance of the purchaser's package by the board of directors and (2) a private interview between the prospective purchasers and the board of directors.
8. To keep subletting from overtaking the building, most cooperatives that allow subletting limit the time frame of the sublet.
9. The rules for the CPS1 statement apply to cooperatives, condominiums, and properties offered by homeowners associations. It sets out the New York attorney general's rules governing how a developer may test the market for a new development before filing the offering plan and before construction is completed. The CPS1 statement includes rules on how the development may be advertised. All advertising must be approved by the attorney general and, during the CPS1 period or phase, the developer cannot declare a firm price.
10. To create a condominium, the owner/developer of the property (the sponsor, or declarant) records a condominium declaration. The declaration includes certain provisions required by statute. The sponsor records the declaration with the county clerk and the offering plan with the New York attorney general.
11. The shareholder's rights and obligations are in the condominium's by-laws. A board of managers (or directors) oversees the finances and decision-making policy regarding the property.
12. The sponsor is the owner or developer of the condominium. He or she appoints the board of directors and the managing agent. There is an inherent limitation on sponsor control of the board of directors.
13. A letter of intent is an agreement to purchase a condominium. The letter is a written offer to reserve a specific unit that may be under construction. Certain sections of the letter may be nonbinding, such as the unit's final price.
14. A lender normally requires at least a temporary CO (TCO) before it will close the loan. If a TCO expires and is not renewed, a new buyer may find it difficult or impossible to renew homeowners' insurance policies or sell or refinance the unit.
15. Flipping may be a problem because it can drive up prices. The investor attempts to buy low and sell high. It can cause major losses for people who buy the flipped property from the investor and end up paying more than if they had bought it from the developer.
16. The title company completes a title search before purchase. The search reveals any defects in the title of the unit along with any problems or liens against the condominium building or the complex.

17. Condominium contracts are similar to other fee simple interest real estate contracts. However, they may contain a right of first refusal clause for the board of managers of a condominium association.
18. Closing costs for the seller include the NYC Real Property Transfer Tax (if applicable) and NYS Real Property Transfer Tax, broker's commission, managing agent's fees, UCC-3 filing fee, and attorney's fees. The cooperative corporation may charge a flip tax and a stock transfer fee. Closing costs for the buyer include the UCC-1 filing fee, mortgage recording tax, title search and title policy, managing agent's fees, credit report fees, attorney's fees, and Mansion Tax (if applicable).

Commercial and Investment Properties/ Real Property Investment

Key Terms

After-tax cash flow The profit from income-producing property, less income taxes, if any, attributable to the property's income

Anchor tenant A well-known commercial retail business, such as a national chain store or regional department store, placed in a shopping center to generate the most customers for all stores in the shopping center

Before tax cash flow Income measured before income taxes are considered

Capitalization rate The annual return that an investor expects to receive; the primary method to estimate the present value of income-producing properties

Cash break even ratio Evaluates the financial performance of an income property to determine the rate of occupancy needed to meet operating expenses and mortgage payments

Cash flow The net proceeds after all expenses are met; may be measured before or after taxes are considered

Cash-on-cash return *See* Equity dividend rate

Common areas Includes the lobby, elevators, corridors, restrooms, and utility closets; tenants may pay a pro rata share for the common areas in addition to their own space

Debt service Mortgage principal and interest payments

Debt service coverage ratio A measure of the cash flow available to pay current debt obligations

Effective gross income Total potential income, less deductions for vacancy and credit losses, plus other income

Equity dividend rate The portion of net operating income that remains after total mortgage debt service is paid but before ordinary income tax on operations is deducted

Feasibility study A detailed economic analysis that considers the cost of site development, construction, financing, tax considerations, rates of return on similar investments, and the benefit to the community

Gross income Income received without subtracting expenses

Gross income multiplier (GIM)/Potential gross income multiplier (PGIM) Found by dividing the property's value by the total income from the property; it is a ratio of the property's value to gross income

Gross rent multiplier (GRM) Found by dividing the asking price of a property by the property's gross rents; used to compare value estimates of other properties by multiplying the GRM of each property by the gross rents to find an estimated price/value for the property

Joint venture An organization formed by two or more parties for the purpose of investing in real estate or other assets

Lease escalation clauses Increased costs to the tenant for different reasons at specified times during the lease term

Leasehold mortgage An instrument that pledges a leasehold estate rather than a freehold estate to secure payment of a note; leaseholds acceptable to lenders are usually long-term estates for years

Leverage The use of borrowed funds in addition to an investor's own funds; allows the investor to accumulate the maximum amount of real estate with the minimum amount of personal funds

Net operating income Gross operating income minus operating expenses and debt service (cash flow)

Net income multiplier (NIM) Used to estimate the market value of income producing properties; equal to the market value of a property divided by the net operating income

Operating expense ratio A measure of costs to operate a piece of property compared to the income that the property brings in; calculated by dividing a property's operating expense by its gross operating income

Operating statement A report of rental property receipts and disbursements, resulting in net income

Overall cap rate (OAR) Also referred to as the going-in capitalization rate; the first year's net operating income divided by the acquisition cost of the property

Participation mortgage A mortgage in which two or more lenders participate in making the loan or one in which the lender participates in the profits generated by a commercial property that secures the mortgage loan

Porter's wage escalation formula Provides that the rent will increase a specific amount per square foot for a specified increase in the porter's hourly wage

Pro-forma schedule An operating statement that reflects a property's income and expenses based upon the investor's expectations about the real estate market

Rate of return Percentage of income that the investor gets back on an investment

Rentable square footage Equals the entire space including the usable square footage and the tenant's pro rata share of the building common areas, such as the lobby, hallways, and restrooms

Sensitivity analysis A study of how a change in one factor can affect a property's income

Short sale A transaction in which the sale proceeds fall short of the balance owed on the property; used when a borrower cannot pay back the mortgage and the lender decides that selling the property at a loss is better than going after the borrower for the full indebtedness

Tax shelter A method of protecting income from taxation; for example, by accelerating allowable depreciation

Time value of money The principle that the passage of time affects the value of a given sum by earning interest and by being eroded by inflation; an investor must consider whether his investment funds will bring the greatest return on dollars invested for a given period

Usable square footage The area contained within the space that the tenant occupies

Key Points

1. Types of investment property include unimproved land, residential buildings, multi-use buildings, retail centers, and offices.
2. The primary purpose of the investor is to generate income (cash flow) without higher than expected risk.
3. A property profile includes the analysis of risk and return, special risks, timing, pricing, rate of return, portfolio development and securitization, sensitivity analysis, and special financing.
4. The rate of return, or percentage of income per dollar amount invested, that the investor receives back on an investment includes a risk factor. The greater the risk of loss, the greater the potential rate of return the investor can expect.
5. An operating statement for a property includes the income and expenses for a property. The costs of business or investment property are tax deductible.
6. The net operating income is the result of deducting operating expenses from gross income.
7. A ground lease is a long-term lease on unimproved land. It is generally for construction purposes.
8. Cash flow, or income received, is the most important consideration in evaluating an investment. The investor evaluates cash flow before and after taxes.
9. There are two types of income to consider: cash flow during the holding period of the investment and cash generated when the property is sold at the end of the holding period.
10. Cash-on-cash return is a value measurement for a property that considers the equity in the property measured against the cash flow. The method looks at the amount of cash required to purchase the equity interest in a property—the difference between the sales price and the mortgage loan. It also measures the cash flow.
11. A capitalization rate is the annual return that an investor expects to receive. The capitalization rate is used in the appraisal income approach. It is the primary method used to estimate the present value

of income-producing properties. The capitalization formula is Value × Capitalization rate = Annual net income.

12. The rentable square footage of most commercial space includes square footage that cannot be used or is sometimes unseen but that the tenant pays rent for anyway. Rentable square footage includes the usable square footage plus the tenant's pro rata share of the building common areas, such as the lobby, hallways, and restrooms.
13. Tenant costs may include common area maintenance (CAM) costs for areas such as the lobby, elevators, corridors, restrooms, and utility closets.
14. A business client is generally committed to a longer lease term and a more expensive lease. Unlike residential leases, there is no standard commercial lease agreement. Each lease conforms to the particular space and tenant.
15. Generally, there are four types of leases for commercial space: gross lease, net lease, percentage lease, and operating stop or expense stop lease. A percentage lease has a base rent plus an additional monthly rent that is a percentage of the lessee's gross monthly sales.
16. Leases based on arrangement for payment are the gross lease and the net lease. Under a gross lease, the landlord pays the real property taxes, insurance, and costs for maintaining the property. Under a net lease, the tenant pays some or all of these expenses. A lessee who contracts for a triple net lease pays all expenses associated with the property in addition to the rent, except for the debt service.
17. Lease clauses include use clauses; subordination, nondisturbance, and attornment clauses; estoppel certificates; sublease/assignment clauses; and electric service clauses.
18. Lease escalation clauses call for increased costs to the tenant for different reasons at specified times during the lease term. These clauses protect the property owner against increases in operating costs.
19. Lease escalation clauses include definitions for proportionate share of occupancy and base year, operating stop and tax stop clauses, real property tax clauses, direct operating costs, the porter's wage escalation formula, and fixed percentage increases.
20. Properties can be purchased below market value through foreclosure, other bank-owned property, government-owned property, or a short sale. These types of purchases offer the real estate investor opportunities to acquire properties at substantial discounts.

Useful Links

Government owned properties for sale

www.hudhomesusa.org

Income Tax Issues in Real Estate Transactions

Key Terms

Active income Salaries or income from a business in which the taxpayer materially participates

Adjusted basis Consists of the price paid for the property and includes expenses incurred during acquisition and the cost of any capital improvements (less depreciation, if applicable); used to determine the amount of gain or loss realized by an owner upon sale of the property

Appreciation An increase in value

Basis Usually the cost of a property

Boot Cash received in a tax-deferred exchange

Capital gain The profit realized from the sale of real property or other investment asset

Capital loss Occurs when an investment property or other type of investment is sold

Cost recovery A type of income tax deduction available for real estate and personal taxes

Deductible expenses Cost of operating a property used in business or held as an investment; these expenses are subtracted from gross income to arrive at net income

Depreciated value The basis of a depreciable asset, used to compute the taxable gain from its sale; the basis is acquisition cost, plus capital improvements, less accrued depreciation

Economic depreciation Loss of value from physical deterioration of property caused by normal use, failure to maintain the property adequately, and natural and other hazards

Passive activity A trade or business in which the taxpayer invests but does not materially participate; income from funds invested in passive activities such as rentals and limited partnerships

Portfolio income Interest, annuities, dividends, royalties, and profits from the sale of portfolio assets

Recaptured depreciation When a property owner disposes of the property, a tax on the income or gain realized because of the allowed depreciation is recaptured as ordinary income up to the amount of the depreciation; recapture means to be included as taxable income; real estate sold is recaptured at a 25% rate

Straight-line depreciation A type of income tax depreciation that allows investment property to be deducted in installments over a number of years; the building and improvements are depreciable over 27.5 years for income-producing residential property; 39 years for nonresidential property

Tax basis Consists of the price paid for the property, plus expenses incurred in acquiring the property (other than those incurred in arranging financing), plus the costs of any capital improvements

Tax depreciation A deduction from a property's income when determining taxable income

Tax-deferred exchange Trading of like-kind properties held as an investment or for business use

Tax shelter A legal method of minimizing or decreasing an investor's taxable income and, therefore, the investor's liability

Key Points

1. The first important reform to the tax code in 31 years is the federal Tax Cuts and Jobs Act (TCJA) of 2017, which is in effect from January 1, 2018 to December 31, 2025. This law has brought significant changes and amendments to the tax code.
2. There are seven tax brackets for federal income tax: 10%, 12%, 22%, 24%, 32%, 35%, and 37%.
3. The mortgage interest deduction on real property, including a personal residence and a second home, is limited to the first $750,000 of the loan.
4. Interest on home equity loans (HELOCs) is not tax deductible, however interest on HELOCs or second mortgages are deductible if the proceeds are used to buy, build, or substantially improve the residence. Mortgage loans of up to $1 million made before the new tax law came about are not limited to the $750,000 amount.
5. Homeowners may refinance mortgage debts existing on 12/14/17, up to $1 million, and still deduct the interest, as long as the new loan does not exceed the amount of the mortgage being refinanced.
6. Taxpayers can deduct up to $10,000 in state and local taxes. However, they must choose between property taxes and income or sales taxes.
7. Under the federal TCJA, there is a cap on the deductibility of state and local income from the federal income taxes. Because of this issue for New Yorkers, the NYS budget for the 2018–2019 fiscal year provides for an optional *employer-side* payroll tax to replace an *employee-side* state income tax. The payroll tax is a deductible business expense by the employer. It is not taxable income for the employee because it is not the employee's income. If the employer lowers the employee's salary by the amount that he/she pays in payroll tax for the employee, although the employee's salary is reduced, he/she would pay no NYS income tax because the employer would pay the amount in payroll tax. The NYS budget also allows for localities to establish charities to funnel property tax payments to education and health care programs, allowing such payments to be deductible on resident's federal tax returns.
8. The long-term capital gains tax—gains on capital assets held for longer than 12 months—are computed according to the taxpayer's income. Filing singly, the capital gains tax rate is 0% for a gain on an investment up to $38,600 and the gain is treated as ordinary income on the taxpayer's income tax return. If the gain is from $38,600 to $425,800, the capital gains tax rate is 15%. If the gain is over $425,800, the capital gains tax rate is 20%. There are other income figures for various categories of income tax filings. Short-term capital gains—assets held for less than 12 months—are taxed at the marginal rate for the taxpayer's income.
9. According to tax regulations, single taxpayers may take up to a $250,000 exclusion from taxation on gain in the sale of their homes. Married taxpayers may take up to a $500,000 exclusion.

10. There are three classifications of income: active income earned through salaries or in a business in which the taxpayer actively participates; portfolio income, which includes interest, annuities, dividends, and royalties; and passive activity income, which includes invested funds.
11. To qualify as a tax-deferred 1031 exchange, like-kind real property must be exchanged. The real property exchanged must have been held for use in business (other than inventory) or as an investment. Taxes may not be deferred from the sale of personal property such as furniture and equipment included with the like-kind exchange of real property.
12. Tax losses from investment property are allowed to offset income only from passive activities.
13. Deductible allowances from property income to arrive at taxable income, and tax losses allowed to offset passive and active income, are income shelters for investors.
14. Tax depreciation (cost recovery) is a deductible allowance from net income used to arrive at taxable income. It provides a tax shelter for the property owner.
15. Depreciation enables the owner of a business or an investment property to recover the cost or other basis of the asset. Land is not depreciable—only structures on the land.
16. Under the TCJA, the deduction for business interest expenses is limited to the sum of business interest income plus 30% of adjusted taxable income. Real estate businesses can elect out of the business interest deduction limitation, but at the cost of longer depreciation recovery periods—30 years for residential real property and 40 years for nonresidential real property. If a real estate business does not elect out of the interest deduction limitation, then residential depreciation recovery depreciation stays at 27.5 years and nonresidential real property depreciation recovery stays at 39 years.

Useful Links

NYS Division of Housing and Community Renewal

www.nyshcr.org

Mortgage Brokerage

Key Terms

Mortgage bankers Individuals and entities licensed by the NYS Department of Financial Services to make residential mortgage loans

Mortgage brokers Individuals and entities registered by the NYS Department of Financial Services to solicit, process, place, or negotiate residential mortgage loans for others; applies to one- to four-unit properties; may employ mortgage loan originators

Mortgage Broker Dual Agency Disclosure Form A form under Article 12-D of the New York Banking Law that must be completed when an individual acts as mortgage broker and real estate broker in the same transaction

Mortgage commitment A promise made by a lending institution to make a certain type of mortgage loan

Mortgage loan originators (MLO) Individuals licensed by the NYS Department of Financial Services who, for compensation or gain, accept a residential mortgage loan application or offers or negotiate terms of a residential mortgage loan

Mortgage loan servicers (MLS) Individuals and entities registered by the NYS Department of Financial Services who service residential mortgage loans by receiving any scheduled periodic payments from a borrower for a mortgage

Nonconforming loan A loan that does not meet Federal Reserve Bank criteria for funding, possibly due to the loan amount being a higher dollar amount than the conforming loan limit

Preapplication and fee agreement According to the banking law, a mortgage broker or mortgage banker must provide certain disclosures to each loan applicant, at or before the time of application; includes the fees payable at the time of application, the conditions for refunding the fee, and whether the mortgage broker is using three or fewer lenders; this form complies with the New York Banking Law

Preapproval A step above prequalification; involves verifying a purchaser's credit, down payment, and employment history

Prequalification Not a commitment by the lender; after the loan officer determines that a purchaser prequalifies, he issues a prequalification letter that is used to make an offer on a property and show the seller that the purchaser qualifies to buy the property

Rate lock A mortgage loan cannot be closed without locking in an interest rate

Service release premium A form of compensation that a lender may pay to a broker for delivering a loan; each loan comes with a servicing right to collect the mortgage payments

Underwriting The process in which the lender evaluates all of the borrower's financial data and determines whether the borrower may obtain the loan

Yield spread premium (lender rebate) The rate at which a mortgage broker is compensated for the difference between the interest rate on a par loan and the interest rate on an above-par loan that a mortgage broker can deliver to the lender; expressed in the number of points paid to a mortgage broker

Key Points

1. In New York, a mortgage broker must register with the NYS Department of Financial Services (NYSDFS).

2. A licensed real estate broker may use his broker license as experience for the mortgage broker registration. The real estate broker license must be current. Licensed salespersons must have actively participated in the residential mortgage business for two years.
3. To obtain a mortgage loan originator license, the applicant must complete 20 hours of prescribed education and pass an exam.
4. According to New York banking regulations, when a mortgage broker representing the buyer/borrower is also the real estate broker representing the seller in the same residential real estate transaction, that information must be disclosed at the first substantive contact between the mortgage broker and the purchaser/borrower.
5. A mortgage broker acting as a real estate broker in the same transaction must use both the disclosure form for real estate transactions and the disclosure form for mortgage broker transactions for covered properties.
6. A mortgage banker is an individual or a company licensed by the NYSDFS to engage in the business of making residential mortgage loans. Mortgage bankers, also called mortgage companies, make mortgage loans for housing construction and the purchase of existing housing.
7. The requirements for a mortgage banker license include having a net worth of at least $250,000 and having an existing line of credit of at least $1 million provided by an unaffiliated banking institution, an insurance company, or a similar credit facility approved by the superintendent of banking.
8. The role of the mortgage broker is to find appropriate financing at the most favorable interest rate and terms for a borrower.
9. A mortgage broker may arrange for a prequalification or preapproval letter. He or she suggests the best financing options, coordinates the appraisal, and helps obtain the mortgage commitment.
10. Mortgage brokers analyze and find mortgage products that may be applicable to a certain borrower. These products include amortized mortgages, adjustable rate mortgages, construction loans, and conforming and nonconforming loans.
11. Some mortgage brokers process loans and close loans in their own name. However, at or about the time of settlement, they transfer these loans to lenders that simultaneously advance funds for the loans. This transaction is known in the lending industry as table funding.
12. Mortgage brokers assist with other closing details such as ensuring the loan is available, the certificate of occupancy is issued, and the bank conditions are satisfied.
13. A mortgage broker chooses from a number of available lenders to secure financing for the borrower. For example, when a purchaser obtains a mortgage loan, it may be possible to lock in a certain interest rate. This lock-in can be achieved with traditional lenders as well.
14. The mortgage broker's commission is paid by the borrower or more likely by the lender. The fee increases the loan balance and is paid through a lender rebate (yield spread premium or service release premium). The mortgage broker's fee must be disclosed to the borrower.

Useful Links

NYS Department of Financial Services

www.dfs.ny.gov

Mortgage Broker Application Resources

www.dfs.ny.gov/banking/mortgage_brokers.htm

Mortgage Loan Servicer Application Resources

www.dfs.ny.gov/banking/mortgage_servicers.htm_

Mortgage Loan Originator Application Resources

www.dfs.ny.gov/banking/mbmlo.htm

Mortgage Banker Application Resources

www.dfs.ny.gov/banking/mortgage_bankers.htm

New York Association of Mortgage Brokers

www.nyamb.org

Property Management

Key Terms

Actual eviction The removal of a tenant by the landlord because the tenant breached a condition of a lease or other rental contract

Anchor store A well-known commercial retail business, such as a national chain store or regional department store, placed in a shopping center to generate the most customers for all stores in the shopping center

Asset manager Focuses on maximizing property values for investment purposes

Capital expense Capital expenses are those required to improve or maintain a building

Capital reserve budget A projected budget over the economic life of the improvements of the property set aside to cover variable expenses such as repairs, decorating, remodeling, and capital improvements

Constructive eviction Results from some action or inaction by the landlord that renders the premises unsuitable for the use agreed to in a lease or other rental contract

Corrective maintenance Work performed to fix a nonfunctioning item that the tenant has reported; for example, repair of a leaky faucet

Eviction A landlord's action that interferes with the tenant's use or possession of the property; eviction may be actual or constructive

Fixed expenses Expenditures such as property taxes, license fees, and property insurance; subtracted from effective gross income to determine net operating income

Insurable interest The legitimate financial interest an insured has in a property that provides eligibility for insurance coverage of any type

Management agreement A contract that creates an agency relationship in which the owner is the principal and the property manager is the agent for the purposes specified in the agreement

Management proposal A document that sets forth the duties of the manager if employed by the owner

Modified gross rent Refers to the apportionment of expenses between a landlord and tenant; landlords are responsible for the major expense items, but tenants are responsible for their directly related expenses

Operating budget An annual budget that includes only the items of income and expense expected for week-to-week operation

Planned Unit Development (PUD) A form of cluster zoning providing for both residential and commercial land uses within a zoned area

Portfolio manager Analyzes decisions about investment purchases and mix and decides how to balance the decisions regarding the investment against the risk

Preventative maintenance A periodic check of mechanical equipment on the premises to minimize wear and tear; for example, changing air filters on air conditioners and furnaces

Property management The leasing, marketing, managing, maintenance, and accounting functions necessary to operate a commercial property

Property management report A periodic (usually monthly) accounting of all funds received and disbursed; contains detailed information of all receipts and expenditures for the period covered (plus the year-to-date) and relates each item to the operating budget for the period

Property manager A person who manages properties as an agent of the owner

Public liability insurance Covers the risks an owner assumes when the public enters his premises

Resident manager A person living on the premises who is a paid employee of the owner; a real estate broker, a management firm, or an owner of a building may employ the resident manager

Risk management Embodies the concern for controlling and limiting risk in property ownership

Site manager May also be the resident manager; one who oversees the day-to-day operations of the property or properties

Stabilized budget A forecast of income and expenses reasonably projected over a short term, typically five years

Vacancy rate The percentage of all available units in a rental property, such as an apartment complex, that are vacant or unoccupied at a particular time

Variable expense An expense that is not specifically predictable and is subject to the needs of a property at any given time

Key Points

1. The property manager strives to produce the greatest net return possible for the owner.
2. When an individual is employed by one owner of real property on a salaried basis to perform any of the functions of a real estate salesperson or broker defined in the New York Real Property Law, he does not require a real estate license.
3. If an individual or a company works for more than one owner, the individual or company should have a real estate license. If the individual or company has a broker license, the people working for the company would have salesperson licenses.
4. A building manager may work for a property management firm or have his own company.
5. Real estate asset managers act as the property owner's advisor for the property. They plan and direct the purchase, development, and sale of real estate on behalf of the business and investors. They focus on long-term financial planning rather than on day-to-day property operations.
6. The property manager acts as the owner's agent and fiduciary in managing renting, leasing, and perhaps selling the property.
7. When a property manager enters into a management agreement, a general agency is created. The manager owes a fiduciary (undivided loyalty) to the owner-principal.
8. Risk management describes the concern for controlling and limiting risk in property ownership. A manager's written specifications to competing agents ensure comparable quotes.
9. Property managers formulate the management plan; handle rentals, tenant relations, and employees; oversee the budget; pay bills; and supervise maintenance.
10. The property manager must be skilled in several areas, including accounting, budgeting, construction and building systems, and owner–tenant relations. Real-estate-related knowledge is essential.
11. Property managers should be familiar with the types of leases used for the property being managed whether it be residential, commercial, industrial, medical office buildings, hotels, or other property type. The lease should protect the landlord as well as the tenant.
12. The property manager should be familiar with the local assessment grievance process and applicable building codes for the property.
13. Properties that may require management are condominiums, cooperatives, apartments, single-family rental houses, mobile home parks, office buildings, shopping malls, industrial property, and farms.

14. The property manager should be familiar with environmental and fair housing laws including the Americans with Disabilities Act and their applicability to the leasing and renting of property.
15. The property manager should have some understanding of the functioning, and energy consumption, of the major mechanical systems of a building, including the plumbing, electrical, heating, and cooling systems.
16. The property manager should have a plan and systems in place in case of various emergencies and when evacuation from the building may be necessary.
17. The property manager's overall goals are to (a) produce the best possible net operating income from the property and (b) increase the value of the principal's investment.
18. The property manager must continuously evaluate rents, budgets, and markets to ensure the best future return on the investment.
19. An operating budget, capital reserve budget, and stabilized budget should be established before rental of a project is organized and structured. The budgets are subject to adjustments, mostly in the first months of a project.
20. The operating statement is a method that property owners use to project net operating income for a property. Net operating income (NOI) is the gross income minus the operating expenses.
21. A tenant option is a right to renew a lease contract at a certain time. The tenant may have to pay upfront for this option and it is generally in writing like any other contract. A lease option to buy provides for the lease of property with an option to buy the property during or upon expiration of the lease. The option may include a right of first refusal allowing the option holder to exercise his or her option before any other parties can contract for the lease.
22. Public relations have a dual role in the property management office. A management company uses public relations to market itself and to market client properties.
23. Many individuals from diverse backgrounds are attracted to the property management profession. Formal education and training are available through various entities, and different professional designations are awarded to individuals demonstrating competence through education and field activity.

Useful Links

The Institute of Real Estate Management

www.irem.org

New York City Chapter of IREM

www.iremnyc.org

Rochester–Western New York Chapter of IREM

www.irem58.org

The BOMI Institute

www.bomi.org

Licensee Safety

Key Terms

Commercial general liability insurance Covers claims for bodily injury and property damage, which are not covered specifically by errors and omissions insurance

Cyber security The state of being protected, or formulating protection, against the criminal and/or unauthorized use of electronic data

Errors and omissions insurance A form of liability insurance that helps protect against claims from service-related liability such as that provided by a real estate office

NYS Penal Code Article 35 This justification defense under NYS law allows an individual to legally use physical force to defend him or herself

Key Points

1. One of the reasons why the real estate licensee must address and cope with safety issues to such a great degree is because they deal with the unknown public. The real estate business also takes place in a variety of places and settings that are unfamiliar to the agent.
2. When an agent has a first contact with a prospective client or customer, the agent should obtain information on the phone that is enough to perform a basic background check on the individual(s) with whom they will be working.
3. A buddy system is recommended for real estate agents who work alone in the office and for all agents while showing a property or performing a listing presentation at someone's home or place of business.
4. It is always best that agents drive themselves to appointments, as well as meet the client or customer at the property at the appointed time.
5. Some real estate offices have abandoned the concept of the open house. If the office policy is such that the open house produces sales and it is the desire of the client, it is best that an open house not be conducted alone especially in a larger property or one with more than several levels.
6. Real estate brokerage firms have a duty to protect the personal information that is shared by clients and customers. Protection begins with a secure computer network system at the real estate office.
7. Commercial general liability insurance covers claims for bodily injury and property damage, which are not covered specifically by errors and omissions insurance. Errors and omissions insurance focuses on issues such as failure to perform on a contract and/or causing financial loss.
8. This *justification defense* under NYS law allows an individual to legally use physical force to defend him or herself or defend another.

General Business Law (Broker Course Only)

Key Terms

Arbitration A form of resolving a dispute that includes two or more opposing parties and a neutral third party; the neutral third party makes a judgment after hearing both sides

Automatic stay Bankruptcy court order that suspends certain actions of creditors against the debtor or the debtor's property

Certificate of deposit Note containing an acknowledgment by a bank that a sum of money has been received; the bank must repay the money together with interest at an agreed upon rate when the CD expires

Chapter 7 Bankruptcy Liquidation form of bankruptcy in which the debtor's nonexempt property is sold for cash

Chapter 11 Bankruptcy Reorganization form of bankruptcy that provides for a method for reorganizing the debtor's financial affairs under the supervision of the bankruptcy court

Chapter 13 Bankruptcy A consumer debt adjustment form of bankruptcy which permits the court to supervise the debtor's plans for the payment of unpaid debts by installments

Check A type of draft and three-party negotiable instrument containing an order to pay

Collateral Property or something of value than can be used as security for repayment of a debt

Defenses Creation of negotiable instruments may give rise to defenses against payment; this means that individuals or entities involved in the payments of an instrument may claim that the instrument is compromised in some way and may refuse payment

Draft A three-party negotiable instrument containing an order to pay

Drawee A person ordered in a draft to make payment

Drawer A person who signs a draft and is identified as the one ordering payment

Endorsement A signature on a negotiable instrument by someone other than a maker, a drawer, or an acceptor that indicates a negotiation or transfer to another

Equitable distribution The theory that governs the division of marital property in New York

Holder of a negotiable instrument One who is in possession of an instrument that is drawn, issued, or endorsed to him or her; subject to all the claims and defenses that can be asserted against the transferor

Holder in due course Holder of a negotiable instrument who takes an instrument for value, in good faith, and without notice that it is defective or overdue

Endorsee The person who is the payee on an endorser

Endorser The person who transfers or endorses a negotiable instrument to another

Litigation Lawsuit

Marital property Property acquired during the marriage and distributed equitably, taking into account various factors

Mediation The use of a neutral third party to discuss and attempt to resolve a dispute

Negotiable instrument An unconditional promise or order to pay a fixed amount with or without interest

Notice of pendency A statement on the public record warning all persons that a title to real property is the subject of a lawsuit and any lien resulting from the suit will attach to the title held by a purchaser from the defendant

Payee A recipient of money

Uniform Commercial Code A federal statute enacted by New York and, in substantially the same form, by most other states, to simplify, clarify, and modernize the laws governing commercial transactions

Key Points

1. The broker should have knowledge of how laws affecting real property apply to the transaction and are enforced at different government levels: federal, state, and local. These laws include federal and New York fair housing laws; federal laws include the Americans with Disabilities Act, the Equal Credit Opportunity Act, (also known the Fair Lending Law), the Residential Lead-based Paint Hazard Disclosure Act, the Foreign Investment in Real Property Tax Act, TILA-RESPA Integrated Disclosure Rule (TRID), the Do-Not-Call Registry, and the CAN_SPAM Act. These laws are briefly described in various sections of this review where they specifically apply to the subject.
2. Also important to the management of the real estate office are various NYS-mandated disclosures that must be made in certain real property transactions. These disclosures include agency disclosure, truth-in-heating disclosure, and agriculture district disclosure. These disclosures are discussed briefly in various sections of this review where they apply to the topic.
3. Another important disclosure includes the mandate by the NYS Secretary of State that real estate agents disclose the difference between an Exclusive Right-to-Sell and Exclusive Agency contract if and when clients enter into these listing contracts with the broker. This explanation applies to the listing of one- to four-unit dwellings but does not apply to condominiums and cooperatives. The explanation should be explained by the broker and must also appear in writing on each of these contracts used in New York. The explanation that appears on the contract must be read and acknowledged by the clients' signatures on the contract.

4. Sales agents and other parties to a transaction may first look to the primary broker for information and compliance regarding local laws affecting the real property transaction. Oversight for compliance will also likely be accomplished by the attorneys for the buyer and seller, any lender's attorneys, title companies, and possibly other NYS-licensed professionals associated with the transaction such as appraisers, home inspectors, surveyors, and others.
5. A broker must understand that a federal law or state law may be less restrictive than a local law dealing with the same issue. The broker should be aware of *if* and *how* federal and state laws are modified on the local level to assure compliance.
6. As mentioned in the topic of leases, in renting property with six or more units, a landlord must establish interest-bearing accounts for security deposits. Further, landlords are entitled to 1% of the security deposit for administrative costs. Tenants have the option of this interest paid to them annually, applied to their rent, or paid to them when the lease term ends.
7. Both real and personal property may be sold as part of the real estate transaction. Real property includes the land and improvements (buildings) that attach to the land. Personal property may include shares of stock evidencing ownership, such as in a cooperative purchase transaction, and items such as equipment, storage sheds, and furnishings, often evidenced by a separate bill of sale at closing.
8. Negotiable instruments include checks and drafts (three-party instruments) as well as promissory notes and certificates of deposit (two-party instruments).
9. Negotiable instruments must comply with the following: be in writing; be signed; contain an order or promise to pay a fixed sum of money; and be payable on demand or by a definite date. If no date is specified, it is payable on demand.
10. Litigation (lawsuit), mediation, and arbitration are methods to resolve disputes.
11. Although arbitration and mediation are both forms of dispute resolution involving a neutral third party, the arbitrator makes a decision, the mediator does not. However, the mediator will make suggestions to resolve the dispute.
12. Bankruptcies must adhere to the federal bankruptcy code and New York bankruptcy laws and are filed in the federal district court. Bankruptcy options include Chapter 7, Chapter 11, and Chapter 13 of the bankruptcy code.
13. For a creditor to possess a secured interest in the personal property of another in a bankruptcy proceeding, the creditor must file a financing statement in a government office. The statement serves constructive notice that the creditor claims an interest in the specified personal property of the debtor. A creditor who extends credit to a consumer to purchase goods under a written security agreement at the time of sales also serves as the creditor's security interest.
14. Unsecured creditors are those who do not have a security agreement or other collateral of the debtor.
15. If a person receives money or property from another, the donor may be subject to a federal gift tax. Money and property owned upon death may be subject to an estate tax. The federal Tax Cuts and Jobs Act (TCJA) of 2017 is in effect from January 1, 2018 to December 31, 2025. Under this law, the federal estate and gift tax exemption is $11.2 million for individuals and $22.4 million for married couples. This means that an individual can leave $11.2 million to heirs and pay no federal

estate or gift tax. These figures will rise yearly due to inflation until 2025 and if a new tax law is not enacted, these figures will revert back to 2017 levels, adjusted for inflation. The federal estate and gift tax rates range from 5% to 40%.

16. The federal annual individual gift tax exemption to any individual is $15,000; $30,000 for married couples. This exemption does not apply to gifts to a spouse who is already exempted by the unlimited interposal exemption. There is no requirement to file a federal gift tax return and this exemption does not use any of the $11.2 million lifetime federal and gift tax exemption.
17. The estate of an individual who was a New York State resident at the time of death must file a New York estate tax return if the total of the federal gross estate plus any taxable gifts made while the individual was a New York resident exceeds the New York basic exclusion amount of $5,250,000. This amount is applicable for dates of death on or after April 1, 2017. This exclusion amount will remain in effect until Dec. 31, 2018. On Jan. 1, 2019, the basic exclusion amount will be indexed for inflation annually and will be equal to the federal exclusion amount.
18. With the estate tax law as enacted in 2014, there is a limited three-year look-back period for gifts made between April 1, 2014, and Jan. 1, 2019. This means that if a New York resident dies within three years of making a taxable gift, the value of the gift will be included in the decedent's estate for purposes of computing the New York estate tax. Taxable estates that exceed 105% of the New York exclusion amount lose the benefit of the exclusion completely, and the entire taxable estate will be subject to the New York estate tax at applicable graduated rates.
19. The theory of equitable distribution is applied by the New York courts as to the division of marital property. Irretrievable breakdown, also known as no-fault divorce, is one cause of action for a divorce in New York.
20. Generally, marital property acquired before the marriage or inherited during the marriage is treated as separate property belonging solely to the spouse who acquired it. Marital property is property acquired during the marriage and is distributed equitably considering various factors.
21. In some divorce actions, spouses may jointly own land or other types of investments. One or the other may bring legal action to have the property partitioned so that the spouses, and possibly another owner, may have a specified and divided portion of the property.
22. Real estate agents may become involved in the sale of the marital property, if and when it may be sold due to a court order to sell the family residence. This is because the spouses may not agree upon who will hold title or who will reside at the property.
23. The Statute of Limitations imposes time limits within which litigation may be commenced. In New York, the time limit by statute to bring legal action against a party based on contract is six years.
24. The Statute of Frauds states that contracts involving the creation of an interest in real property or the conveyance of an interest in real property must be written to be enforceable.
25. A mechanic's lien for a single-family dwelling must be filed with the clerk of the county where the property is situated within four months from the date of completion of the contract. For other types of property, the liens must be filed in the public records within eight months after the completion date of the contract.
26. A judgment is a court decree resulting from a lawsuit. It attaches as a lien to the real property the debtor currently owns or acquires after the judgment and before satisfaction of the judgment. The

lien is enforced by an execution of the judgment. This is a court order instructing the sheriff to attach and seize the debtor's property. Proceeds from the sale are used to satisfy the judgment.

27. When a deed restriction is violated, it comes back into force after the restriction is reinstituted. This might result from compliance with the restriction willingly by a homeowner or by a court order. For example, a subdivision deed restriction does not allow a fence between the properties and a neighbor installs a fence; the violated restriction is back in force when the fence is removed.

Achieving Agreements through Transaction Analysis (Broker Course Only)

Key Terms

Agreement A meeting of two or more minds; a real property transaction, the consent of two or more parties concurring regarding the transmission, rights to, and benefits of real property

Analysis A detailed examination of the elements or structure of the transaction that serves as the basis for the discussion and interpretation of the agreement

Designated agent A salesperson or associate broker, supervised by a broker, who is assigned to represent a client when a different client is also represented by said real estate broker in the same transaction

Interest rate lock A buyer of real property may negotiate for a closing date on or before a given date so that the desired locked-in interest rate applies

Market value The most probable price of a property as of a specific date, in cash or in other terms, for which the property should be sold after reasonable exposure in a competitive market under conditions requisite to a fair sale, with the buyer and seller acting prudently and knowledgeably and for self-interest and assuming that neither is under undue duress

Negotiation To bargain, conduct, communicate, and/or conference with others regarding the transaction

Seller concessions Occur when buyers request that a seller pay certain costs at closing for them

Stacking of contingent sales Occurs when the buyer, who is under a contingency contract to a seller, has a sale pending with the same contingency on the buyer's own property; it is also possible that the purchaser of that buyer's property also has the same contingency, and so on down the line

Transactional agreement An agreement to transact real property that is the end result of a successful transaction analysis

Transaction analysis The design and achievement of a real estate transaction that is mutually beneficial to the parties involved, who may be the seller, buyer, landlord, or tenant

User-friendly confidentiality agreement Either a listing agreement between a broker and seller or a buyer agency representation agreement between a buyer and a broker

Wants and needs Wants are the untempered desires of the transaction party; untempered refers to the fact that the wants are not moderated or lessened by anything but are the desires of and secondary to the needs of the client; needs of a transaction party are the essential ingredients of a transactional agreement and are the "must haves" of the negotiation

Key Points

1. The purpose of transaction analysis is for the real estate agent to design and achieve a transactional agreement that is mutually beneficial to the parties, who may include the seller, buyer, landlord, and tenant.
2. A real estate transaction occurs during the act of conducting an agreement for the purchase and sale of real estate between two or more parties. This act is in the form of a negotiation which is to bargain, conduct, communicate, and/or conference with others regarding the transaction.
3. A transactional agreement is the result of a successful transaction analysis. In light of these definitions, transaction analysis is the design and achievement of an agreement that is mutually beneficial to the parties involved in the transaction.
4. Every agency creates a fiduciary relationship between principal and agent. The agent has certain obligations to the principal, as required of every agent by law. The agent's fiduciary duties and responsibilities include confidentiality; reasonable care, skill, and diligence; loyalty; obedience; disclosure of information; and accountability.
5. The inclusion of the fiduciary duty of confidentiality opens the way for the necessary incorporation of all of the other fiduciary duties especially reasonable care, skill, and diligence, and loyalty. In offering services to the principal, agents assert that they possess the necessary skills and training to perform the requested services. An agent must demonstrate loyalty to the principal and must work diligently to serve the best interests of the principal under the terms of the employment contract creating the agency. The agent may not work for personal interest or the interest of others adverse to the principal's interest.
6. A user-friendly confidentiality agreement is a listing agreement that includes the obligations that a broker has to a client and the obligations that a client has to the broker. It forms the basis of the fiduciary relationship between the client and the broker.
7. An alternative for handling a dual agency in a brokerage firm, according to New York law, is the designated agent. With disclosure and informed consent in writing of the buyer and seller, one sales agent in the firm is designated to represent the buyer. Another agent is designated to represent the seller. Designated agents are expected to represent the best interests of, and advocate for, the party that each represents. Therefore, the designated sales associate and representative broker cannot provide the fiduciary duty of undivided loyalty.
8. Wants are the untempered desires of the transaction party. The word *untempered* refers to the fact that the wants are not moderated or lessened by anything. They are the desires of the client but are secondary to the needs of the client.
9. The needs of a transaction party are the essential factors of a transactional agreement.
10. To achieve a transactional agreement, an awareness of potentially adverse objectives of one party must be molded into an understanding of the other party's needs.

11. In a real estate transaction, the needs of the parties are the driving force that are the least likely and most difficult to be negotiated, if at all. And if they do end up being negotiated, they are often the most difficult to concede by either party. This is because needs constitute the "must haves" that a seller or buyer believes must happen to make the deal. The untempered wants or desires of a party to the transaction are secondary to needs and often comprise part of a secondary negotiation.
12. Needs and wants are variable, interchangeable, and dependent on the individual situation and/or preferences, as well as the type of real property being transferred.
13. It is the broker's job as part of the analyses to estimate the market value of the property to offer the client a range of value that a seller can expect to obtain and a buyer can expect to pay. Since estimating market value is not an exact science, estimating a range of value is necessary.
14. The overall objective is to reach a transactional agreement on fair terms within a reasonable period of time.
15. Fair terms can be defined as terms that are equitable for all parties. It does not mean that all parties received everything that they needed or wanted. But the goal of the broker is to ensure that the client leaves the transaction with the belief that the terms were in the client's best interest to the best of the broker's abilities and that the best possible deal was made under the varied circumstances. A reasonable period of time means different time frames depending on the transaction.
16. Certain viable factors can play a role in achieving a transactional agreement. First and foremost is the factor of the price, which is usually the most important to the parties. Price is the amount a particular purchaser agrees to pay and a particular seller agrees to accept under the circumstances surrounding the transaction. This amount may or may not equal the value.
17. Other viable factors that require negotiation for a transactional agreement to take place include but are not limited to occupancy considerations; whether an appraisal or market value range (comparative market analysis) is required; timing of the closing; financial positions of the parties; stacking of contingent sales; multiple offers on the property; interest rate deadlines; the attorney's unconditional approval; home inspection corrections; and seller concessions.
18. A contingency is a method through which a buyer or seller can be released from a contract. If a certain event does not occur, then the party who has a contingency can be released from the contract.
19. Because of rate lock deadlines, a buyer may negotiate for a closing date on or before a given date so that the desired locked-in interest rate applies. A mortgage loan cannot be closed without locking in an interest rate. There are four components to a rate lock: the loan program; interest rate; points; and length of the lock.
20. Generally, a seller concession amount is used to pay for closing costs, but sellers may concede money if they agree that certain maintenance or repairs need to be made to the property that the seller does not want to do.
21. Discussion, dialogue, and conferencing between and among the parties are the communication methods by which a successful negotiation can take place.

22. The ability to listen is as important to a discussion or dialogue as is the verbal response. Listening and carefully paying attention to what an individual is saying opens up a dialogue in which important information is shared among the parties.
23. An agreement attitude can be attained by validating all parties' needs or wants, and not dismissing them as if they are not important or relevant. Validation does not mean agreeing with the other party.
24. For the transactional agreement to take place, there should be an understanding of the other parties' wants and needs, which a broker can communicate to his or her client. Understanding by the client can bring about compromise and successful negotiation.

Quick View Tables

The following quick view tables contain important study information from each of the subjects in the salesperson 75-hour course and the broker 45-hour course.

License Law and Regulations/Operating a Real Estate Office

Table 1.A Summary of License Requirements

Requirement	Salesperson	Broker/Associate Broker
Age	18 ✓	20
Citizenship/permanent residency	Yes, other choices ✓	Yes
Qualifying course	75 hours ✓	120 hours total
Experience	None ✓	2 years as salesperson or 3 years' equivalent
Fee/term of license	$55/2 years ✓	$155/2 years
Continuing Education	22.5/every 2 years	22.5/every 2 years
Licensing agency	Dept. of State	Dept. of State
License Law	Article 12-A of the Real Property Law	Article 12-A of the Real Property Law

Table 1.B Broker's Responsibility

Form/Online Application	Kept by	Displayed	DOS fee
Broker initial license and renewal	Broker	Yes	$155
Change of association	N/A	No	$20
Change of name, personal address	N/A	No	$10
New branch office	N/A	No	$155
Salesperson initial license and renewal	Broker	No	$55
Termination of association	N/A	No	$0

Law of Agency

Table 2.A Types of Agents

Type of Agent	Representation	Definition	Limitations
1. Single agent	Buyer or seller	The agent works for the buyer or seller.	The agent never represents both. Firms that represent solely the buyer or seller may reject subagency and dual agency. The broker should counsel, but not advise, the principal as to the limitations of this relationship. If a situation arises to compromise the relationship, the broker could suggest that another broker from a referral firm be utilized.
2. Seller's agent	Seller	A listing agent who acts alone or cooperates with other agents as a subagent or broker's agent.	The agent works in the best interests of the seller but must deal fairly and honestly with buyers.
3. Subagent	Seller or buyer	An agent of the principal under the agency relationship of the primary broker.	The agent must be hired with the principal's informed consent. The principal may be vicariously liable for the subagent's acts.
4. Buyer's agent	Buyer	The agent represents the buyer as principal and enters into a listing agreement with the buyer. Locates a property and negotiates for the buyer.	The agent works in the best interests of the buyer but must deal fairly and honestly with sellers.
5. Dual agent	Buyer and seller	Represents both buyer and seller in the same transaction; undisclosed dual agency is a breach of fiduciary duty and violation of license law.	This arrangement is allowable only with disclosure and written informed consent. The agent cannot give undivided loyalty to either party.

6. Broker's agent	Broker (who may represent either buyer or seller)	A broker's agent cooperates with or is engaged by a listing agent, buyer's agent, or tenant's agent. The seller, buyer, landlord, or tenant does not have vicarious liability for the acts of the broker's agent.	The broker's agent does not have a direct relationship with the seller, buyer, landlord, or tenant.
7. Cooperating agent	Buyer or seller	Representation includes seller's agents, subagents, buyer's agents, and broker's agents. These agents work to assist the listing broker in the sale of the property. Cooperating agents may or may not work through MLS.	The principal can designate those agents that work as broker's agents, subagents, or buyer's agents. The principal may choose to reject subagency arrangements.

Table 2.B Express and Implied Agency

Type of Agency	**How Communicated**	**Form**
Express	In writing/orally	Listing agreement/conversation
Implied	Action of parties	Ratification/estoppel*

***Agency by ratification** confirms an earlier implied agency agreement such as when a principal signs a contract of sale.

Agency by estoppel exists when a principal does not stop an individual from representing his interests, therefore creating an agency relationship between the two.

Independent Contractor/Antitrust

Table 2.C Requirements for Salesperson Independent Contractor Status

Requirement	**Parties involved**
NYS salesperson or broker license	Regulated by NYS Department of State (NYSDOS)
Independent contractor agreement	Between salesperson and broker
Termination of relationship	Agreement between salesperson and broker at any time

Table 2.D Antitrust Violations

Violation	When it occurs	Laws it violates
Price fixing	Competitors in the same industry conspire to charge the same or similar price for goods and services	Sherman and Clayton Antitrust Acts; NYS Antitrust Laws
Group boycott	A person or group is persuaded to not do business with another person or group	Sherman and Clayton Antitrust Acts; NYS Antitrust Laws
Market allocation agreement	Agreement between competitors who divide or assign a certain territory for sales	Sherman and Clayton Antitrust Acts; NYS Antitrust Laws
Tie-in arrangements	Agreement between a buyer and seller that as a condition of sale, the buyer will do business with another party	Sherman and Clayton Antitrust Acts; NYS Antitrust Laws

Legal Issues

Estates and Interests

Table 3.A Types of Ownership

Type	Owners	Right of Survivorship
In severalty	One owner	No
Tenancy in common	Two or more	No
Joint tenancy	Two or more	Yes

Liens and Easements

Table 3.B Types of Liens

Type	Specific/General	Voluntary/Involuntary
Mortgage	Specific	Voluntary
Real property tax	Specific	Involuntary
Mechanic's	Specific	Involuntary
Judgment	General	Involuntary
Income tax	General	Involuntary

Table 3.C Types of Easements

Type	Purpose	Owner
Easement in gross	Utilities	Government/public company
Easement appurtenant	Ingress/egress	Private parties
Negative easement appurtenant	View easements	Private parties

Deeds/Conveyances

Table 3.D Forms of Deeds

Type	Description
Full covenant and warranty	Fullest guarantee of title
Quitclaim	No warranties of title
Bargain and sale with covenants	Contains warranties of title
Judicial deed	Results from a court order

Table 3.E A Valid Deed or Conveyance

Requirement	Clarification
In Writing	Required by the Statute of Frauds
Competent grantor	Grantee need not be competent but must be living
Legal description	Must have formal legal description
Consideration	Something of value; minimum nominal consideration ($1.00)
Words of conveyance	Demonstrates grantor's intent to convey title
Acknowledgment	Grantor's signature before a notary to allow recording
Delivery and acceptance	Grantor must deliver the deed and grantee must accept

Title Closing and Costs

Table 3.F Closing Preparations

Required for Closing	Definition
Closing statement	Prepared by attorneys for buyer, seller, and lender
Licensee assistance	Inspection of property with purchaser before closing
Marketable title	Includes title search, check for chain of title, abstract of title
Payment of broker commission	Paid at closing; may include all or part of deposit
Perc, soil, water flow tests	New construction and other property that have wastewater treatment or well
Place of closing	Lender, attorney office, title company, county clerk
Structural inspection	Performed by NYS-licensed home inspector, other professionals
Title insurance	Insures the policy owner against financial loss if title is not good

Table 3.G Closing Costs

Seller Closing Costs	Purchaser Closing Costs
Real property transfer tax	Appraisal and credit report fees
Broker commission	Mortgage recording tax
Discharging liens	Lender fees
Discount points	Mortgage and homeowner's insurance
Survey (may be buyer)	Pest inspection

Contract of Sale and Leases

Table 4.A Lease Agreements

Term	Definition
Assignment	Full transfer of lease by lessee to another who pays owner
Sublease	Sublessee pays leaseholder who pays owner

Actual eviction	Illegal forcible eviction of tenant
Constructive eviction	Tenant may withhold rent if necessary services not provided (requires court order)
Eviction	Legal proceeding to evict a tenant

Table 4.B Types of Leasehold Estates

Type of Estate	Definition	Inheritable
Tenancy for years	Exists for a fixed time period	Yes
Periodic estate	Automatically renews itself for another period unless notice is given	Yes
Month-to-month tenancy	Lease terminates at any time	No
Estate at sufferance	Tenant who refuses to leave after right to possession ends	No

Contracts

Table 4.C Types of Contracts

Contract type	Description
Express	Oral or written agreement
Implied	Inferred from behavior of the parties
Unilateral	One party is obligated under the contract
Bilateral	Two parties are obligated under the contract
Executory	Not fully performed contract
Executed	Fully performed contract
Valid	Binding and enforceable
Void	No legal force or effect
Voidable	May or may not be enforceable

Contract Preparation

Table 4.D Data Required for Contract Preparation

Data	Supplied By
Certificate of Occupancy	Building Department
Personal data	Buyer, seller, real estate agent
Prior deed	Seller
Prior title insurance policy	Seller, lender
Survey	Seller or buyer (new survey may be required)
Tax, water, fuel bills	Seller through his agent

Real Estate Finance

Table 5.A Mortgage Summary

Mortgage Type	Definition	Participants
Primary mortgage market	Mortgage obtained from lender	Any bank or other lending institution
Secondary mortgage market	Mortgage purchased from lender by secondary market agencies	Fannie Mae, Ginnie Mae, Freddie Mac
Conventional loan	Loan not insured by a government agency	Any bank or other lending institution
Government loan	Loan insured by a government agency	Lenders that process FHA, VA, RHS, SONYMA loans
Conforming loan	Loan application that conforms to secondary market guidelines	Fannie Mae, Ginnie Mae, Freddie Mac
Seller financing	Seller takes a mortgage for all or part of the purchase price	Sellers that participate in purchase money, wraparound mortgages, installment land contracts, or sale leaseback

Table 5.B Types of Seller Financing

Type of financing	Title transfer	Payment arrangement
Installment land contract	Remains with seller until full payment is made	Down payment may be required; monthly installment payments
Purchase money mortgage	Conveyed to buyer	Title used as security for loan; monthly amortized loan
Sale leaseback	Buyer takes title; leases property back to seller	Seller makes lease payments to buyer
Wraparound	Conveyed to buyer	Buyer takes title subject to existing first mortgage; monthly amortized loan payment to seller

Land Use Regulations/Development

Table 6.A Public Control of Land

Control	Definition	Method
Eminent domain	Government right to take property for public good	Condemnation—act of taking
Escheat	Right of government to seize property if there are no heirs	Government follows protocol to locate heirs
Police power	Right of government to act for public welfare	All public laws, regulations, and agencies
Taxation	Levy against property value	Lien against property

Table 6.B Types of Zoning

Type of Zoning	Definition	Legal?
Cluster	Grouped development that allows for open space	Yes
Cumulative use	May permit higher priority uses that are not designated for that zone	Yes
Exclusive use	Property to be used only as designated in zone	Yes

Nonconforming use	When a preexisting use is different from that specified by the zoning code	Yes
Spot	A property is rezoned to permit a different use than the zoning requirements	No
Transfer of development rights	A transfer of zoning rights from one property to another property	Yes

Construction

Table 7.A Main Building Systems Defined

System	Purpose
Electrical system	Begins outside with service entrance cables that connect to the main panel board; branch circuit wires bring electrical power to receptacles
Heating system	Consists of hot water, steam, forced warm air, or electric furnaces; fueled by oil, gas, solar, or electricity
HVAC system	Heating, ventilating, and cooling system
Insulation System	Insulation is applied to the warm (inside) of exterior walls such as roofs, ceilings, floors, and foundation walls
Plumbing system	Actually, two piping systems; one delivers clean water into the structure; the other processes wastewater
Private wastewater system	Also called a septic system, it processes and treats wastewater on site
Private water supply system	Consists of well or wells pumping water from the ground to a pressurized holding tank

Environmental Issues

Table 7.B The Residential Lead-based Paint Hazard Reduction Act

Main Point	Explanation
Property types	Sale or lease of residential properties built before 1978
Who must comply	Seller and seller's agents

Forms needed	Lead hazard pamphlet, reports of lead-based paint, contingency for 10-day lead paint assessment, disclosure form
Penalty for noncompliance	Payment of up to three times the amount of damage incurred by lessor or purchaser; up to $10,000 fine

Valuation Process and Pricing Properties

Table 8 Comparing Market Value, Price, and Cost

Type of Value	Definition
Cost	The dollar expenditure for labor, materials, and other items
Market value	The price a property will bring in a competitive market with neither party under duress
Price	The amount of money a purchaser and seller agree upon

Human Rights, Fair Housing/Advanced Fair Housing, and Fair Lending

Table 9.A Human Rights Law Violations

Violation	Definition	Possible Violator
Blockbusting	Behavior that causes panic selling by announcing that people of certain protected classes are moving to the neighborhood; an attempt to gain listings	Salespersons, brokers
Redlining	Certain neighborhoods are targeted as ones that are not eligible for mortgages or other home loans based on the community's membership in certain protected classes	Lenders
Steering	Behavior that encourages prospects either toward or away from certain communities based on membership in certain protected classes	Salespersons, brokers

Table 9.B Important Human Rights Laws and Enforcement Agencies

Law or Agency	Purpose
Federal Fair Housing Act and amendments	Makes discrimination illegal through establishment of protected classes through the initial law and subsequent amendments in the sale and rental of residential housing; prohibits discriminatory lending practices such as redlining
New York City Commission on Human Rights	Protects NYC residents against discrimination and adds more protected classes for housing than NYS laws
NYS Division of Human Rights (NYSDHR)	Pursues and enforces human rights complaints
NYS Human Rights Law	Added more protected classes for housing than the federal law and covers discrimination in the sale or rental of commercial property, consumer credit, and employment
Equal Credit Opportunity Act (Fair Lending Law)	Makes it unlawful for creditors to discriminate in lending policies and other forms of consumer credit transactions
Community Reinvestment Act	Encourages lending institutions to meet the credit needs of communities including neighborhoods with moderate- and low-income housing
U.S. Dept. of Housing and Urban Development (HUD)	HUD enforces fair housing violations on the federal level
U.S. Department of Justice	U.S. Department of Justice has a civil rights division

Real Estate Mathematics

Table 10.A Important Measures and Formulas

Measure	Formula
Acre	43,560 sq. ft.
Area of rectangle	Width × depth
Area of a triangle	1/2 base × height
Commission	Sales price paid × percentage of commission = commission
Interest	Loan balance x interest rate = annual interest

Table 10.B Useful Mathematical Formulas for Income Property Valuation

Name of Formula	Formula
Cash break-even ratio or default ratio	Calculate the annual operating income of the property, then add debt service to operating expenses and divide by the gross operating income
Debt service coverage ratio (DSCR)	Divide the net operating income by the annual debt service
Effective gross income multiplier (EGIM) (Broker course only)	Divide the property's asking price or market value by the annual effective gross income
Equity dividend rate (also known as cash-on-cash return)	Divide the annual before tax cash flow by the total cash invested
Gross income multiplier (GIM) (Broker course only)	Divide the property's asking price or market value by the total income from the property
Gross rent multiplier (GRM) (Broker course only)	Divide the property's asking price or market value by the property's annual gross rent (income)
Loan to value ratio (LTV)	Divide the loan amount by the market or sales price x 100
Net operating income multiplier (NOIM)	Divide the market value by the annual net operating income
Operating expense ratio (OER)	Divide the property's operating expense by its effective gross income
Overall capitalization rate or cap rate	Divide the net operating income by the acquisition cost of the property
Potential gross income multiplier (PGIM) (Broker course only)	Divide the property's asking price or market value by the annual potential gross income

Municipal Agencies

Table 11 List of Municipal Agencies

Agency	Level of Government
Architectural Review Board	City, Town, Village
Building Department	City, Town, Village
City/Town Council	City/Town
Conservational Advisory Council	County, City, Town
Engineer	City, Town, Village
Health Department	City, County
Planning Board	County, City, Town, Village
Tax Assessor	City, Town, Village
Village Board of Trustees	Village
Wetlands Commission	County, City, Town, Village
Zoning Board of Appeals	City, Town, Village

Property Insurance

Table 12 Types of Insurance Policy

Insurance Type	Purpose
Commercial	Liability and property insurance and possible business suspension insurance
Contents	Issued on an actual cash basis, must pay extra for replacement cost
Flood	Issued to property owners in coastal and other flood-prone areas
Homeowner's	Varying levels of coverage insuring the home and contents
Tenant's/Renter's	Generally, applies to improvements within the unit, not the building
Umbrella	Excess liability policy for additional coverage above primary policy

Taxes and Assessments

Table 13.A When Reassessment May Occur

Reassessment	Explanation
Community-wide reassessment	Periodically to restore fairness within the community
Illegal/legal assessment	Taxpayer may protest unequal or unlawful assessment
Obtaining a building permit	Improvement made to property, finished basement, pool, garage
Reassessment upon sale	Property may not be reassessed immediately upon purchase but at a later date for fairness
Undeclared improvements discovered	Assessor cross-checks building permits

*Table 13.B Grounds for Protesting Residential Property Assessments**

Grounds	Definition
Excessive assessment	Owner believes that assessed value of property is greater than full value of property
Misclassification of homestead and nonhomestead classes	Property designated in the wrong class or the allocation of the total assessed value between the homestead and nonhomestead is incorrect
Unequal assessment	Owner believes that property is assessed at higher percentage of value than others
Unlawful assessment	Property is fully exempt from property taxation

*Protests are made by the property owner or a representative such as an attorney.

Condominiums and Cooperatives

Table 14 Ownership Differences and Similarities between a Condominium and a Cooperative

Cooperatives	Condominiums
Board package and interview	Purchaser documents and interview but may not be as strict as co-op
By-laws and house rules	Covenants, conditions, and restrictions, and by-laws
Common areas owned by cooperative cooperation	Common area owned in common by owners of individual units
Monthly maintenance fee to cooperative for underlying mortgage, other expenses	Common charges for upkeep, insurance, and salaries
Offering plan must be approved by attorney general	Offering plan must be approved by attorney general
Ownership: Leasehold	Ownership: Fee simple
Possible flip tax at closing	No flip tax
Proprietary lease and shares of stock in cooperative corporation	Deed

Commercial and Investment Real Estate/ Property Management

Table 15.A Commercial Lease Clauses

Lease Clause	Purpose
Building amenities	Moving allowances, parking, other incentives
Escalation clauses	Various types of clauses indicating terms of lease payment increases
Estoppel certificate	Tenant's statement pertaining to the lease term, rent, security, and other issues
Lease duration	Short-term leases generally 3–5 years; long term, 5 or more years

On-site management	Degree of maintenance coverage
Subordination, nondisturbance, and attornment agreement	Legal agreements pertaining to the lease
Tenant mix	Variety of businesses in the building
Type of lease	Triple net, net, gross, percentage
Use clause	Limitations as to how the space can be used

Table 15.B Types of Value

Type of Value	**Definition**
Assessed value	Value to which a tax rate is applied
Investment	Amount of return produced
Mortgage loan value	Amount a lender believes a property will bring in a foreclosure sale
Value in use	Based on usefulness to investor

Income Tax Issues in Real Estate Transactions

Table 16 Like-Kind (Tax-Deferred) Exchange

Issues for a like-kind exchange	**Explanation**
Closing of new property	Must close within 180 days from the date exchangor sold the original property
Must be business or investment property	Personal residences, stocks, cars, not allowed
Must be real property for tax deferment	Personal property such as equipment or furniture in property not subject to tax deferment
Purchase of replacement property	Investor must contract for replacement property within 45 days
Qualified Intermediary (QI)	The QI accepts funds and handles contracts

Mortgage Brokerage

Table 17 The Differences and Similarities between a Mortgage Broker and a Mortgage Banker

Mortgage Broker	Mortgage Banker
Cannot act as a mortgage banker	Can act as a mortgage broker
Does not collect payments	May collect payments
Finds financing	Provides financing
Receives a fee for finding financing (through borrower, mortgage banker)	Receives payment (points, interest) for providing financing (from borrower)
Registered by NYS Department of Financial Services	Licensed by NYS Department of Financial Services

Property Management

Table 18.A Property Manager's Obligations to the Owner

Obligations	Explanation
Budget	Operating budget, capital reserve budget, variable expenses, stabilized budget
Future of the project	Analyze business trends
Maintenance	Preventative maintenance, corrective maintenance, construction
Rents space, collects rent, pays expenses, oversees maintenance	Basic functions
Reporting	A periodic accounting of all funds received and disbursed
Tenant relations	Tenant problems, evictions, subletting

Table 19 Licensee Safety

Possible Safety Issue	Remediation
Agent in real estate office alone	Park in a well-lit location; lock office doors; let buddy know you are in the office; have buddy check on you; and advise buddy when you leave
General safety tips	Have properly functioning car and mobile phone; always notify a buddy as to your whereabouts; do not pick up clients or prospects at hotels, train stations, or other public places; vet all those with whom you will do business; have prospects sign in upon arrival at the office; have another agent at the office be able to identify prospects
Open house	Conduct with one or more agents
Showing property	Meet prospects in the office and vet before showing; notify buddy; meet prospects at the property; have them enter a room first; know exits to the property
Showing vacant, remote, or foreclosed properties	Show with another agent; carefully examine interior and exterior; look for broken windows and broken locks; leave if you suspect someone is in or around property; call police if necessary

General Business Law (Broker Course Only)

Table 20 Federal and NYS Laws and Disclosures Important to Real Estate Brokers

Law/Disclosure	Federal or NYS	Definition
Agency Disclosure	NYS	Disclosure of who the agent represents in 1–4-unit residential properties and condos and coops in any size building
Agricultural District Disclosure	NYS	Disclosure as to whether a property lies in a designated NYS Agricultural District
Americans with Disabilities Act	Federal	Protection against those with disabilities in public accommodations and residential buildings
CAN SPAM Act	Federal	Protection against fraudulent commercial emails

Do-not-call Registry	Federal	Registry maintained by the Federal Trade Commission
Equal Credit Opportunity Act	Federal	Protections against discrimination in lending practices
Exclusive-right-to sell/Exclusive agency	NYS	Agent must present written explanation and obtain acknowledgment from listing seller of differences between the two contracts for 1–3-unit residential properties
Foreign Investment in Real Property Tax Act	Federal	Imposes a tax on capital gains derived by foreign people from the sale of their U.S. property
NYS Human Rights Law	NYS	Protects NYS residents against discrimination
Residential Lead-based Paint Hazard Reduction Act	Federal	Disclosure of the presence of lead-based paint in pre-1978 target properties
TILA-RESPA Integrated Disclosure Rule	Federal	Disclosure by lender to consumer for costs and other requirements for most residential mortgage loans; lenders must provide loan estimate and closing disclosure forms
Truth-in-Heating Disclosure	NYS	Disclosure of heating and cooling bills by the landlord through a summary of the bills for the life of the structure or the preceding two years

Achieving Transactional Agreements through Transaction Analysis (Broker Course Only)

Table 21 Agent's Role in Transaction Analysis

Agent's Role	Explanation
Agent is a fiduciary	Owes full range of agency fiduciary duties to the client
User-friendly confidentiality agreement	Either a listing agreement with a seller or a buyer agency representation agreement with a buyer
Untempered wants or desires of the transaction party	Must ultimately be realistic to the other party; secondary to the needs
Needs of the transaction party	Essential ingredient of a transactional agreement and constitutes the "must haves," which may still be subject to negotiation
Representation of client	Agent must always work in the best interests of the client

Transaction analysis	Must consider the motivations of the parties and various negotiation points including price, timing, occupancy, interest rate lock-in, seller concession, multiple offers, financial positions of the parties, and other viable factors
Negotiation skills	Good listener, creates discussion and dialogue, communicates an agreement attitude
Transactional Agreement	Beneficial to all parties to the transaction

There are many "ors" and "ees" in real estate law. If the word ends in *or*, think of this party as the *initiator* of something. If the word ends in *ee*, think of the party as the *receiver* of something.

Table 22 Remembering the "ors" and "ees" and what they mean

"or"	**"ee"**
Grantor—gives deed	Grantee—receives deed
Lessor—gives lease	Lessee—receives lease
Optionor—gives option	Optionee—receives option
Mortgagor—gives mortgage (note)	Mortgagee—receives mortgage (note)
Vendor—sells item	Vendee—receives or purchases item

Marcia's List

A Study Guide Summary

The following is a quick abbreviated overview of the most important key terms and concepts from each of the topics in the 75-hour salesperson and the 45-hour broker qualifying courses. Check off the items you are unsure of and look them up in this ***Cram, New York Real Estate for Salespersons, 6th e* Revised** or ***New York Real Estate for Brokers, 6th e***. Check out the comments for helpful explanations for certain key concepts.

License Law and Regulations/Operating a Real Estate Office

Key Term	Comment
Article 12-A	**Article 12-A** of the New York Real Property Law addresses the licensure of salespersons and brokers. Also, NYSDOS regulations govern the licensure process.
Broker price opinion (BPO)	A **broker price opinion** is not as detailed as an appraisal. Generally, a BPO is based on the real estate broker's inspection of the subject property and recent listings and sales near the property. The difference between a CMA and BPO is that with a comparative market analysis, the broker needs to state a price or price range for the subject property.
Blind ad	
Commingling	**Commingling** of funds is prohibited by the New York license law. Brokers must keep personal and business accounts separate to avoid *commingling* personal and business monies.
eAccessNY	
Exemptions to licensure	There are several **exemptions to licensure**. An important one is that NYS licensed attorneys admitted to the New York Bar may also serve as real estate brokers. Should the attorney want to open an office and hire salespeople, the attorney must obtain a real estate broker license from the NYSDOS (but does not have to take a course or exam).
Kickback	
Mandatory seller property disclosure form	
Misdemeanor	

Net listing	A **net listing** contract is illegal in New York. It can occur if a broker arranges to keep as a commission any money obtained from the property sale above a price specified by the seller. Commissions for the sale of real property are generally a percentage of the entire selling price.
Relationship and supervision responsibilities for salespersons and associate brokers	
Requirements for licensure	
Salesperson/broker/ associate broker	
Team as it relates to real estate advertising	A **team** refers to two or more people associated with the same brokerage firm, one of whom must be an associate broker or salesperson, that operate as a pair or group
Types of business organizations for broker licensure	

Law of Agency (Includes Independent Contractor and Antitrust)

Key Term	Comment
Advance informed consent to dual agency	**Advance informed consent to dual agency** allows buyers or sellers to consent to dual agency on the NYS agency disclosure form in advance of it occurring. *Dual agency* occurs when a real estate broker or salesperson attempts to represent the buyer and seller in the same transaction. It is allowable in New York with disclosure and informed consent.
Agency Disclosure Form for Buyer/Seller and Landlord/Tenant (two separate forms)	
Broker's agent/seller's agent/buyer's agent/dual agent/subagent/designated agent	
Client/principal/customer	
Fiduciary	

First substantive contact or meeting	The **first substantive contact** occurs when some detail and information about the property is shared with parties who express interest in the real estate transaction. Examples of this contact include the signing of the listing agreement with the seller or a showing of the property with the buyer.
Group boycott/market allocation agreement/price fixing/tie-in arrangement	A **group boycott**, **market allocation agreement**, **price fixing**, or **tie-in arrangement** are all illegal restraints of trade activities and violations of antitrust law that are counter to free competition in the marketplace.
Independent contractor/independent contractor agreement	
Internal Revenue Code Section 3508 (a) (b)	
Meaning and difference between exclusive agency and exclusive-right-to-sell	The difference between an **exclusive agency** and an **exclusive-right-to-sell** listing agreement is that with an *exclusive agency* contract, the broker is legally entitled to the commission if the exclusive broker or another broker effects sale of the property, but not if the owner sells the property without the assistance of any broker. With the *exclusive-right-to-sell contract*, the exclusive broker is entitled to the commission no matter who effects the sale, including the owner.
Open listing	
Special agent/general agent	A real estate agent is a **special agent** who has narrow authorization to act on behalf of the principal or client. An example is a listing broker who represents a client for the sale of his or her property. A **general agent** is one who is authorized to handle all affairs of the principal concerning a specified matter or property. An example is a property manager who has varied duties to perform for his or her principal or client.
Sherman and Clayton Antitrust Acts	
Undivided loyalty	As part of their fiduciary duties, agents must remain loyal to the principal and work in the best interest of the principal. It is important to note that when a real estate agent enters into a dual agency relationship with the buyer and seller, the client or principal must give up the fiduciary duty of **undivided loyalty** that is not possible in a dual agency relationship.
Vicarious liability	

Legal Issues

Part I Estates and Interests

Key Term	Comment
Corporation/general partnership/limited partnership/S corporation	A **corporation** is a taxable legal entity, with tax rates separate from individual income tax rates. A corporation is formed in New York by the filing of a certificate of incorporation. A **general partnership**, formed by agreement, is made up of partners who are personally liable for partnership debts exceeding partnership assets. With a **limited partnership**, there are one or more partners who are liable for partnership debts, and one or more silent, or limited, partners who contribute money or other assets to the extent of their ownership interest. An S corporation is taxed like a partnership.
Differences between joint tenancy and tenancy in common	Ownership in **joint tenancy** requires all four unities of time, title, interest, and possession. Should one of the owners die, the other owners acquire the decedent's rights to the real property. This is known as the *right of survivorship.* With a **tenancy in common**, the only unity is that of possession. The tenant in common can devise this ownership right to another outside of the tenancy in common. There is no right of survivorship for the other owners.
Fee simple absolute	The **fee simple absolute estate** in real property provides the most complete form of ownership and bundle of rights in real property. There are other estates in real property that do not provide this complete form of ownership and are known as *defeasible estates.*
Fixture/trade fixture	
Leasehold estate	A **leasehold estate** is one for a limited time. It is useful to think of a leasehold estate as a rental of real property.
Life estate	
Right of survivorship	
Severalty	**Severalty** means that the title to real property is held in the name of only one person or entity. Do not think of the word "several," but rather that the interest is severed from *all others.*

Part II Liens and Easements

Key Term	Comment
Easement appurtenant	
Easement in gross	All easements that are not *easements appurtenant* are **easements in gross**, which are commercial easements. They are usually owned by government agencies or utility companies. Think of electrical or cable lines.
Encroachment	
Encumbrance	
Judgment	
Lien	
Lis pendens	***Lis pendens*** is a Latin term meaning a notice that a lawsuit has been filed and litigation may be pending. Sometimes a property cannot transfer if a *lis pendens* has been filed.
Mechanic's lien	

Part III Deeds/Conveyance of Real Property

Key Term	Comment
Accession/alluvion/ avulsion rights	
Adverse possession	
Deed/conveyance	
Dedication	
Delivery and acceptance	To transfer title by a deed, the grantor (seller) must **deliver** a deed to the grantee (buyer) and the grantee must **accept** the deed.
Executor/executrix	
Full covenant and warranty deed	A **full covenant and warranty deed** contains the strongest and broadest form of guarantee of title of any type of deed and the greatest protection to the grantee. Most residential title transfers use this type of deed.
Grantor/grantee	

Metes and bounds description	
Quitclaim deed	A **quitclaim deed** releases or conveys to the grantee any interest, including title, that the grantor may have and contains no warranties of title. It is sometimes used when there is a "cloud on the title" and the seller cannot warrant clear title to the buyer.
Testate/intestate	
Voluntary and involuntary alienation	**Voluntary** and **involuntary alienation** may occur during the life of an owner. *Voluntary alienation* occurs when there is a willing transfer of title during life. An example is if a grantor transfers title to a grantee while both are alive such as with a deed. *Involuntary alienation* occurs when an individual must give up title to real property against his/her will because of bankruptcy, adverse possession, or foreclosure.

Part IV Title Closing and Costs

Key Term	Comment
Abstract of title/chain of title/marketable/title search	An **abstract of title** is a condensed history of the title that summarizes all links in the **chain of title** (continuous title with no breaks) plus any public records affecting the title. This process is called a **title search** and is performed before a real estate closing. If there are no problems found during the title search, a property is said to have **marketable title**, that is, the property is reasonably free and clear of encumbrances.
Closing disclosure form	
Commission Escrow Act	
Debits/credits	
Flip tax	
Loan estimate form	
Proration	
Survey	
TILA-RESPA Integrated Disclosure Rule (TRID)	The **TILA-RESPA Integrated Disclosure Rule** replaces the **Real Estate Settlement Procedures Act** and the **Truth-in-Lending Act** as they apply to most, but not all, real estate closings for residential federally financed properties; not commercial properties or owner-

	financed loans. The law regulates lending institutions in making mortgage loans and replaces the Good Faith Estimate (GFE) and HUD Form No. 1 with the **Loan Estimate Form and the Closing Disclosure Form**. The *Loan Estimate Form* indicates the loan's interest rate and monthly payment and must be provided within three days of a buyer submitting a loan application. The *Closing Disclosure Form* provides all transaction and closing costs for the loan and must be provided three days before closing.

The Contract of Sale and Leases

Part I Leases

Key Term	Comment
Assignment/Sublease	An **assignment** involves the transfer of a contract such as a lease from the present tenant to the assignee. The assignee (the person who is now responsible for the contract) then must make lease payments to the landlord. With a **sublease**, a tenant leases a property to a third party, the sublessee. The original tenant, however, is still responsible to the landlord for the lease payments under the original lease.
Estate at sufferance/estate at will/tenancy for years/periodic estate	
Eviction/actual eviction/constructive eviction	
Gross/net lease	
Lessor/lessee	
Quiet enjoyment	

Part II Contracts

Key Term	Comment
Caveat emptor	**Caveat emptor** is a Latin term meaning "buyer beware." Although brokers have certain duties and responsibilities toward buyer customers, in New York, the theory of "buyer beware" may apply in certain situations.
Contingencies	
Counteroffer	
Executory/executed contract	An **executory contract** is one that is not fully completed. An example would be a listing contract in which the property is still on the market. An **executed contract** is one that has been performed and the terms of the contract have been met.
Meeting of the minds	
Offer and acceptance	
Ready, willing, and able buyer	A **ready, willing, and able buyer** leads to a **meeting of the minds** when the **offer and acceptance** takes place. At this point, the broker has performed on the listing contract and is generally entitled to his or her commission.
Statute of Frauds	In New York, the **Statute of Frauds** is within the General Obligations Law. The law requires that real estate contracts such as contracts for purchase must be in writing to be enforceable in court. Leases and listing contracts for more than one year must also be in writing.
Statute of Limitations	
Time is of the essence	
Void/voidable/valid contract	

Part III Contract Preparation

Key Term	Comment
Attorney review clause	
Binder	In certain areas of New York, a written document called a **binder** is used by real estate agents for the purchase and sale of real property instead of an offer to purchase contract. Generally, when a binder is used, the attorney for the buyer will use the information in the binder to create a contract of sale.
Down payment	
Lawyer's Fund for Client Protection	
Mortgage contingency clause	

Real Estate Finance

Key Term	Comment
Adjustable rate mortgage/ fixed rate mortgage	An **adjustable rate mortgage** includes a mortgage interest rate that varies, depending on fluctuations of a standard financial index. With a **fixed rate mortgage,** the interest rate stays the same throughout the mortgage term. When interest rates are low, fixed rate mortgages are generally predictable and preferable.
Amortization	
Balloon/blanket/construction/ wraparound mortgage	
Buydown	
Conventional mortgage	
Discount points	
Fannie Mae/Ginnie Mae/FreddieMac/secondary mortgage market	
FHA and VA insured loans	
Foreclosure	

Jumbo mortgage	
Loan-to-value ratio	
Mortgagor/mortgagee	The terms **mortgagor** and **mortgagee** can be misleading. The *mortgagor* or borrower is *giving* the lender a note or promise to pay back the mortgage monies (therefore the mortgagor). The *mortgagee* is the lender, the party who is *receiving* payment on the mortgage note (therefore the mortgag*ee*).
Mortgage	Mortgage loans that meet Fannie Mae and Freddie Mac criteria such as loan amount limits for a certain area are known as *conforming loans*. Loans that exceed the loan limit are *nonconforming loans* also called *jumbo mortgages.*
Note or bond	
Prepayment penalty	
Regulation Z of the Truth-in-Lending Act	**Regulation Z of the Truth-in-Lending Act (TILA)** addresses the accurate advertising of credit terms to consumers by lenders or others advertising credit terms including real estate brokers. Also see comment on the TILA-RESPA Integrated Disclosure Rule above.
Sale-leaseback	
Satisfaction of mortgage	
Seller concessions	**Seller concessions** or contributions are an arrangement in which the seller pays certain financing or closing costs for the buyer. If there is a seller concession in place, the seller pays for part or all of these costs that may be thousands of dollars.
Subprime lenders/predatory lending practices	**Subprime lenders** are companies that provide loans to homebuyers who do not have good credit histories or who are risky candidates for loans because of their incomes. Subprime lenders engage in **predatory lending practices** such as providing mortgage loans to unqualified buyers and also encouraging borrowers to increase their debt as the equity in their homes increases.

Land Use Regulations/Development

Key Term	Comment
Article 9-A of the Real Property Law	
Condemnation/eminent domain/escheat	Government may act to acquire private property. **Eminent domain** is the right or power of government and its agencies to take private property for public use. **Condemnation** is the actual taking of property under the power of eminent domain. **Escheat** is the power of the state to take title to a deceased person's property when no one else is qualified to receive the title.
Feasibility study	
Infrastructure	
Interstate Land Sales Full Disclosure Act	
Moratorium	
Nonconforming use	
Police power	**Police power** is a very encompassing right of government to fulfill its responsibility to provide for public health, safety, and welfare. Police power enables government to enact laws and regulations in the name of the public good.
Spot zoning	**Spot zoning** is illegal in New York. It occurs when local government allows rezoning of a specific property to permit a use different from the zoning requirements for that area. This sometimes is implemented to raise property tax revenues for the municipality. An example might be an industrial spot zone that allows an industrial plant in a residential community.
Transfer of development rights	
Variance/area variance/use variance	
Zoning/Zoning Board of Appeals	

Construction

Key Term	Comment
Flashing	
Footing/foundation	
Headers	
Joist	
NYS General Business Law: Warranties on new home sales and home improvements	According to Article 36-B of the New York General Business Law, implied in all contracts of sale for new housing is a one-year builder's warranty against defects in construction; a two-year warranty for all plumbing, electrical, and heating and air conditioning systems; and a six-year warranty covering material defects.
Outlots	
Platform and slab-on-grade construction	
Roofing terms—eave/fascia/frieze board/pitch/ridge beam/sheathing/soffit	See **Marcia's List Figure 1** that illustrates roofing components and where they are located on the structure of a typical residential house. Look up any of the terms that you are unsure of in the subject review (key terms) section of this *Cram* under the heading, *Construction.*
Smoke alarm and carbon monoxide detector affidavit	
Voltage/amperage	

Marcia's List

Figure 1 Roof components

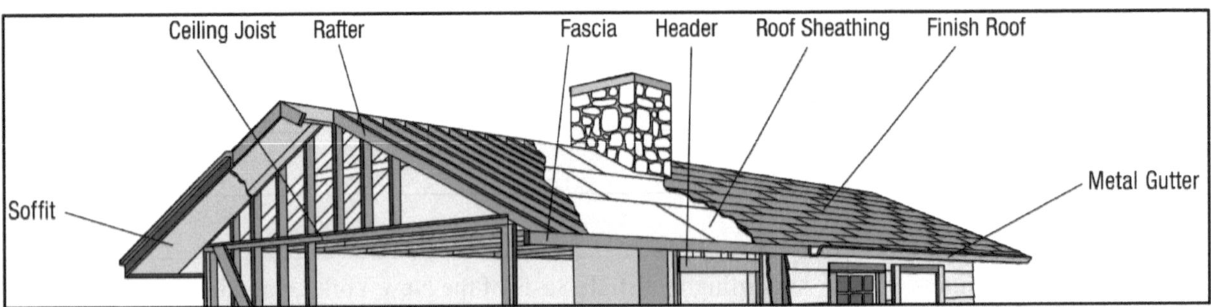

Source: The Home Inspection Book: A Guide for Professionals by Marcia Darvin Spada.

Environmental Issues

Key Term	Comment
Asbestos/friability	In older building construction, **asbestos** was widely used because it is strong, durable, fire retardant, and an efficient insulator. The problem with asbestos is its **friability** or its ability to crumble when it is displaced. The asbestos particles can cause lung disease in those who handle it without training and proper protection. It is no longer used in building products.
Comprehensive Environmental Response, Compensation and Liability Act (CERCLA) (1980)/Superfund Amendment (1986)	The **Comprehensive Environmental Response, Compensation and Liability Act (CERCLA)** is a federal law to correct environmental problems created by uncontrolled waste disposal. The **Superfund Amendments and Reauthorization Act (SARA),** enacted later, strengthened CERCLA by imposing stringent clean-up standards and expanding the definition of persons liable for clean-up costs including the "innocent landowner" defense.
Due diligence	
Environmental impact statement	
Lead	
Radon	

Residential Lead-based Paint Hazard Reduction Act	The federal **Residential Lead-based Hazard Reduction Act** calls for a mutually agreeable 10-day period for a lead paint assessment before a purchaser becomes obligated under a contract. The Act applies to target properties built before 1978. Disclosure is the key. Buyers can still purchase a property that has lead-based paint with disclosure by the seller and agreement by the buyer.
Responsibilities of the NYS Department of Health and NYS Department of Environmental Conservation	
State Environmental Quality Review Act	
Urea formaldehyde foam insulation (UFFI)	

Valuation Process and Pricing Properties

Key Term	Comment
Absorption rate	**The absorption rate** is the time it would take to sell properties in a given area if no other properties are put up for sale in the meantime. The absorption rate is related to the law of supply and demand in that the more properties in the marketplace (supply) the lower the absorption rate will be.
Difference between a comparative market analysis (CMA) and an appraisal	A **comparative market analysis (CMA)** is not an appraisal. Rather, it is an analysis of the competition in the marketplace that a property will face upon sale attempts and uses current competing listings, sold properties, and expired listings to analyze the market and arrive at a price. An **appraisal** is an unbiased estimate of a property's value as of a certain date. The sales comparison approach is an appraisal approach that most closely resembles a CMA.
Direct/indirect costs/ price	**Direct costs** are also called *hard costs* and include the cost of labor and materials for construction of the building. **Indirect costs** support the project including architectural and engineering fees, professional fees such as surveyors, attorneys, and appraisers, and financing costs. The **price** that is paid for the property may be above or below the cost depending on the market and whether or not the building costs exceed the market value of the building because of delays or other construction problems.

Evaluation	An **evaluation** does not necessarily find a price for a property. It is a study of the nature, quality, or utility of certain property interests in which a value estimate is not always required. Evaluations include land use, highest and best use, and feasibility studies and look at the supply and demand in the community.
Market value	
Paired sales analysis	**Paired sales analysis** is used to compare two separate items in two different properties to determine the adjustments for the sales comparison approach. Results are more accurate with more than one comparison.
Sales comparison, income, cost approaches to value	
Supply and demand	

Human Rights and Fair Housing/Advanced Fair Housing and Fair Lending

Key Term	Comment
Americans with Disabilities Act	
Blockbusting, steering, redlining	It is important to understand the meaning of these illegal discriminatory practices. Illegal **blockbusting** occurs when real estate salespersons induce owners to list property for sale or rent by telling them that persons of a particular protected class are moving into the area. This may cause panic selling, giving the broker new listings and eventually new sales. Illegal **steering** occurs when brokers or others direct prospective minority purchasers to presently integrated areas to avoid integration of nonintegrated areas. Illegal **redlining** occurs when lenders refuse to make loans to purchase, construct, or repair a dwelling by discriminating against any of the protected classes.
Cease and desist list	
Civil Rights Act of 1866	
Gentrification	**Gentrification** is a process through which renovation in a deteriorated urban neighborhood attracts more affluent homeowners and often displaces lower-income residents. This process can be devastating to residents who are pushed out of neighborhoods that they have called home for perhaps many years or generations of families.

Jones v. Mayer Supreme Court decision	
NYS Human Rights Law	
Non-solicitation order	
Protected classes	**Protected classes** are groups of individuals for whom it is illegal to discriminate against under federal, state, and local laws. Protected classes in New York State for housing include race, color, religion, national origin, sex, disability, familial status, age, marital status, military status, gender identity, and sexual orientation. Municipalities may have other protected classes such as in New York City.
Testers	

Real Estate Mathematics

Key Term	Comment
Acre	An **acre** is 43,560 square feet. You will not be able to compute an acreage question if you do not know the square footage of an acre.
Appreciation/ Depreciation	
Area formulas	Formula for area of a rectangle or square: Area = Length × Width, or A = L × W Formula for area of a triangle: Area = (0.5 × Base) × Height
Income, Rate, Value (IRV) formula	See **Marcia's List Figure 2** that explains how to use the IRV formula.
Interest	
Percentage formulas	**Commission**: Sales price × Rate of commission = Total commission **Mortgage and interest**: Principal × Rate = Annual interest **Appreciation and depreciation**: Original value × Percent of appreciated value = New value **Points**: Loan × Number of points (%) = Dollars in points

Marcia's List

Figure 2 IRV Formula

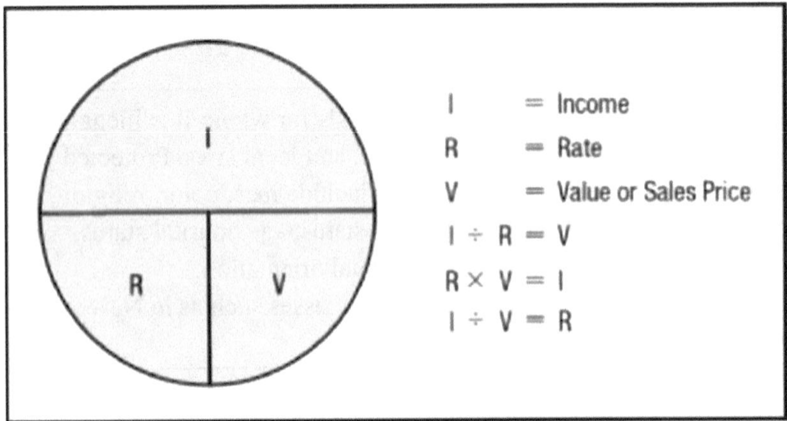

Source: © 2021 Mbition LLC

Municipal Agencies

Architectural Review Board
Conservation Advisory Council
Historic Preservation/Landmark Commission/Planning board
Receiver of Taxes
Village Board of Trustees

Property Insurance

Key Term	Comment
Actual cash value/replacement cost	The **actual cash value (ACV)** for insurance purposes means that the insured is reimbursed for the replacement cost *minus* the physical depreciation of the lost or damaged property. In contrast, the **replacement cost** means that the insured is covered and reimbursed for the actual cost of replacing the damaged property. For example, if a refrigerator is destroyed in a fire, the replacement cost will be the cost of buying another refrigerator.
Deductible	
Liability insurance	
Package policy	
Umbrella policy	

Taxes and Assessments

Key Term	Comment
Ad valorem/In rem	Ad valorem and in rem are Latin terms. **Ad valorem** means according to the value. In New York, the real property tax is based on the fair market value of real property. **In rem** refers to a legal proceeding brought against the real property and not against an individual and his personal property. An example is a property tax lien.
Assessed value	
Assessing unit/approved assessing unit	
Assessment/assessor	
Board of Assessment Review (BAR)	
Grievance	
Homestead	
NYS Office of Real Property Tax Services	
Residential Assessment Ratio (RAR)	
Special assessment/special assessment districts	
Tax levy/tax rate	The **tax levy** is the amount that a municipality must raise to meet budgetary requirements by taxing real property. The **tax rate** is determined by the amount of the tax levy and expressed either in dollars per $100 of assessed value or in mills (one mill is one-tenth of a cent) per $1,000 of assessed value. The formula for computing a property tax bill is: Assessed value x tax rate = annual taxes.
Tax certiorari proceeding	

Condominiums and Cooperatives

Key Term	Comment
Alteration agreement	
By-laws	
Common elements	**Common elements** are areas and utilities in a condominium or cooperative building shared by the owners. These items can include the elevators and hallways as well as recreational facilities.
Condominium/cooperative	
Covenants, Conditions, and Restrictions (CCRs)	
Declaration House Rules	
Maintenance	
Offering statement	
Proprietary lease/shares of stock	Instead of a deed at transfer of a cooperative apartment, the seller delivers to the buyer a **proprietary lease,** a long-term lease creating an estate for years to the apartment. A cooperative ownership is not a fee simple ownership. The shareholders do not own real estate, but a proportionate number of **shares of stock** in a cooperative corporation.
Sponsor	

Commercial and Investment Properties/Real Property Investment

Key Term	Comment
Capitalization rate	
Cash flow	
Cash-on-cash return	
Common areas	
Debt service	
Gross income multiplier	
Gross rent multiplier	

Lease escalation clauses and other lease clauses	**Lease escalation clauses** call for increased costs to the tenant for different reasons at specified times during the lease term. These clauses are favorable to the property owner as they protect the property owner against increases in operating costs. During the past several decades, especially when vacancy rates are low, escalation clauses can generate a hidden profit for the owner, often at a large and not always justified cost to the tenant. There are **other lease clauses** including those that address sublease and assignment.
Leverage	
Net operating income/gross income	
Proforma statement	
Rate of return	
Sensitivity analysis	
Short sale	A **short sale** is a transaction in which the sale proceeds fall short of the balance owed on the property. It is used when a borrower cannot pay back the mortgage and the lender decides that selling the property at a loss is better than going after the borrower for the full indebtedness. In a short sale, the lender agrees to discount the balance due on the mortgage because of a financial hardship on the part of the borrower.
Tax shelter	
Time value of money	
Triple net lease	
Usable square footage/rentable square footage/loss factor	The **usable square footage** is the area contained within the space that the tenant occupies. Property owners quote rent in terms of rentable, not usable, square footage. The **rentable square footage** equals the entire space including the usable square footage and the tenant's pro rata share of the building's common areas such as the lobby. A property owner views the difference between the rentable and usable area in a commercial space as the **loss factor** such as hallways and other common areas.

Income Tax Issues in Real Estate Transactions

Key Term	Comment
Active income/passive activity income/portfolio income	
Basis/adjusted basis	The **basis** of a property, for income tax purposes, is usually its cost. The **adjusted basis** is the original cost of the property or other basis plus certain additions and minus certain deductions such as depreciation and casualty losses (some kind of damage).
Capital gain/$250,000/$500,000 IRS Code special exclusion	**Capital gain** is the profit realized from the sale of any capital investment including real estate. A capital gain occurs when an investor sells the asset for more than the basis. For income tax purposes, capital gain may be taxed at a lower rate than other income. For example, a **special exclusion in the IRS Code** gives home sellers a tax break on capital gains when they are selling their home. Home sellers may be eligible to exclude up to **$250,000** if single, or up to **$500,000,** if married, of the capital gain on the sale of their residence.
Recaptured depreciation	
Straight-line depreciation	The building and improvements are depreciable over 27½ years for income-producing residential property on a straight-line depreciation basis. The basis normally is the cost of acquiring the property reduced by the estimated salvage value of the property at the end of its useful life. **Straight-line depreciation** means that the portion allocated to the building is divided by 27.5 to determine an equal amount of depreciation allowance each year.
Tax depreciation	
Tax-deferred exchange/boot	Performing a 1031 **tax-deferred exchange** allows an individual to defer capital gains taxes on real property bought and sold for investment purposes and does not include the exchange of personal residences. If an exchangor receives cash or some other type of nonqualifying property in the exchange, this is called the **boot**.

Mortgage Brokerage

Key Term	Comment
Difference among mortgage banker/mortgage broker/mortgage loan originator/mortgage loan servicer	A **mortgage broker** is an individual or a company registered by the NYSDFS that is in the business of offering, soliciting, processing, placing, or negotiating mortgage loans for others. *A mortgage broker does not make loans.* A **mortgage loan originator (MLO)** is an individual licensed by the NYSDFS who *works for* a mortgage broker or banker, and for compensation or gain, takes a residential mortgage loan application or offers or negotiates terms of a residential mortgage loan. A **mortgage banker** is an individual or a company licensed by the NYSDFS to engage in the business of *making* residential mortgage loans. A **mortgage loan servicer (MLS)** is registered by the NYSDFS to service mortgage loans as in receiving scheduled periodic payments from a borrower for a mortgage, including amounts for escrow.
Lender rebate	
Mortgage Broker Dual Agency Disclosure Form	
NYS Department of Financial Services (NYSDFS)	
Prequalification/ preapproval	
Rate lock	

Property Management

Key Term	Comment
Capital expense/variable expense	
Corrective maintenance/preventive maintenance	

Landlord concessions/tenant options	**Landlord concessions** are offered by the lessor to the lessee as an inducement for a longer term on a lease. The concession may include reduced rent for a specific time; a shorter lease duration, a higher tenant improvement allowance, a move-in allowance, or a consent to sublease. **Tenant options** may be in the form of a lease with an option to buy including a right of first refusal if another party comes along wanting to lease the optioned property.
Management agreement	The property **management agreement** or contract creates a general agency relationship in which the owner is the principal and the property manager is the agent for the purposes specified in the agreement.
Management proposal	
Modified rent	
Operating budget/capital reserve budget/stabilized budget	
Property management report	The **property management report**, provided by the property manager to the owner, is a periodic (usually monthly) accounting of all funds received and disbursed. The report contains detailed information about receipts and expenditures for the period covered (in addition to the year-to-date figures).
Resident manager	
Vacancy rate	

Licensee Safety

Key Term	Comment
Buddy system	The **buddy system** and the prospect information form are back-up safety measures. To protect the agent, at least one buddy should know the whereabouts of the real estate agent at all times. The **prospect information form** gives the agent valuable upfront information about the individuals with whom the agent will be working.
Commercial general liability insurance	**Commercial general liability insurance** helps protect for claims such as bodily injury, property damage, or advertising injury. The real estate firm should have both types of insurance.
Cyber security	

Errors and omissions insurance	**Errors and omissions insurance** is a form of liability insurance that helps protect against claims from service-related liability.
NYS Penal Code Article 35	
Prospect information form	

General Business Law (Broker Course Only)

Key Term	Comment
Agricultural District Disclosure	
Arbitration/mediation/ litigation	
Chapter 7, Chapter 11, Chapter 13 of the Bankruptcy Code	
Deed restrictions	
Difference between real and personal property	
Drawer/drawee	
Endorsement	
Equitable distribution	
Foreign Investment in Real Property Tax Act (FIRPTA)	
Mediation/arbitration/ litigation	
Negotiable instruments	A **negotiable instrument** is an unconditional promise or order to pay a fixed amount with or without interest. It must satisfy the requirements of negotiability defined in the Uniform Commercial Code (UCC). Negotiable instruments include drafts, checks, promissory notes, and certificates of deposit.

Uniform Commercial Code (UCC)	The **Uniform Commercial Code (UCC)** is a set of uniform acts adopted individually by the states including New York to simplify, clarify, and modernize the laws governing commercial transactions, including laws and regulations regarding negotiable instruments.

Achieving Agreements through Transaction Analysis (Broker Course Only)

Key Term	Comment
Transactional agreement	**Transaction analysis** offers a method through which a real estate agent can systematically evaluate the many components of a **transactional agreement** to achieve success in making the agreement happen once there are parties willing to negotiate to sell and buy real property. The needs and wants of each party must be prioritized and evaluated as to their importance to the parties involved. With information regarding all facets of the transaction, including the marketplace and the individual considerations of the parties, the agent can achieve success in negotiating a transaction that is mutually beneficial to all parties to the transaction.
Transaction analysis	
Concept of needs and wants	
Fiduciary duties	
User-friendly confidentiality agreement	A **user-friendly confidentiality agreement** is a listing agreement in which the obligations of the real estate broker and the client are stated and agreed upon. This agreement services opens the way for the fiduciary duties that the real estate broker owes to the client through the transaction analysis.

Questions for Your Review

This section provides 380 review questions for topics that appear in the salesperson and broker qualifying courses. The topic titles indicate the name of the relevant section as it appears in both the salesperson and broker course if they are not the same. Some topics below are not in both courses. However, real estate broker applicants must know all background content for the salesperson course as well as the content in the broker course to prepare for their classroom and NYS exams.

Tear out the Answer Sheet on the following pages and use it to record your responses to the Review Questions. You may want to photocopy the blank answer sheet so that you can use it repeatedly to review the questions.

To complete the review questions, choose the letter that best answers the question and record that answer using the Answer Sheet. Check your responses using the "Answer Key for Review Questions" at the back of this guide. The explanation for the correct answer is in the Answer Key. Review all incorrect answers. For further explanation, refer to *New York Real Estate for Salespersons, 6th e* Revised and *New York Real Estate for Brokers 6th e.*

Answer Sheet for Review Questions

1. ______________
2. ______________
3. ______________
4. ______________
5. ______________
6. ______________
7. ______________
8. ______________
9. ______________
10. ______________
11. ______________
12. ______________
13. ______________
14. ______________
15. ______________
16. ______________
17. ______________
18. ______________
19. ______________
20. ______________
21. ______________
22. ______________
23. ______________
24. ______________
25. ______________
26. ______________
27. ______________
28. ______________
29. ______________
30. ______________
31. ______________
32. ______________
33. ______________
34. ______________
35. ______________
36. ______________
37. ______________
38. ______________
39. ______________
40. ______________
41. ______________
42. ______________
43. ______________
44. ______________
45. ______________
46. ______________
47. ______________
48. ______________
49. ______________
50. ______________
51. ______________
52. ______________
53. ______________
54. ______________
55. ______________
56. ______________
57. ______________
58. ______________
59. ______________
60. ______________
61. ______________
62. ______________
63. ______________
64. ______________
65. ______________
66. ______________
67. ______________
68. ______________
69. ______________
70. ______________
71. ______________
72. ______________
73. ______________
74. ______________
75. ______________
76. ______________
77. ______________
78. ______________
79. ______________
80. ______________
81. ______________
82. ______________
83. ______________
84. ______________
85. ______________
86. ______________
87. ______________
88. ______________
89. ______________
90. ______________
91. ______________
92. ______________
93. ______________
94. ______________
95. ______________
96. ______________
97. ______________
98. ______________
99. ______________
100. ______________
101. ______________
102. ______________
103. ______________
104. ______________
105. ______________
106. ______________
107. ______________
108. ______________

Answer Sheet for Review Questions (continued)

109. ____	136. ____	163. ____	190. ____
110. ____	137. ____	164. ____	191. ____
111. ____	138. ____	165. ____	192. ____
112. ____	139. ____	166. ____	193. ____
113. ____	140. ____	167. ____	194. ____
114. ____	141. ____	168. ____	195. ____
115. ____	142. ____	169. ____	196. ____
116. ____	143. ____	170. ____	197. ____
117. ____	144. ____	171. ____	198. ____
118. ____	145. ____	172. ____	199. ____
119. ____	146. ____	173. ____	200. ____
120. ____	147. ____	174. ____	201. ____
121. ____	148. ____	175. ____	202. ____
122. ____	149. ____	176. ____	203. ____
123. ____	150. ____	177. ____	204. ____
124. ____	151. ____	178. ____	205. ____
125. ____	152. ____	179. ____	206. ____
126. ____	153. ____	180. ____	207. ____
127. ____	154. ____	181. ____	208. ____
128. ____	155. ____	182. ____	209. ____
129. ____	156. ____	183. ____	210. ____
130. ____	157. ____	184. ____	211. ____
131. ____	158. ____	185. ____	212. ____
132. ____	159. ____	186. ____	213. ____
133. ____	160. ____	187. ____	214. ____
134. ____	161. ____	188. ____	215. ____
135. ____	162. ____	189. ____	216. ____

Answer Sheet for Review Questions (continued)

217. ______
218. ______
219. ______
220. ______
221. ______
222. ______
223. ______
224. ______
225. ______
226. ______
227. ______
228. ______
229. ______
230. ______
231. ______
232. ______
233. ______
234. ______
235. ______
236. ______
237. ______
238. ______
239. ______
240. ______
241. ______
242. ______
243. ______
244. ______
245. ______
246. ______
247. ______
248. ______
249. ______
250. ______
251. ______
252. ______
253. ______
254. ______
255. ______
256. ______
257. ______
258. ______
259. ______
260. ______
261. ______
262. ______
263. ______
264. ______
265. ______
266. ______
267. ______
268. ______
269. ______
270. ______
271. ______
272. ______
273. ______
274. ______
275. ______
276. ______
277. ______
278. ______
279. ______
280. ______
281. ______
282. ______
283. ______
284. ______
285. ______
286. ______
287. ______
288. ______
289. ______
290. ______
291. ______
292. ______
293. ______
294. ______
295. ______
296. ______
297. ______
298. ______
299. ______
300. ______
301. ______
302. ______
303. ______
304. ______
305. ______
306. ______
307. ______
308. ______
309. ______
310. ______
311. ______
312. ______
313. ______
314. ______
315. ______
316. ______
317. ______
318. ______
319. ______
320. ______
321. ______
322. ______
323. ______
324. ______

Answer Sheet for Review Questions (continued)

325. ____________
326. ____________
327. ____________
328. ____________
329. ____________
330. ____________
331. ____________
332. ____________
333. ____________
334. ____________
335. ____________
336. ____________
337. ____________
338. ____________
339. ____________
340. ____________
341. ____________
342. ____________
343. ____________
344. ____________
345. ____________
346. ____________
347. ____________
348. ____________
349. ____________
350. ____________
351. ____________
352. ____________
353. ____________
354. ____________
355. ____________
356. ____________
357. ____________
358. ____________
359. ____________
360. ____________
361. ____________
362. ____________
363. ____________
364. ____________
365. ____________
366. ____________
367. ____________
368. ____________
369. ____________
370. ____________
371. ____________
372. ____________
373. ____________
374. ____________
375. ____________
376. ____________
377. ____________
378. ____________
379. ____________
380. ____________

Review Questions

License Law and Regulations/ Operating a Real Estate Office

1. Which of the following would NOT result in license suspension or revocation?
   A. engaging in fraudulent practices
   B. accepting compensation from more than one party in a transaction without making a full disclosure to all parties
   C. licensees who are not attorneys giving legal advice
   D. licensees accepting a commission from their sponsoring broker

2. Which of the following requires a real estate license to engage in real estate practices?
   A. building superintendent for one owner
   B. public officers representing government interests
   C. attorneys licensed in New York
   D. auctioneers selling real property

3. A licensee who deposits an earnest money deposit in his personal checking account instead of in the broker's trust account is guilty of:
   A. conversion
   B. commingling
   C. escheat
   D. prescription

4. A major purpose of the real estate license law is to:
   A. protect the profitability of the real estate brokerage profession
   B. establish minimum standards for multiple listing services
   C. protect the public
   D. protect licensees from dishonest real estate investors

5. How many hours of qualifying education must a broker complete?
   A. 75
   B. 90
   C. 120
   D. 150

6. The regulatory agency that oversees the licensure process in New York is the:
   A. Department of Law
   B. Department of State
   C. Department of Housing and Urban Development
   D. Attorney General's Office

7. The minimum age for salesperson licensure is:
   A. 16
   B. 18
   C. 19
   D. 21

8. Which of the following is NOT a mandatory requirement for salesperson licensure in New York?
   A. successful completion of the 75-hour qualifying course
   B. broker sponsorship
   C. U.S. citizenship
   D. passing the NYS licensure examination

9. When transacting real estate business, the document that must be carried by the licensee is a:
   A. listing form
   B. driver's license
   C. photo ID card
   D. business card

10. Licensees must complete continuing education requirements:
    A. every two years upon license renewal unless exempt
    B. every four years upon license renewal
    C. only if they are salespersons
    D. only if they have been in business for less than 10 years

11. Casey, a real estate broker, hired Jamie to help with answering the phone, making appointments, and typing contract forms. What type of license does Jamie need?
   A. salesperson license
   B. associate broker license
   C. broker license
   D. no license

12. Bill decides to open his own brokerage firm. What must he do first?
   A. join a multiple listing service
   B. decide what type of business organization he wants
   C. join the local board of REALTORS®
   D. hire at least two sales associates

13. A legal requirement for the operation of a broker's office does NOT include:
   A. a sign visible from the sidewalk or in the lobby stating that the individual or company is a licensed real estate broker
   B. a separate bank account for escrow deposits
   C. submission of all contract forms for DOS approval
   D. DOS approval of a firm name

14. The NYS Department of State's occupational licensing management system is called:
   A. TRID
   B. *eAccessNY*
   C. Mortgage Nationwide Licensing System
   D. TILA

15. If a broker moves a principal or branch office, DOS must be notified online within how many days?
   A. 5
   B. 10
   C. 15
   D. 20

16. To obtain exam results for the salesperson or broker NYS licensure exams, applicants should:
   A. call the DOS
   B. wait for a "passed" slip to arrive in the mail
   C. view exam results through their accounts in *eAccessNY*
   D. obtain immediate exam results upon completion of the licensure exam

17. Andy, a broker, negotiated the sale of a single-family house. The buyer and seller signed the contract of sale that was reviewed and approved by attorneys for both parties, and financing was approved. A day before closing, the buyers want to back out. Andy:
   A. must forfeit his commission because it is unearned
   B. takes a lesser commission than arranged because of the new circumstances
   C. is entitled to the full commission as originally agreed upon
   D. must forfeit his commission because the transaction involves residential real estate and, if it does not close, the broker cannot be compensated

18. The Harrisons, working with a buyer broker, want to purchase an income property, but they do not like the contract of sale presented by the seller's broker. The buyer broker decides to draw the contract. Which of the following is CORRECT?
   A. The buyer broker can legally do this.
   B. The buyers must agree to the contract form presented to the sellers.
   C. The seller's broker can offer to rewrite the contract form.
   D. Neither the seller broker nor buyer broker can write or rewrite any form of contract.

19. A broker wrote a newspaper ad stating: Spacious house, 1 acre, $100,000, vicinity Catskill Mountains, John Jones, Broker, 914.777.7777. This ad violates DOS regulations because it does not mention:
    A. the name of the geographical area in which the property is located
    B. the terms of available financing
    C. the reason the client is selling
    D. enough detail about the house itself

20. To coordinate market and other critical activities in the real estate office, the office should have a:
    A. daily oversight meeting
    B. written policy and procedures manual
    C. posted copy of Article 12-A
    D. weekly interview with the licensees

Law of Agency

Includes Independent Contractor and Antitrust

21. A broker's commission is determined by:
    A. reference to guidelines established by the Division of Licensing Services
    B. agreement between the broker and principal
    C. reference to the multiple listing service fee schedule
    D. reference to the Department of State's fee schedule

22. In the sale of one- to four-unit residential real estate and condominiums and cooperatives in any size building, a listing agent must first disclose his or her status to a prospective buyer:
    A. when a buyer calls the office
    B. only when instructed to do so by her broker
    C. only when the parties enter into a contract of sale
    D. at the first substantive contact

23. When recruiting licensees to work in a brokerage firm, the broker should first:
    A. review the high school education transcripts
    B. administer a critical thinking skills and personality profile test
    C. inquire into the licensee's family status
    D. view the financial data of the licensee

24. Danielle listed her home with broker Robert. Danielle, however, sold her home without any assistance from broker Robert. A court ruled that Danielle owed Robert a full commission on the sale of her home. This is because Robert:
    A. had an exclusive agency listing agreement
    B. was a seller broker rather than a buyer broker
    C. had an exclusive-right-to-sell listing agreement
    D. had an open listing agreement

25. A buyer broker CANNOT receive compensation for services through which of the following methods? As a:
    A. subagent of the seller
    B. flat fee from the buyer
    C. commission split from a listing broker
    D. combination of a partial flat fee from the buyer and a commission split from the listing broker

26. The agency relationship:
    A. requires the principal to compensate the agent
    B. must be the result of a written agreement
    C. makes the agent responsible for all acts of the principal
    D. is consensual

27. The most common agency relationship between brokers and principals is:
    A. special
    B. general
    C. universal
    D. power of attorney

28. In the sale of one- to four-unit residential property, and residential condominiums and cooperatives in any size building, which situation does NOT require the presentation of a disclosure form to a buyer or seller:
    A. when a buyer makes an appointment to see a property
    B. when entering into a listing agreement with a seller
    C. when a seller agent shows a property to a prospective buyer
    D. when prospects walk-through an open house without any specific contact with the agent

29. If Sell-It-Quick Real Estate arranges with Country Lane Realty to charge the same commission to all prospective sellers, this is called an illegal:
    A. group boycott
    B. price-fixing agreement
    C. market allocation agreement
    D. tie-in arrangement

30. If Give You A Mortgage Company and Sell It Now Realty arrange that customers who purchase a home from Sell It Now will be required to apply for a mortgage through Give You A Mortgage Company, this is called an illegal:
    A. group boycott
    B. price fixing agreement
    C. market allocation agreement
    D. tie-in arrangement

31. In general, most real estate agents are:
    A. independent contractors
    B. employees
    C. free agents
    D. statutory employees

32. In an independent contractor relationship:
    A. Salespersons only receive their commissions twice yearly.
    B. Salespersons can work for any number of different brokers at the same time without permission of the other sponsoring broker.
    C. Salespersons are compensated according to hours worked.
    D. An associate broker-independent contractor can be an office manager.

33. Which of the following regarding the duties of the independent contractor is FALSE? Independent contractors may:
    A. work any hours they choose
    B. terminate the relationship at any time
    C. work from their homes
    D. not show a property without the presence of the sponsoring broker

34. In order to comply with federal and state independent contractor law, what must the broker and salesperson do?
    A. They enter into a written independent contractor agreement.
    B. They enter into a general agency agreement.
    C. They sign a disclosure statement.
    D. The salesperson must show the broker evidence that he does not have other outside employment.

35. In order to qualify under the independent contractor relationship, the agent must:
    A. be a broker or associate broker
    B. be licensed
    C. have been licensed for at least one year
    D. work at least 25 hours per week

36. Which IRS form must a broker prepare if an independent contractor earns more than $600 per year?
    A. Form 1040
    B. Schedule C
    C. Form 1099-MISC
    D. Form 3508 (a) (b)

37. An independent contractor who earns over $600 per year must file:
    A. yearly federal tax returns only
    B. yearly state tax returns only
    C. no tax returns as the broker will take care of the filing
    D. yearly federal and state tax returns

38. How many years must a broker keep records as to the sale or mortgage of one- to four-unit properties?
    A. one year
    B. two years
    C. three years
    D. four years

39. If a salesperson is classified as an independent contractor, which of the following is TRUE?
    A. The broker has no duty to supervise the salesperson's activities.
    B. The broker has a duty to supervise the salesperson's activities.
    C. The broker can only supervise those salespersons who are classified as employees.
    D. The broker can only supervise work that is performed in the real estate office.

40. If a salesperson is classified as an independent contractor, who pays withholding taxes? The:
    A. broker, as it is withheld from the salesperson's commission
    B. seller, who pays the commission
    C. salesperson's pension plan
    D. salesperson must take care of withholding and other tax obligations

41. A broker engaged to act on behalf of a principal as a listing agent for a property is what type of agent?
    A. general
    B. universal
    C. special
    D. unilateral

42. Which of the following is FALSE regarding an exclusive agency listing agreement?
    A. The property is listed with one broker only.
    B. The owner does not have to pay the broker a commission if the owner sells the property.
    C. The broker has a right to his commission if he sells the property.
    D. The property is listed with one or more brokers.

43. In the rental of one- to four-unit residential properties and condominiums and cooperatives in any size building, at the first substantive contact, which of the following is TRUE?
    A. An agent must present the disclosure form to prospective tenants when showing the premises.
    B. No disclosure form is needed at the time that the property is being shown.
    C. The disclosure form need only be presented when signing the lease and at no other time.
    D. The disclosure form need only be used in rental properties that have more than four units.

44. Katy lists her condominium with Broker Beth for $150,000. Broker Beth tells a prospective buyer to submit a low offer because seller Katy is going through a divorce. Broker Beth:
    A. violated the fiduciary relationship
    B. did nothing wrong since an offer came through that Katy was happy with
    C. acted properly as long as Katy does not complain
    D. was correct to tell the buyers this information under her duty to disclose

45. One who is hired through a broker to work for that broker, and the principal is not vicariously liable for the acts of that agent, is called a:
   A. dual agent
   B. broker's agent
   C. subagent
   D. facilitator

46. In New York, dual agency is:
   A. illegal under all circumstances
   B. legal only in commercial transactions
   C. legal with timely disclosure and informed consent
   D. legal only with regard to sales but not rentals

47. What do subagents, listing agents, seller agents, and single agents have in common?
   A. They are all dual agents.
   B. They all represent the seller.
   C. They all must belong to MLS.
   D. They are all cooperating agents.

48. In an exclusive-right-to-sell contract, under what conditions is the listing broker entitled to a commission?
   A. only when the broker sells the property
   B. when the broker or the owner sells the property, but no one else
   C. when anyone including the broker, owner, or other brokers sell the property
   D. only if the listing broker's firm sells the property

49. Excluded from Section 443 of the Real Property Law covering the use of the disclosure form is:
   A. single-family home sales
   B. rentals in one- to four-unit properties and condos and coops in any size building
   C. vacant land
   D. sales of duplex property

50. Sellers, buyers, landlords, and tenants may consent to dual agency:
   A. only at a first substantive contact
   B. under no circumstances
   C. only in the sale or rental of single-family homes
   D. in advance of it occurring

Legal Issues

Part I Estates and Interests

51. The term estate *pur autre vie* refers to a(n):
   A. estate of a former tenant
   B. estate owned by the government
   C. estate managed by an agent
   D. life estate measured by the life of someone other than the life tenant

52. Which of the following is NOT a characteristic of real property?
   A. indestructibility
   B. uniqueness
   C. mobility
   D. limited availability

53. Ownership as tenants by the entirety is limited to:
   A. families with children
   B. a married couple
   C. any two individuals whose names appear on a deed
   D. ownership of commercial properties

54. Public parks and historical monuments are examples of which type of real property?
   A. agricultural
   B. residential
   C. commercial
   D. special purpose

55. A life estate can be defined as:
   A. ownership or possession for someone's lifetime
   B. a measure of profit of the estate
   C. the absorption of one estate into another
   D. a leasehold estate

56. Which of the following is NOT a freehold estate?
   A. fee simple absolute
   B. leasehold
   C. fee simple defeasible
   D. fee simple on condition

57. A grantor conveys 100 acres to his daughter, but if the daughter uses the property for a commercial purpose, her ownership terminates. This is an example of a(n):
   A. fee simple on condition
   B. estate *pur autre vie*
   C. leasehold estate
   D. fee simple absolute

58. Ownership in severalty refers to:
   A. ownership by one owner
   B. co-ownership
   C. a financing charge
   D. purchase of optioned property

59. Chattel refers to:
   A. property pledged as security for payment of a debt
   B. personal property
   C. field for cattle to graze
   D. a type of monetary exchange

60. An interest in land allowing for possession for a definite and limited time is called:
   A. an estate for years
   B. long-term estate
   C. joint tenancy
   D. usury

Part II Liens and Easements

61. A lien is:
   A. a privilege to do a particular act
   B. the right to enter a parcel of land
   C. a claim that one person has against the property of another for a debt
   D. money paid for compensation to use one's land

62. An easement is a(n):
   A. parcel of land
   B. nonpossessory use of land by another
   C. easier route through a property
   D. structure that facilitates drainage

63. The meaning of the term *lis pendens* is:
   A. a legal notice that a lawsuit is pending
   B. Latin for "lease period"
   C. a lien against a property
   D. the extent of authority of a court

64. Mortgages are:
   A. involuntary general liens
   B. voluntary general liens
   C. voluntary specific liens
   D. involuntary specific liens

65. A mechanic's lien is a(n):
   A. involuntary general lien
   B. voluntary general lien
   C. voluntary specific lien
   D. involuntary specific lien

66. Although certain types of liens have priority over other types, what other factor determines the priority of payment of the lien?
   A. the dollar value of the lien
   B. the time and date of filing
   C. the credit history of the person who is responsible for payment
   D. the type of property to which the lien is attached

67. Utility companies generally must obtain which type of easement to run electrical cables or pipe through a property?
    A. easement in gross
    B. easement appurtenant
    C. easement by prescription
    D. easement by grant

68. The land that benefits from an easement appurtenant is called the:
    A. servient tenement
    B. easement in gross
    C. dominant tenement
    D. encumbered property

69. Tree branches that extend over the boundary of one property into another's are called:
    A. easements
    B. created nuisances
    C. acts of nature
    D. encroachments

70. A characteristic of a license to use another's land is that it is:
    A. similar to a lien
    B. the same as an easement
    C. a temporary privilege
    D. a permanent privilege

Legal Issues

Part III Deeds/Conveyance of Real Property

71. A deed is:
    A. a note payable on demand
    B. an agreement between parties to do certain things
    C. a document in writing, executed and delivered, that conveys title to real property
    D. to bequeath by a will

72. The *habendum* clause in a deed is the:
    A. forfeiture clause
    B. defeasance clause
    C. "to have and to hold" clause
    D. mortgaging clause

73. A deed that conveys to a grantee an interest in real estate with no warranty of title is called a(n):
    A. full covenant and warranty deed
    B. executor's deed in the form of a full covenant and warranty deed
    C. special deed
    D. quitclaim deed

74. When a deed is executed, this means that it is:
    A. delivered
    B. acknowledged
    C. signed by the grantor
    D. corrected

75. The party that conveys title to real property is called the:
    A. grantee
    B. grantor
    C. trustee
    D. party of the second part

76. The legal term for the transfer of property is called:
    A. alienation
    B. subrogation
    C. *lis pendens*
    D. execution

77. Which of the following is NOT a judicial deed?
    A. sheriff's deed
    B. binder
    C. executor's deed
    D. referee's deed

78. A deed description that starts with a point or place of beginning is called a:
    A. description by monument
    B. description by reference
    C. metes and bounds description
    D. description by lot and block

79. When a landowner donates a parcel of land for public use, this is called:
    A. dedication
    B. adverse possession
    C. the right of accession
    D. forced grant

80. A male person appointed in a will to carry out its provisions is called the:
    A. testator
    B. legatee
    C. devisor
    D. executor

81. Alienation after death is by:
    A. deed
    B. will
    C. adverse possession
    D. bankruptcy

82. Which of the following is NOT a type of involuntary alienation?
    A. adverse possession
    B. dedication
    C. lien foreclosure sale
    D. bankruptcy

83. The law requiring all deeds be in writing is the:
    A. Statute of Frauds
    B. Statute of Limitations
    C. law of agency
    D. real property law

84. A person may NOT receive title under adverse possession in New York unless the individual:
    A. is at least 25 years of age
    B. has been in possession of the property for a period of at least five years
    C. has secretly lived on the property for eight years
    D. has met all legal requirements and a court confirms what has already taken place

85. If a person dies and leaves a valid will, he is said to die:
    A. intestate
    B. devised
    C. testate
    D. probate

86. To make a gift of real property by will is to:
    A. devise
    B. administer
    C. assign
    D. litigate

87. The term "accretion" refers to the:
    A. taking of private property for public use
    B. dedication of land by a developer
    C. gradual buildup of land in a water course
    D. the wearing away of land by water, wind, or other processes of nature

88. A quitclaim deed is most generally used when:
    A. the strongest form of guarantee of title is required
    B. an attorney is not involved in the transaction
    C. there are only two parties to the transaction
    D. the grantor's rights or interests and nothing more are conveyed

89. A tenancy in common:
   A. does not require the unity of possession
   B. requires that each tenant holds an undivided interest in the entire property
   C. includes the right of survivorship
   D. is the same as a joint tenancy

90. Evidence that something of value is present in a deed is known as:
   A. earnest money
   B. consideration
   C. chattel
   D. devise

Legal Issues

Part IV Title Closing and Costs

91. Title to real estate is transferred:
   A. when a contract for purchase and sale is executed by buyer and seller
   B. when financing for the purchaser is approved by the lending institution
   C. upon execution and delivery of a valid deed
   D. after the broker receives his or her commission

92. Generally, in the closing process, attorneys for a lender represent the best interests of the:
   A. lending institution
   B. purchaser
   C. seller
   D. real estate licensee

93. A federal statute that regulates disclosure and closing requirements relative to a mortgage loan on residential property is the:
   A. Fair Housing Act
   B. Interstate Land Sales Disclosure Act
   C. Mortgage Forgiveness Debt Relief Act
   D. TILA-RESPA Integrated Disclosure Rule

94. An unbroken transfer of successive titles to real property is called:
   A. movable title
   B. conveyable title
   C. chain of title
   D. attorney's opinion of title

95. The document that shows the measurements, boundaries, and area of property is called a(n):
   A. feasibility study
   B. survey
   C. architectural rendering
   D. plat

96. A condensed history pertaining to the title of a property is called a(n):
   A. abstract of title
   B. chain of title
   C. title insurance
   D. intestate succession search

97. One of the most important roles of a licensee before closing is to:
   A. examine the deed to make sure it is valid
   B. prepare the closing statement
   C. examine the abstract of title
   D. arrange and accompany a prospective purchaser through a final inspection of the property

98. A New York tax on the conveyance of title to real property is called the:
   A. mortgage recording tax
   B. real estate transfer tax
   C. capital gains tax
   D. sales tax

99. Which of the following is NOT a buyer debit at closing?
   A. unpaid utility bills
   B. purchase price
   C. discount points
   D. homeowner's insurance

100. Which of the following is NOT a seller debit at closing?
   A. delinquent property taxes
   B. existing mortgage
   C. mortgage insurance
   D. purchase money mortgage taken back from buyer

101. When all interested parties to a title closing meet, their main purpose is to:
   A. remove all clouds on title to the property
   B. transfer title to real property from seller to buyer
   C. arrange financing
   D. draw the deed and other legal documents

102. A deed for a given property is recorded in January 20xx. A subsequent deed is drawn on the same property in June 20xx in the same year, but is not recorded. Which of the following is TRUE?
   A. The June 20xx deed takes priority over the January deed.
   B. The January 20xx takes priority over the June 20xx deed.
   C. The June 20xx deed would only take priority over the January deed if it were a quitclaim deed.
   D. Priority of deeds is not established by the date they are filed.

103. The Commission Escrow Act is a law that protects compensation for a:
   A. seller
   B. buyer
   C. real estate broker
   D. board of REALTORS®

104. Grantor A conveys a certain property to Grantee B; Grantor B then conveys this same property to Grantee C; Grantor D then conveys this same property to Grantee E. Based on this information, which of the following applies?
   A. There is a break in the chain of title.
   B. There is no break in the chain of title.
   C. The chain of title is not a valid method of searching records pertaining to a property's history.
   D. The above illustrates a clear title to the property.

105. A title insurance policy:
   A. is only issued upon receipt of an acceptable abstract or title opinion
   B. is not generally required by lenders
   C. is routinely issued even without an acceptable abstract of title
   D. can only be issued by the NYS Department of Financial Services after an examination of all records pertaining to the property

106. The TILA-RESPA Integrated Disclosure Rule:
   A. provides guidelines to protect sellers with regard to the sale of residential property
   B. requires disclosure of settlement costs before closing
   C. protects banks from lending to individuals who are questionable credit risks
   D. ensures that banks do not have an overabundance of mortgages in their portfolios

107. Which of the following is NOT a buyer debit on a closing statement?
   A. purchase price
   B. loan origination fee
   C. discount points
   D. earnest money deposit

108. Which of the following is NOT a seller debit on a closing statement?
   A. delinquent real property taxes
   B. purchase money mortgage taken back from buyer
   C. purchase price
   D. broker commission

109. A federal tax on capital gains derived by foreign people from the sale of their U.S. property is called:
   A. FIRPTA
   B. flip tax
   C. sales tax
   D. escrow tax

110. A type of purchase that involves the transfer of shares of stock rather than conveyance through a deed is that of a(n):
   A. condominium
   B. industrial property
   C. cooperative
   D. vacant parcel of land

The Contract of Sale and Leases

Part I Leases

111. A key feature of a periodic lease is:
   A. it automatically renews for another period unless notice is given to terminate
   B. is never for more than one year's duration
   C. is only used for commercial leases
   D. the death of the landlord or tenant, and the heirs of the deceased are not bound by the lease terms

112. A definition of a leasehold estate:
   A. provides title to real property
   B. provides possession, but not title to real property
   C. is conveyed by deed
   D. never exists for a fixed period

113. When the duration of the lease is completely unknown when the lease is signed, this is called a:
   A. fixed estate
   B. periodic estate
   C. month-to-month tenancy
   D. freehold estate

114. A tenant who was originally in lawful possession of a premises but refuses to leave after his right to possession terminates is legally called a:
   A. month-to-month tenant
   B. holdover tenant
   C. squatter
   D. trespasser

115. A lease is most generally a type of:
   A. deed
   B. promissory note
   C. contract
   D. option agreement

116. Which of the following is NOT a standard lease provision?
   A. identification of the premises
   B. competency of the parties to contract
   C. specification of rent and payment
   D. specification of a minimum one-year term

117. When Heath looked over the lease to his apartment, it had so many legal terms and unclear language that he had to have his attorney explain it. This lease:
   A. is perfectly acceptable
   B. should always be read by an attorney before signing
   C. should appear in at least two languages
   D. should be written in a clear and coherent manner using everyday terminology

118. A right of a landlord that does not have to be specified in the lease is a right to:
   A. inspect the leased premises for any reason
   B. remove a tenant from a premises at any time during the lease
   C. enter the premises in an emergency such as a fire
   D. send repair persons to the premises without permission from the tenant

119. If a tenant must leave a leased premise because of lack of heat, he may be able to forfeit his lease obligations and claim:
   A. constructive eviction
   B. actual eviction
   C. forfeiture
   D. *lis pendens*

120. If a landlord sells a building containing rental properties, the new owner may:
   A. evict any of the current tenants without cause
   B. raise the rents on the leased premises before termination of the lease
   C. inspect all of the leased premises without permission from the lessees
   D. none of the above

Part II Contracts

121. Consideration is:
   A. a promise of quiet enjoyment
   B. the giving of something, which need not be monetary value, as an inducement to contract
   C. always expressed as a dollar value
   D. a power of attorney

122. A *meeting of the minds*:
   A. is a contract between an agent and a buyer
   B. means that the agency relationship is confirmed
   C. means that a seller and a buyer have agreed to the contract terms
   D. has nothing to do with offer and acceptance

123. The law that places a time limit on the years allowed to commence a lawsuit is the:
   A. Statute of Limitations
   B. TILA-RESPA Integrated Disclosure Rule
   C. Statute of Frauds
   D. Uniform Commercial Code

124. A contract between two parties who have definitely agreed to the contract terms is called an:
   A. express unilateral contract
   B. express bilateral contract
   C. implied bilateral contract
   D. implied unilateral contract

125. Under an installment land contract, which of the following does NOT apply?
   A. The purchaser has immediate legal title to the property.
   B. It is an express bilateral executory contract.
   C. The purchaser is given possession of the property.
   D. The purchaser must maintain the property.

126. The substitution of a new contract for a prior contract is called:
   A. sublet
   B. novation
   C. rescission
   D. release

127. In general, a valid written listing agreement between a seller and a real estate agent in which a buyer is not yet found is a(n):
   A. implied contract
   B. void contract
   C. unenforceable contract
   D. executory contract

128. If a sales contract states that "time is of the essence," this means that the contract must be performed:
   A. within a reasonable time period
   B. within one year
   C. on or before the date stipulated on the contract
   D. within three months

129. Which of the following is FALSE regarding an earnest money deposit?
   A. It shows the sincerity of buyer.
   B. It legally must accompany an offer to purchase.
   C. It demonstrates financial capability to raise the money called for in the purchase offer.
   D. It may serve as possible liquidated damages to the seller if the buyer defaults.

130. A contract with a minor is:
   A. automatically void
   B. illegal
   C. always invalid
   D. voidable by the minor

Part III Contract Preparation

131. A form of seller financing is a(n):
   A. assumable mortgage
   B. home equity line of credit
   C. FHA loan
   D. purchase money mortgage

132. A portion of the property's purchase price that is paid in cash and NOT part of the mortgage is the:
   A. binder
   B. down payment
   C. assumable mortgage
   D. mortgage commitment

133. Which of the following is generally the first to sign the contract of sale?
   A. purchaser
   B. seller
   C. seller's attorney
   D. real estate broker or salesperson

134. Rafael, a real estate salesperson, advises his buyer clients not to sign a contract of sale prepared by their attorney because he believes that the "as is" clause in the contract will cause them trouble later. Which of the following is TRUE?
   A. Raphael can advise his clients as to legal matters as long as they don't have an attorney.
   B. Raphael can advise his clients about any matters as long as they have signed the agency disclosure form.
   C. Raphael can advise his clients on all contract matters.
   D. Raphael is engaging in the illegal practice of law.

135. An IOLA account is one held by:
   A. real estate brokers
   B. attorneys
   C. apartment sharing agents
   D. mortgage brokers

136. The Lawyer's Fund for Client Protection has to do with attorney:
   A. escrow accounts
   B. licensure
   C. relationships with real estate brokers
   D. court appearances

137. In certain upstate areas, if a real estate salesperson takes a deposit, which of the following is TRUE?
   A. He must keep it in his checking account.
   B. He must lock it in a safe place until the closing.
   C. He must turn it over to his broker.
   D. He can keep it as his commission.

138. Keri is buying a residential single-family property for $450,000. Generally, what would be the customary deposit?
   A. $15,000
   B. $30,000
   C. $45,000
   D. $75,000

139. At what point is a real estate contract of sale binding?
   A. when it is signed by buyer and seller
   B. when it is signed by buyer and seller and agents for each
   C. when it is reviewed and approved by the attorneys for buyer and seller
   D. at closing

140. A document NOT required for closing is a:
   A. survey
   B. certificate of occupancy
   C. prior deed
   D. census statement

Real Estate Finance

141. The mortgagor is the:
   A. lender
   B. broker
   C. borrower
   D. trustee

142. The mortgagee is the:
   A. lender
   B. broker
   C. borrower
   D. trustee

143. A mortgage is a(n):
   A. unilateral implied contract for repayment of a loan
   B. written document pledging a property as security for the repayment of a loan
   C. insurance policy to protect against a variety of hazards
   D. conveyance used to transfer title to real property

144. Which of the following best describes down payments for VA loans?
   A. They are always 5% of the appraised value.
   B. They are typically $5,000.
   C. They are always 10% of the sales price.
   D. They do not always require a minimum down payment.

145. A balloon mortgage is best described as:
   A. based on the borrower's ability to pay
   B. having a larger payment due at the end of its term
   C. covering more than one parcel of real property
   D. an amortized loan

146. When a lender is willing to lower the interest rate at the time the loan is made in return for extra payments of points upfront, this is called:
   A. buydown
   B. usury
   C. apportionment
   D. satisfaction of mortgage

147. An amortized mortgage loan is one that is paid in monthly payments:
   A. with a balloon payment at the end
   B. of interest only
   C. of principal only
   D. of principal and interest

148. A wraparound mortgage:
   A. covers both the mortgaged property and mortgage insurance
   B. covers more than one parcel of real estate
   C. is a subordinate mortgage which includes the same principal obligation secured by a first mortgage against the same property
   D. is not a type of seller financing

149. A document for recording and acknowledging that a mortgage is paid in full is called a:
   A. payoff statement
   B. satisfaction
   C. closing disclosure form
   D. certificate of title

150. The New York agency that raises money from tax-free bonds and applies the money to mortgage loans is called:
   A. Fannie Mae
   B. SONYMA
   C. FDIC
   D. RHS

151. A conventional loan:
   A. involves participation by an agency of the federal government
   B. is always an amortized loan
   C. involves no participation by any agency of the federal government
   D. is an FHA loan

152. A blanket mortgage is one:
   A. that has matured and is open to foreclosure
   B. on personal property as opposed to real property
   C. in which two or more parcels are pledged as security for the mortgage debt
   D. that is junior in lien priority to a previous mortgage

153. One of the most difficult loans for a lender to underwrite because it requires funds to create a project that does not exist is a:
   A. commercial loan of any type
   B. construction loan
   C. home equity line of credit
   D. purchase money mortgage

154. When the monthly payment on a mortgage is less than the full interest amount and does not pay any of the principal, which of the following occurs?
   A. negative amortization
   B. a nonconforming loan
   C. deficiency
   D. default

155. A purchase money mortgage is:
   A. given by a purchaser to the seller to cover part of the purchase price
   B. given by the seller to the purchaser to cover part of the purchase price
   C. a type of swing loan
   D. the same as an installment land contract

156. The clause in a mortgage entitling the lender to declare the principal balance due and payable if the borrower sells the property during the mortgage term is the:
   A. defeasance clause
   B. alienation clause
   C. prepayment penalty clause
   D. granting clause

157. The process by which loan documentation is reviewed and the borrower's ability and willingness to repay the loan is evaluated is:
   A. investment analysis
   B. loan underwriting
   C. loan-to-value ratio analysis
   D. income qualification

158. A short-term loan that may provide funds over and above an already existing loan until permanent financing is in place is known as:
   A. convertible financing
   B. blanket financing
   C. gap financing
   D. flexible payment financing

159. A type of mortgage that gives the lender the option to convert the outstanding balance into an agreed upon percentage of ownership in the property is known as a:
    A. subordinate mortgage
    B. convertible mortgage
    C. flexible payment plan
    D. bridge loan

160. A transaction in which a property owner sells a property to an investor who immediately leases back the property to the seller is known as:
    A. release land subdivision financing
    B. ground lease
    C. conversion mortgaging
    D. sale leaseback

Land Use Regulations/ Development

161. Which of the following is generally TRUE?
    A. Escheat is the power of government to take private property for public purposes.
    B. Zoning ordinances are private land use controls.
    C. Deed restrictions are examples of the government's right to control land use.
    D. Eminent domain allows government to take property for public use only if it is for the use and benefit of the public.

162. The doctrine of laches refers to:
    A. loss of legal rights because of failure to assert them
    B. a special real estate lockbox
    C. government restrictions on land use
    D. a lessor's interest in leased property

163. The New York law that protects residents in the purchase of vacant subdivided land sold on the installment plan is:
    A. Article 12-A of the Real Property Law
    B. Article 9-A of the Real Property Law
    C. General Business Law
    D. Statute of Frauds

164. When property reverts to the state due to the lack of heirs, it is called:
    A. eminent domain
    B. equity
    C. escheat
    D. reversion

165. The agency that coordinates information relevant to an environmental impact statement is called the:
    A. Office of the County Clerk
    B. Zoning Board of Appeals
    C. lead agency
    D. coordinating agency

166. Zoning ordinances are an example of the use of a government's:
    A. police power
    B. health regulatory power
    C. right of eminent domain
    D. private restrictions

167. The government agency that sends inspectors onsite to ensure construction code compliance is the:
    A. Zoning Board of Appeals
    B. U.S. Department of HUD
    C. Department of Environmental Conservation
    D. Building Department

168. An in-law apartment that is connected to a residential home is called a(n):
    A. annexation
    B. accessory use
    C. home occupation
    D. group home

169. Hospitals, schools, and courthouses are examples of which type of zoning?
   A. institutional
   B. industrial
   C. public open space
   D. commercial

170. A municipality that imposes a delay in developing property in a given area has issued a(n):
   A. transfer of development rights
   B. moratorium
   C. demographic evaluation
   D. infrastructure assessment

171. A subdivision plat is generally recorded with the:
   A. Department of State
   B. local zoning board
   C. county clerk
   D. assessor's office

172. The study of the physical features and contours of land is known as:
   A. topography
   B. infrastructure
   C. demography
   D. geology

173. The purpose of planning is to:
   A. provide for the orderly growth of a community
   B. create the greatest allowable density patterns
   C. create a larger tax base
   D. protect developers from excessive building code requirements

174. The agency that has the statutory authority to review and approve plans for subdivision development is the:
   A. local building department
   B. local planning board or commission
   C. Department of Environmental Conservation
   D. county assessor's office

175. The New York law that requires local government to assess the environmental significance of actions that it must approve is the:
   A. Superfund Amendment
   B. State Environmental Quality Review Act
   C. Clean Air Act
   D. EPA

176. If a property owner is denied a request for a variance, he:
   A. must accept the decision
   B. may petition the county assessor's office for a new ruling
   C. may petition the New York Supreme Court through an Article 78 proceeding
   D. may request a new hearing before the planning board within 30 days

177. Vincent wants to use part of his house as a broker's office. This use is not allowed in his neighborhood. Vincent must:
   A. apply for use variance
   B. apply for an area variance
   C. forget about the idea, as New York residents cannot change the use of their homes for any reason
   D. apply for a special zone

178. One of the differences between a request for a variance and a special use permit is that special use permits:
   A. do not require that the applicant demonstrate undue hardship
   B. are illegal in New York
   C. are only allowed for large commercial projects
   D. require an Article 78 proceeding

179. The New York agency that oversees wetland protection is the:
   A. Department of Health
   B. Department of Agriculture
   C. Department of State
   D. Department of Environmental Conservation

180. A type of loan that provides interim financing for subdivision development is known as:
   A. sale leaseback
   B. mini-perm
   C. package mortgage
   D. junior mortgage

Construction

181. Guidelines for minimum separation distances between a well and a septic system are furnished by the:
   A. Environmental Protection Agency
   B. NYS Department of Environmental Conservation
   C. U.S. Department of HUD
   D. NYS Department of Health

182. Which of the following is NOT a consideration in the design and development of a construction site?
   A. drainage
   B. appurtenances
   C. insulation requirements
   D. zoning

183. The concrete base below the frost line that supports the foundation of a structure is called the:
   A. foundation wall
   B. footing
   C. slab
   D. girder

184. The wooden skeleton of a residential property is called the:
   A. frame
   B. walls
   C. sheetrock
   D. foundation

185. Openings for doors and windows in a residential property are supported by:
   A. lally columns
   B. rafters
   C. headers
   D. sill plates

186. Which of the following is TRUE?
   A. The lesser the degree of insulation, the greater the R-factor.
   B. The greater the degree of insulation, the greater the R-factor.
   C. R-factor ratings apply only to blanket insulation.
   D. The R-factor has nothing to do with insulation.

187. A type of heating system that heats water in a boiler and then uses circulator pumps to allow the heated water to travel through pipes to convectors is called a(n):
   A. forced warm air system
   B. electric heating system
   C. heat pump
   D. hot water system

188. Which of the following is FALSE regarding the plumbing system?
   A. The systems for water supply and wastewater are combined.
   B. It must follow local code guidelines as to materials used.
   C. Private systems must adhere to minimum separation distances for wells and septic systems.
   D. If no local code guidelines are available, systems must comply with the New York Fire Prevention and Building Code.

189. The minimum electrical service installed in a residential home must be:
   A. 50 amps
   B. 100 amps
   C. 150 amps
   D. 200 amps

190. A device that melts and opens a circuit to stop electrical power when overheating occurs is called a:
   A. fuse
   B. distribution panel
   C. service drop
   D. voltmeter

191. The first wooden member of the house that is used as the nailing surface for the floor system is the:
   A. foundation wall
   B. sill plate
   C. fascia
   D. ridge beam

192. The Act administered by the Consumer Financial Protection Bureau that regulates the sale of unimproved lots across state lines is known as the:
   A. Superfund Amendment and Reauthorization Act
   B. Interstate Land Sales Full Disclosure Act
   C. Uniform Building Code
   D. Residential Warranty Corporation Act

193. The National Electric Code:
   A. only applies to commercial structures
   B. is not valid in New York
   C. offers minimum guidelines and standards for electrical installations
   D. is overseen by the NYS Office of General Services

194. The law that is the guideline for New York's drinking water regulations is the:
   A. Superfund Amendments and Reauthorizations Act
   B. Residential Lead-based Paint Hazard Reduction Act
   C. Safe Drinking Water Act
   D. Department of Environmental Conservation regulations

195. The New York law that provides minimum standards for construction materials and safety is:
   A. General Business Law
   B. not state law since only local statutes are used
   C. Article 9-A of the Real Property Law
   D. NYS Fire Prevention and Building Code

196. According to the New York General Business Law, how many years must a builder warrant new construction against defects in construction?
   A. one
   B. two
   C. three
   D. five

197. After signing a home improvement contract, an owner has up to how many days to cancel it?
   A. one business day after the contract was signed
   B. three business days after the contract was signed
   C. one week after the contract was signed
   D. one month after the contract was signed

198. The water supply system in New York is regulated by the:
   A. Army Corp of Engineers
   B. Department of Agriculture
   C. State Department of Public Works
   D. Department of Health

199. The New York law that sets minimum energy efficiency requirements for the design of new buildings and renovations and additions to existing buildings is:
   A. Article 9-A of the Real Property Law
   B. Energy Conservation Construction Code
   C. General Business Law
   D. Human Rights Law

200. A seller must sign an affidavit indicating the presence of a smoke alarm and carbon monoxide detector in the sale of:
A. commercial properties
B. one- and two-family residential properties and residential condominiums and cooperatives
C. apartment units only
D. only properties used by the public

Environmental Issues

201. Which of the following acts imposed stringent cleanup standards and expanded the definition of those responsible for cleanup?
A. National Environmental Policy Act
B. State Environmental Quality Review Act
C. Clean Air Act
D. Superfund Amendments and Reauthorization Act

202. Local drinking water problems are remediated by the:
A. Department of Environmental Conservation
B. local departments of health
C. Department of Agriculture
D. Department of State

203. One of the biggest dangers in highly corrosive water is that it may contain large amounts of:
A. radon
B. PCBs
C. lead
D. CFCs

204. The regulatory agency that licenses individuals to apply termiticide in New York is the:
A. Department of Environmental Conservation
B. Department of Health
C. Department of Parks
D. Department of State

205. A fibrous mineral formerly used in many construction applications such as ceiling tiles and roof shingles is called:
A. lead
B. asbestos
C. radon
D. UFFI

206. The Residential Lead-based Hazard Reduction Act calls for:
A. a ban on the sale of all homes that contain lead paint
B. homeowners to remove all lead paint before the property is put up for sale
C. funding for homeowners to remove all lead paint from their home
D. a mutually agreeable 10-day period for a lead paint assessment before a purchaser becomes obligated under a contract

207. Radon most generally enters the home:
A. through openings in the attic or roof area
B. when people leave their windows open for long periods of time
C. when there is a heavy rainstorm
D. through small cracks in the foundation wall

208. According to the EPA, which level of radon concentration is considered safe?
A. no level
B. 1 picocurie
C. 2 picocuries
D. 4 picocuries

209. If the indoor air quality of a commercial building causes large numbers of people to fall ill, this is called:
A. an unhappy event
B. sick building syndrome
C. radon toxicity
D. commercial building syndrome

210. A toxic liquid organic compound that was used as an insulating medium for electrical transformers and which has polluted both the soil and waterways in New York is:
A. radon
B. UFFI
C. chlorofluorocarbons
D. PCBs

Valuation Process and Pricing Properties

211. An analysis of the competition in the market place that a property will face upon sale attempts is called a(n):
A. appraisal
B. evaluation
C. comparative market analysis
D. cost approach to value

212. Which of the following methods are NOT used for appraisal purposes?
A. income approach
B. sales comparison approach
C. cost approach
D. comparative market analysis

213. An owner who uses a residential property for vacation purposes only may attribute which type of value to this property?
A. assessed value
B. insurance value
C. value in use
D. investment value

214. A market value estimate of real property is a(n):
A. appraisal of a single-family home
B. feasibility study
C. highest and best use study
D. land utilization study

215. A property will probably NOT sell for market value if:
A. buyer and seller are equally motivated
B. a reasonable time is allowed for exposure in the market place
C. the buyer and seller are related to each other
D. it is an arms-length transaction

216. Which of the following is TRUE?
A. Price always equals cost.
B. Price is always more than the cost.
C. Price is always equivalent to the market value of a property.
D. Price is not always equivalent to the market value of a property.

217. In the construction of a property, if time schedules are not met or other construction problems occur, most likely the:
A. market value will equal the cost
B. cost may exceed the market value
C. cost will be below the market value
D. price will definitely have to equal the cost

218. In the construction of a property, the costs of architectural and engineering fees are called:
A. direct costs
B. hard costs
C. payment schedule
D. indirect costs

219. Comparables used in the creation of a comparative market analysis should be:
A. as similar as possible to the subject property
B. exactly the same as the subject property
C. as different as possible from the subject property
D. located in a different neighborhood from the subject property

220. Which of the following is NOT an appropriate comparable for a comparative market analysis?
  A. expired listings
  B. current competing properties
  C. properties yet to be built
  D. sold properties

Human Rights and Fair Housing/Advanced Fair Housing and Fair Lending

221. Redlining is:
  A. steering home seekers to a particular neighborhood
  B. drawing red circles on a zoning map indicating what areas are prime housing markets
  C. denying or restricting loans in a certain area by a lending institution
  D. a zoning procedure

222. The Civil Rights Act of 1866:
  A. prohibits all discrimination based on race
  B. prohibits discrimination in federally funded housing only
  C. allows an exception to racial discrimination for an owner-occupied two-family dwelling
  D. does not apply to nonlicensed persons

223. For violation of the Federal Fair Housing Act, a first-time civil monetary penalty may be:
  A. up to $10,000
  B. up to $75,000
  C. not more than $1 million
  D. The penalty is not limited by statute and may be determined by the court.

224. Illegal blockbusting is described as:
  A. purchase of a home in a neighborhood by a member of a minority group
  B. directing home seekers into an area to change its character
  C. directing certain home seekers away from an area in order to maintain its character
  D. homeowners being told by real estate salespeople that a member of a protected class is moving into their neighborhood, causing them to panic and place their homes for sale

225. What is illegal steering?
  A. leading prospective homeowners toward or away from certain areas
  B. refusing to make loans to persons in certain areas
  C. a requirement to join MLS
  D. a practice of fixing commission rates by an MLS steering committee

226. What is one of the differences between the federal Fair Housing Law and the New York Human Rights Law?
  A. Federal law does not cover rental housing.
  B. New York law does not have exemptions as in the federal law.
  C. New York law covers commercial property as well as residential.
  D. Federal law lacks monetary penalties for violation.

227. The Americans with Disabilities Act covers:
  A. single-family homes
  B. vacant land
  C. places of amusement only
  D. buildings open to the public as well as multi-family dwellings

228. In addition to federal law, protected classes under the New York Human Rights Law include:
   A. familial status and race
   B. age and marital status
   C. race and religion
   D. disability and familial status

229. Nancy owns and lives in a duplex in Rochester, New York. She wishes to rent the other apartment. Nancy:
   A. must rent her home to any person who is financially qualified
   B. may not discriminate against individuals because they are a certain race
   C. must rent her home to families with children, if approached
   D. must place her property for rent in a local newspaper if she does not use the services of a salesperson

230. An area designated by the NYS Department of State where salespeople and brokers may not solicit listings is called a(n):
   A. cease and desist zone
   B. area under moratorium
   C. quarantined zone
   D. market allocation area

Real Estate Mathematics

231. A real estate broker earns a $12,500 commission in the sale of a condominium. His commission rate is 7%. What is the selling price of the condo? (Round to the nearest dollar.)
   A. $158,600
   B. $178,571
   C. $357,269
   D. $458,213

232. A broker earns a commission of $8,250. His commission rate is 7.5%. What is the selling price of the property?
   A. $80,000
   B. $90,000
   C. $100,000
   D. $110,000

233. A property valued at $475,000 appreciates 2% per year. How much is the property worth after two years?
   A. $484,500
   B. $493,175
   C. $494,190
   D. $501,160

234. An office space is 52 feet wide × 162 feet long and leases for $75,000 per year. What is the price per square foot?
   A. $8.90
   B. $14.50
   C. $20
   D. $25

235. An acre of land has a width of 425 feet. If this acre of land is rectangular in shape, what is its length?
   A. 85.5 feet
   B. 93 feet
   C. 102.5 feet
   D. 120 feet

236. The purchase price of a property is $175,000. The bank authorizes a loan-to-value ratio of 90%. What is the amount of the loan authorized?
   A. $90,000
   B. $100,000
   C. $125,000
   D. $157,500

237. A property closes on November 15. The yearly property taxes are $2,500. What is the credit to the seller on the closing statement?
   A. $256
   B. $312.50
   C. $375
   D. $476.89

238. A property sells for $120,000. The buyer obtains an 80% loan. If the bank charges 3 points at closing, how much in points must the buyer pay?
   A. $1,589
   B. $2,245
   C. $2,880
   D. $3,496

239. A loan of $50,000 is repaid in full one year after the loan is made. If the interest rate on the loan is 9.5%, what amount of interest is owed?
   A. $4,750
   B. $5,000
   C. $5,765
   D. $6,987

240. A property sells at the assessed value. The annual real property tax is $2,304 at a tax rate of $24 per thousand of tax value. The property is taxed at 80% of assessed value. What is the selling price?
   A. $110,000
   B. $120,000
   C. $130,000
   D. $140,000

Municipal Agencies

241. The legislative power of a city is vested in:
   A. the mayor
   B. its city council
   C. the state legislature
   D. the zoning board of appeals

242. The main function of a city or town planning board is to advise on:
   A. environmental issues
   B. wetland regulation
   C. school policy
   D. land use matters

243. The government agency that may grant a variance is the:
   A. citizen's advisory council
   B. town board
   C. zoning board of appeals
   D. planning board

244. Jonas is seeking information about constructing a property near a wetland. He can find information and guidance from the:
   A. conservation advisory council
   B. architectural review board
   C. zoning board of appeals
   D. county legislature

245. Building departments CANNOT:
   A. issue building permits
   B. issue certificates of occupancies
   C. inspect ongoing construction
   D. rule on variance applications

246. The document containing each property's assessment in a municipality is the:
   A. title register
   B. city or town budget
   C. assessment roll
   D. tax map

247. In some cities and towns, the official or agency that collects fees for water usage and other permits is the:
   A. tax assessor
   B. receiver of taxes
   C. engineer
   D. building department

248. The NYS agency that oversees the placement of a property in or near a wetland is the:
   A. Department of Environmental Conservation
   B. Department of Health
   C. Department of Public Works
   D. Department of State

249. A town or village planning board consists of how many members?
   A. two to four
   B. five to seven
   C. seven to nine
   D. any number as decided by the town board or village board of trustees

250. Meri wants more information about renovating a historic property. Which agency would be LEAST likely to be involved in this process?
   A. historic preservation commission
   B. zoning board of appeals
   C. building department
   D. conservation advisory council

Property Insurance

251. A clause in an insurance policy that modifies or changes the insurance policy in some way is known as a(n):
   A. endorsement
   B. peril
   C. deductible
   D. umbrella

252. Insurance obtained through the New York Property Insurance Underwriting Association can be undesirable because:
   A. it is unreliable
   B. the premiums are higher than those obtained through the voluntary market
   C. only certain areas of New York are insured
   D. there is a long waiting list

253. The National Flood Insurance Program is administered by:
   A. the NYS Insurance Department
   B. FEMA
   C. HUD
   D. the U.S. Army Corps of Engineers

254. According to New York law, which of the following deductibles must be disclosed to the insured?
   A. personal property
   B. fire
   C. flood
   D. windstorm

255. As long as the insurance company states the reason for the cancellation, an insurance policy may be cancelled within how many days?
   A. 25
   B. 30
   C. 60
   D. 90

256. The cost of a homeowner's policy is directly related to the:
   A. policy holder only
   B. property only
   C. statewide fee schedule
   D. both A and B

257. The amount the insured must pay toward a claim before receiving any policy benefits is called the:
   A. premium
   B. peril
   C. deductible
   D. endorsement

258. An excess liability policy, providing additional coverage above that offered by primary policies is called a(n):
   A. replacement cost premium
   B. umbrella policy
   C. luxury coverage
   D. homeowner's special form policy

259. In the insurance policy contract, the basic coverage is outlined in which part of the policy?
    A. declarations page
    B. actual cost section
    C. contingency plan endorsement section
    D. statement of liability

260. Which of the following is NOT a type of coverage in an insurance policy?
    A. dwelling
    B. personal property
    C. loss of use
    D. functional obsolescence

Taxes and Assessments

261. Which of the following is an example of a property that is NOT tax exempt?
    A. VA hospital
    B. synagogue
    C. gas station
    D. state office building

262. The tax rate is determined by the:
    A. city or town council
    B. assessor
    C. amount of the tax levy
    D. census

263. The percentage at which properties are assessed in a locality is called the:
    A. tax levy
    B. level of assessment
    C. residential assessment ratio
    D. tax rate

264. Reassessments can be performed on properties:
    A. when improvements are made only
    B. on a regular prescribed basis only
    C. as a random spot check on any property in the locality
    D. both A and B

265. Which of the following CANNOT collect real property taxes in New York?
    A. cities
    B. towns
    C. villages
    D. the state

266. Which of the following CANNOT receive an exemption from paying real property taxes?
    A. those with disabilities
    B. property owners under 25 years old
    C. seniors
    D. veterans

267. The purpose of the board of assessment review is to:
    A. levy taxes
    B. set uniform percentages
    C. develop the equalization rate
    D. hear grievances

268. If a property owner believes that his property's assessed value is greater than the property's full value, he may claim that he has been subject to:
    A. unequal assessment
    B. excessive assessment
    C. unlawful assessment
    D. misclassification

269. A judicial review of a tax protest in the New York Supreme Court is called a(n):
    A. tax certiorari proceeding
    B. grievance
    C. Article 78 proceeding
    D. tax hearing

270. The first task in determining the assessment for tax purposes is to:
    A. hold a referendum to decide who is exempt
    B. evaluate the zoning regulations for the community
    C. establish the market value of each parcel of land within the taxing unit
    D. file a petition of appeal

271. Which of the following is generally completely exempt from property taxes?
   A. all private hospitals
   B. all industrial properties
   C. government-owned properties
   D. factories

272. Local governments in New York have the option of offering a reduction of property taxes to:
   A. senior citizens
   B. state employees
   C. condominium and cooperative owners
   D. minors who own real property

273. An *in rem* legal proceeding takes place:
   A. only in assessing units of more than one million people
   B. against the real property directly and not the individual
   C. only if the assessing unit has full value assessment
   D. if the mortgage payment is overdue for more than three months

274. Tax maps for a tax unit are maintained by the:
   A. local planning board
   B. zoning board of appeals
   C. tax assessor
   D. mayor or town supervisor's office

275. The residential assessment ratio (RAR) is NOT used for:
   A. the grievance process
   B. a small claims assessment review
   C. municipalities conducting revaluation projects
   D. a general measure of assessment equity

276. An appraisal for tax purposes and an appraisal for mortgage purposes are:
   A. exactly the same
   B. different in that a tax assessment takes the market value from the appraisal and applies a uniform percentage
   C. different only in that one is completed by an assessor and the other is completed by an appraiser
   D. different because an appraisal for mortgage purposes endeavors to find market value and a tax appraisal endeavors to find value in use

277. The New York agency that certifies the residential assessment ratios is the:
   A. Department of State
   B. Department of Financial Services
   C. Office of Accounting
   D. State Board of Real Property Tax Services

278. Which of the following is classified as non-homestead property?
   A. farm dwelling
   B. factory
   C. condominium
   D. duplex

279. A written complaint filed with the board of assessment review to protest an assessment is known as a(n):
   A. *in rem* legal proceeding
   B. summons and affidavit of complaint
   C. grievance
   D. legal protest

280. The NYS agency that oversees property taxes in New York is the:
   A. Office of Real Property Tax Services
   B. Department of State
   C. Department of Financial Services
   D. Department of Law

Condominiums and Cooperatives

281. Ownership in a cooperative is evidenced by:
   A. shares of stock
   B. a deed
   C. a recognition agreement
   D. an alteration agreement

282. Which type of ownership interest does a cooperative owner have in his real property?
   A. freehold
   B. leasehold
   C. fee simple absolute
   D. tenant-at-will

283. Which of the following is NOT included in a condominium offering plan?
   A. initial declaration
   B. prospectus
   C. initial price of the units
   D. proprietary lease

284. With regard to a condominium or cooperative, whether or not a tenant can advertise from their apartment window, is included in the:
   A. alteration agreement
   B. house rules
   C. recognition agreement
   D. letter of intent

285. A board package, submitted to the cooperative board of directors, consists mainly of:
   A. societal status information
   B. family history
   C. financial data
   D. reasons for purchase

286. An agreement that outlines the responsibilities between the cooperative corporation and the lender is called a(n):
   A. CPS1 statement
   B. subordination agreement
   C. alteration agreement
   D. recognition agreement

287. Which of the following describes a condop?
   A. a cooperative that does not have board interviews
   B. a building that has both condominium and cooperative ownership
   C. a condominium that has no board of directors
   D. a condominium or cooperative that does not have an offering plan adopted by the attorney general

288. Pet restrictions, repair obligations, and use of the common elements are disclosed in a condominium's:
   A. by-laws
   B. letter of intent
   C. CPS1 statement
   D. tenant declaration

289. During the CPS1 period or phase, which of the following is TRUE in the marketing of condominiums or cooperatives?
   A. The developer need not follow any attorney general rules governing advertising.
   B. Only the attorney general can set the price for the units.
   C. The developer may set the market price for the units.
   D. No firm price can be declared by the developer for individual units.

290. Which of the following is TRUE regarding the mansion tax?
   A. The tax applies to all residential properties sold for $1 million or more.
   B. The tax applies only to condominiums and cooperatives when the units are over 5,000 square feet.
   C. It applies to one-, two-, and three-unit residential properties as well as condominiums and cooperatives sold for $1 million or more.
   D. It only applies in New York City.

Commercial and Investment Real Estate/Real Property Investment

291. A benefit that depreciation provides is tax:
   A. credit
   B. deduction
   C. evasion
   D. basis

292. A tax-deductible expense for a business property does NOT include:
   A. advertising
   B. utilities
   C. mortgage principal
   D. insurance

293. An investor purchases a $2,000,000 multi-family apartment complex with a $500,000 down payment. Each month, the cash flow from rentals, less expenses, is $15,000. What is the cash-on-cash return?
   A. 28%
   B. 31%
   C. 36%
   D. 42%

294. The value of an income property is $850,000 and the capitalization rate is 12%. What is the projected annual net income?
   A. $82,500
   B. $87,000
   C. $98,000
   D. $102,000

295. When offering available square footage to tenants, property owners generally charge for:
   A. usable square footage
   B. rentable square footage
   C. carpetable area
   D. effective square footage

296. Which of the following defines when an investment will generate a positive return?
   A. attornment
   B. expense stop
   C. point of no return
   D. natural breakeven point

297. A lease clause that states that the landlord's lender and future owners of the building cannot terminate the lease as long as the tenant fulfills lease obligations is called a(n):
   A. escalation clause
   B. estoppel
   C. subordination clause
   D. nondisturbance clause

298. A type of lease escalation clause is known as:
   A. porter's wage formula
   B. estoppel
   C. a use clause
   D. subordination

299. Generally, with a real estate investment, the greater the risk of loss means:
   A. the greater the return on investment
   B. the less the return on investment
   C. risk has nothing to do with return
   D. risk and return are always equal

300. The use of OPM, or other people's money, involves:
   A. risk
   B. return
   C. leverage
   D. debt service

301. Valid reasons to consider investment in real property might NOT include:
   A. a hedge against an inflationary economic trend
   B. tax savings generated by passive losses
   C. a means of providing cash flow
   D. a means of providing liquidity to one's investment portfolio

302. A real estate investor may defer capital gains taxes by:
   A. investing in income shelters
   B. dealing in cash transactions only
   C. exchanging like-kind properties
   D. selling high-end properties over $500,000 because capital gains may be deferred

303. An economic analysis of all data related to a project including its costs, rates of return, and benefit to the community is known as a(n):
   A. operating statement
   B. feasibility study
   C. potential gross income
   D. pro forma schedule

304. A short sale is a transaction in which:
   A. closing includes "time is of the essence"
   B. there is seller financing
   C. the sale proceeds fall short of the balance owed on the property
   D. there is always lender financing

305. Foreclosed properties are generally sold at:
   A. a short sale
   B. an auction
   C. the time of listing
   D. the request of the owner

306. A short sale is a:
   A. debt service
   B. financial loss for the lender
   C. foreclosure
   D. credit loss

307. An operating statement adjusted to reflect a potential change in income and expenses based on the investor's assessment of the real estate market is known as:
   A. a feasibility study
   B. investment strategy
   C. timing planning
   D. a proforma schedule

308. Foreclosed properties are usually offered:
   A. "as is"
   B. by a lender
   C. when the borrower is in default on the mortgage
   D. all of the above

309. The percentage of income that the investor realizes on an investment is known as:
   A. loan-to-value ratio
   B. rate of return
   C. leverage
   D. time value of money

310. The study of how a change in one factor affecting a real estate investment can affect the income to the property is known as:
   A. a feasibility study
   B. risk analysis
   C. sensitivity analysis
   D. securitization

Income Tax Issues in Real Estate

311. According to IRS rules, real property taxes are deductible for:
    A. a single-family home personal residence
    B. a second home personal residence
    C. a condominium personal residence
    D. all of the above

312. Gains held on assets held for less than 12 months are known as:
    A. cost recovery
    B. capital loss
    C. short-term capital gains
    D. long-term capital gains

313. Petros lost $15,000 of his personal funds in the stock market in the taxable year 20xx. Under what circumstances can he deduct this amount from his yearly income taxes?
    A. Only if he earned under $25,000 for 20xx
    B. Only if he is in the 15% tax bracket
    C. Only if he is unemployed
    D. Under no circumstances

314. Property eligible for a tax-deferred exchange does NOT include:
    A. industrial property
    B. commercial property
    C. a personal residence
    D. a hotel or motel

315. Which of the following may be deducted on a real property purchaser's income tax return under certain conditions?
    A. appraisal fees
    B. points
    C. notary fees
    D. preparation fee for the mortgage

316. The main housing credit agency in New York is:
    A. NYS Division of Housing and Community Renewal
    B. HUD
    C. FEMA
    D. NYS Division of Human Rights

317. In reference to the straight-line method for depreciating nonresidential property, it may be depreciated over how many years?
    A. 15 years
    B. 27.5 years
    C. 35.5 years
    D. 39 years

318. Which of the following is NOT a tax bracket for income tax obligations?
    A. 10%
    B. 25%
    C. 32%
    D. 35%

319. How many days from the day of closing does a real estate exchanger have to contract for another (replacement) property?
    A. 15 days
    B. 30 days
    C. 45 days
    D. 60 days

320. In a tax-deferred exchange, any cash in the exchange is called the:
    A. equity
    B. collateral
    C. cache
    D. boot

Mortgage Brokerage

321. The New York agency that registers mortgage brokers is the:
   A. Department of Financial Services
   B. Insurance Department
   C. Department of State
   D. Attorney General's Office

322. An experience requirement for a NYS-licensed real estate broker to obtain a mortgage broker registration includes:
   A. one year in the mortgage business
   B. two years in the mortgage business
   C. a current real estate broker's license
   D. a real estate salesperson who has been licensed for at least one year

323. A mortgage broker who represents a purchaser in negotiating a mortgage loan is a(n):
   A. agent
   B. intermediary
   C. facilitator
   D. none of the above

324. A mortgage broker who represents the purchasers in negotiating a mortgage while also representing the sellers as a real estate broker in the same transaction is acting as a:
   A. general agent
   B. facilitator
   C. dual agent
   D. single agent

325. The minimum line of credit required to be licensed in New York as a mortgage banker is:
   A. $250,000
   B. $500,000
   C. $1 million
   D. $2 million

326. In applying for a mortgage, the document needed to verify a purchaser's credit and employment history is a(n):
   A. appraisal
   B. validation
   C. preapproval
   D. statement of net worth

327. A request by a purchaser to reserve a certain loan interest rate for a specified time is called a(n):
   A. rate lock
   B. commitment
   C. rate cap
   D. interest reserve

328. The process in which the lender evaluates all of the borrower's financial data and determines if the borrower will obtain the loan is called:
   A. alienation
   B. preapproval
   C. clarification
   D. loan underwriting

329. A lender's rebate is payment to the:
   A. loan underwriter
   B. seller
   C. purchaser
   D. mortgage broker

330. A loan that does NOT meet the Federal Reserve Bank loan criteria for funding is known as:
   A. illegal
   B. secondary
   C. nonconforming
   D. straight term

Property Management

331. If a property manager works for one owner, which of the following is TRUE? The property manager:
   A. must have a broker license
   B. must have a minimum of a salesperson license
   C. does not need a real estate license
   D. is always an independent contractor

332. The document that is used to create an agency relationship between the property manager and the owner is a:
   A. management agreement
   B. management proposal
   C. listing agreement
   D. letter of intent

333. In managing a property, risk management has to do with:
   A. financial risk
   B. liability when the public enters the property
   C. managing the activities of employees
   D. tenant behavior

334. If a building is 98% occupied, the property manager may feel justified in:
   A. believing that the laws of supply and demand are not in favor of the property
   B. rewriting the leases during the lease term
   C. lowering the rents
   D. raising the rents

335. Property income and expenses for week-to-week operations are computed in which type of budget?
   A. cash flow
   B. capital reserve
   C. stabilized
   D. operating

336. Randy rents six apartments in his building for $750 per month and seven apartments for $1,050 per month. Figuring in a 5% vacancy rate, what is the annual projected rent roll?
   A. $135,090
   B. $139,500
   C. $142,200
   D. $185,300

337. Which document prepared by a property manager relates expense items to the operating budget for the period?
   A. property management agreement
   B. property management report
   C. rent roll
   D. stabilized budget

338. Lydia, a property manager, enlisted her maintenance team to go through the building and assess and repair all items. This is an example of:
   A. excessive oversight
   B. due diligence
   C. preventative maintenance
   D. corrective maintenance

339. In New York, if a property management company works for more than one owner, the principal requires a(n):
   A. real estate broker license
   B. BOMI affiliation
   C. IREM designation
   D. none of the above

340. As managing agent for an apartment complex, Alexa, a real estate broker, accepts a small bonus from the landscapers since she hired them. She does not tell the owners about the bonus. Alexa:
   A. is violating her fiduciary duty to the owners
   B. may accept the bonus
   C. may be illegally accepting payment
   D. both A and C

341. A site manager who is a salaried employee of the owner and only manages the property where she lives needs:
   A. a salesperson license
   B. an associate broker license
   C. a broker license
   D. no license

342. A management agreement most often creates which type of agency relationship?
   A. special agency
   B. agency by proxy
   C. general agency
   D. no agency relationship

343. The primary goal of a property manager should be:
   A. to produce the highest possible net operating income from the property
   B. collecting rents
   C. residing on the property
   D. screening tenants

344. To save on payroll and employee costs, some property managers are:
   A. performing maintenance functions themselves
   B. cutting costs by not allowing preventative maintenance activities
   C. subcontracting individuals to perform maintenance tasks
   D. attempting to allow items to break in hopes of collecting insurance coverage

345. A forecast of expected income and expenses projected over, for example, a five-year term is known as a(n):
   A. operating budget
   B. capital reserve budget
   C. stabilized budget
   D. variable expense budget predictable but subject to the needs of the property at any time

346. A manager's strategy for marketing available rental space should not be influenced by:
   A. present demand for space
   B. racial composition of the neighborhood
   C. tenant selection process
   D. newness of the project

347. The type of property where a manager may be more involved with the physical management of the property than with other types of management responsibilities is:
   A. storefronts
   B. office buildings
   C. industrial property
   D. condominiums and cooperatives

348. A designation given by the Institute of Real Estate Management is:
   A. NYARM
   B. BOMI
   C. CPM
   D. ABO

349. A consideration for the property manager in setting rental rates must NOT include:
   A. setting higher rates for families with children
   B. the owner's goals
   C. supply and demand
   D. present vacancy rental rates

350. Adequate insurance coverage has to do with:
   A. selecting tenants who will pay the rent on time and not need to be evicted
   B. controlling and limiting financial risk by purchasing adequate insurance coverage
   C. preventative maintenance
   D. corrective maintenance

Licensee Safety

351. The main reason why licensee safety measures are extremely important to the real estate profession is that agents:
   A. are dealing with other people's property
   B. are on the road a great deal
   C. often work alone and in unfamiliar surroundings
   D. receive assistance from unknown cyber systems

352. The initial method of screening new prospects when they come to the office includes:
   A. having visitors sign into a log at the reception desk identifying themselves
   B. having another staff member, other than the agent, be able to meet and identify the prospect
   C. performing a full investigation into the individual prior to the first meeting
   D. a and b only

353. The initial meeting with prospects should take place at:
   A. the prospect's home
   B. the real estate office
   C. at the first substantive contact wherever that is
   D. at the first property showing

354. An intake sheet published by the National Association of REALTORS® that helps the agent to profile a prospect for identity purposes is called a(n):
   A. prospect identification form
   B. agency disclosure form
   C. needs and wants checklist
   D. binder

355. The purpose of the buddy system is to:
   A. serve as a backup check-in system while the agent works alone in the office or while showing a property
   B. assist with clerical duties that the agent must perform
   C. serve as a social support system for the busy agent
   D. help protect the agent from harm by accompanying the agent to all property showings

356. Which of the following activities can cause a safety issue for the real estate agent?
   A. conducting an open house without the assistance of at least one other agent
   B. walking into a room at a showing first and having the prospects follow the agent in
   C. showing abandoned or foreclosed property without the assistance of at least one other agent
   D. all of the above

357. The most efficient method of protecting documents while sending them electronically is to:
   A. send a copy of the document to someone on your buddy network
   B. encrypt the document
   C. make a hard copy and store it in your file for that transaction
   D. send a copy of the document to your broker

358. An insurance policy that helps protect a real estate office against claims that focus on failure to perform on a contract is called:
   A. an umbrella policy
   B. a fidelity policy
   C. a package policy
   D. errors and omissions insurance

359. In New York, a person may legally use physical force in self-defense under which NYS law:
    A. Article 12-A of the Real Property Law
    B. Article 15 of the Real Property Action and Proceedings Law
    C. NYS Penal Code, Article 35
    D. Article 9-A of the Real Property Law

360. A method of risk reduction that a real estate office can employ to induce safety is to:
    A. create a written policies and procedures manual
    B. insist that all agents carry pepper spray
    C. hire agents that have at least five years' experience in the real estate profession
    D. require all agents to commit to at least two years' employment with the firm

General Business Law (Broker course only)

361. Negotiable instruments are a substitute for:
    A. contracts
    B. money
    C. deferred credit
    D. mortgages

362. Real estate brokers must explain and have buyers acknowledge the difference between which two brokerage contracts?
    A. exclusive-right-to-sell and exclusive agency
    B. binder and contract of sale
    C. exclusive agency and open listing
    D. exclusive right-to-sell and open listing

363. The signer of a check is known as the:
    A. drawer
    B. drawee
    C. payee
    D. borrower

364. When renting a property with six or more units, a landlord has which of the following options for tenants regarding paying a tenant's interest on the security deposit?
    A. pay the interest annually to the tenant
    B. apply the interest to the tenant's rent
    C. pay the interest to the tenant when the lease term ends
    D. any of the above

365. An exemption to the Chapter 7 bankruptcy filing is a(n):
    A. *in rem*
    B. homestead
    C. unified credit
    D. tuition

366. A legal method of dividing land investment property in some actions for divorce is:
    A. partition
    B. escheat
    C. eminent domain
    D. sale leaseback

367. According to the Statute of Limitations in New York, the time frame to bring legal action in a contract dispute is:
    A. one year
    B. three years
    C. six years
    D. ten years

368. In New York, judgments against a debtor are enforced by:
    A. the person to whom the debt is owed
    B. a court order instructing the sheriff to attach and seize the debtor's property
    C. the local assessor's office
    D. an Article 78 proceeding

369. A legal dispute CANNOT be resolved by:
    A. litigation
    B. mediation
    C. arbitration
    D. stagnation

370. The type of bankruptcy in which the debtor's nonexempt property is sold for cash, the proceeds distributed to creditors, and unpaid debts discharged is called:
   A. Chapter 13
   B. Chapter 11
   C. Chapter 7
   D. Chapter 10

Achieving Transactional Agreements through Transaction Analysis (Broker Course only)

371. Dual agency can occur when:
   A. a buyer and a seller meet at the showing of a property
   B. a real estate agent represents both seller and buyer in the same transaction
   C. two buyers bid on the same property
   D. there is no listing agreement

372. A transactional agreement to sell and purchase real property should:
   A. benefit only the client of the selling broker
   B. fulfill only the buyer's wants and needs
   C. be mutually beneficial to all parties to the transaction
   D. be a unilateral agreement

373. Which of the following is FALSE? A transactional agreement:
   A. is the end result of a transaction analysis
   B. should be mutually beneficial to all parties to the transaction
   C. should be in the best interests of the broker and the client
   D. should be entered into without sacrificing the interests of the client simply to reach an agreement

374. Which of the fiduciary duties can an agent NOT offer to a client if there is a dual agency arrangement?
   A. competence
   B. skill
   C. diligence
   D. undivided loyalty

375. Which of the following is NOT a fiduciary duty that an agent has to the client?
   A. power of attorney
   B. loyalty
   C. obedience
   D. accountability

376. In any real estate transactional agreement, a real estate broker can be best described as a(n):
   A. agent
   B. manager
   C. negotiator
   D. principal

377. The first step in transaction analysis is to:
   A. identify what is most beneficial to the client
   B. identify the needs and wants of the parties to the transaction
   C. identify the best interests of the broker and the client
   D. have the seller complete the property condition disclosure form

378. A user-friendly confidentiality agreement could be a(n):
   A. listing agreement
   B. both A and C
   C. buyer agency representation agreement
   D. agency disclosure form

379. The services to be performed by an agent representing a seller in a transactional agreement are documented in the:
   A. property condition disclosure form
   B. agency disclosure form
   C. listing contract
   D. contract of sale

380. The role of a real estate agent in transaction analysis includes:
   A. good listening skills
   B. creating discussion and dialogue between the parties
   C. communicating an "agreement attitude"
   D. all of the above

Sample Licensing Exams

The following four practice exams—two for the salesperson and two for the broker—are formatted to match the New York State licensing exam. That is, the topics and the number of questions for each topic are similar to that of the actual test. The total number of exam questions, 75 for the salesperson and 100 for the broker, are the same quantity as on the state licensing exam. Because the practice exams are weighted to match the actual test, your performance on these should be a good indicator of your performance on the state exam. Note that these practice exams follow as closely as possible to the weightage of topics to the New York State licensing exam. For your classroom exam, after you complete the broker 45-hour qualifying course, whether online or in a classroom, there will be a two-hour local concerns topic so that test will include several local concerns questions. Therefore, there are a few less curriculum content questions in the classroom/online exams than the NYS exam and the practice exams in this guide.

Tear out the Answer Sheet on the next pages and use it to record your responses. You may want to copy the blank answer sheet so that you can use it a second time.

Complete the practice exams under exam conditions. Find a quiet place and allow an uninterrupted 1.5 hours for each salesperson exam and 2.5 hours for each broker exam. This is the same amount of time allotted to the state exams.

After completing the exam, check your answers with the "Answer Key for Practice Exams" at the back of this guide. Review all incorrect answers. The rationale for the correct answer appears in the Answer Key. For further study, refer to the textbooks, *New York Real Estate for Salespersons, 6th e* Revised or *New York Real Estate for Brokers, 6th e.*

Salesperson Practice Exam 1

1. ______
2. ______
3. ______
4. ______
5. ______
6. ______
7. ______
8. ______
9. ______
10. ______
11. ______
12. ______
13. ______
14. ______
15. ______
16. ______
17. ______
18. ______
19. ______
20. ______
21. ______
22. ______
23. ______
24. ______
25. ______
26. ______
27. ______
28. ______
29. ______
30. ______
31. ______
32. ______
33. ______
34. ______
35. ______
36. ______
37. ______
38. ______
39. ______
40. ______
41. ______
42. ______
43. ______
44. ______
45. ______
46. ______
47. ______
48. ______
49. ______
50. ______
51. ______
52. ______
53. ______
54. ______
55. ______
56. ______
57. ______
58. ______
59. ______
60. ______
61. ______
62. ______
63. ______
64. ______
65. ______
66. ______
67. ______
68. ______
69. ______
70. ______
71. ______
72. ______
73. ______
74. ______
75. ______

Salesperson Practice Exam 2

1. ______	26. ______	51. ______
2. ______	27. ______	52. ______
3. ______	28. ______	53. ______
4. ______	29. ______	54. ______
5. ______	30. ______	55. ______
6. ______	31. ______	56. ______
7. ______	32. ______	57. ______
8. ______	33. ______	58. ______
9. ______	34. ______	59. ______
10. ______	35. ______	60. ______
11. ______	36. ______	61. ______
12. ______	37. ______	62. ______
13. ______	38. ______	63. ______
14. ______	39. ______	64. ______
15. ______	40. ______	65. ______
16. ______	41. ______	66. ______
17. ______	42. ______	67. ______
18. ______	43. ______	68. ______
19. ______	44. ______	69. ______
20. ______	45. ______	70. ______
21. ______	46. ______	71. ______
22. ______	47. ______	72. ______
23. ______	48. ______	73. ______
24. ______	49. ______	74. ______
25. ______	50. ______	75. ______

Broker Practice Exam 1

1. ____________
2. ____________
3. ____________
4. ____________
5. ____________
6. ____________
7. ____________
8. ____________
9. ____________
10. ____________
11. ____________
12. ____________
13. ____________
14. ____________
15. ____________
16. ____________
17. ____________
18. ____________
19. ____________
20. ____________
21. ____________
22. ____________
23. ____________
24. ____________
25. ____________
26. ____________
27. ____________
28. ____________
29. ____________
30. ____________
31. ____________
32. ____________
33. ____________
34. ____________
35. ____________
36. ____________
37. ____________
38. ____________
39. ____________
40. ____________
41. ____________
42. ____________
43. ____________
44. ____________
45. ____________
46. ____________
47. ____________
48. ____________
49. ____________
50. ____________
51. ____________
52. ____________
53. ____________
54. ____________
55. ____________
56. ____________
57. ____________
58. ____________
59. ____________
60. ____________
61. ____________
62. ____________
63. ____________
64. ____________
65. ____________
66. ____________
67. ____________
68. ____________
69. ____________
70. ____________
71. ____________
72. ____________
73. ____________
74. ____________
75. ____________
76. ____________
77. ____________
78. ____________
79. ____________
80. ____________
81. ____________
82. ____________
83. ____________
84. ____________
85. ____________
86. ____________
87. ____________
88. ____________
89. ____________
90. ____________
91. ____________
92. ____________
93. ____________
94. ____________
95. ____________
96. ____________
97. ____________
98. ____________
99. ____________
100. ____________

Broker Practice Exam 2

1. ____	26. ____	51. ____	76. ____
2. ____	27. ____	52. ____	77. ____
3. ____	28. ____	53. ____	78. ____
4. ____	29. ____	54. ____	79. ____
5. ____	30. ____	55. ____	80. ____
6. ____	31. ____	56. ____	81. ____
7. ____	32. ____	57. ____	82. ____
8. ____	33. ____	58. ____	83. ____
9. ____	34. ____	59. ____	84. ____
10. ____	35. ____	60. ____	85. ____
11. ____	36. ____	61. ____	86. ____
12. ____	37. ____	62. ____	87. ____
13. ____	38. ____	63. ____	88. ____
14. ____	39. ____	64. ____	89. ____
15. ____	40. ____	65. ____	90. ____
16. ____	41. ____	66. ____	91. ____
17. ____	42. ____	67. ____	92. ____
18. ____	43. ____	68. ____	93. ____
19. ____	44. ____	69. ____	94. ____
20. ____	45. ____	70. ____	95. ____
21. ____	46. ____	71. ____	96. ____
22. ____	47. ____	72. ____	97. ____
23. ____	48. ____	73. ____	98. ____
24. ____	49. ____	74. ____	99. ____
25. ____	50. ____	75. ____	100. ____

Salesperson Practice Exam 1

License Law and Regulations (3 hours) (3 questions)

1. The licensure term for real estate salespersons and brokers is:
   A. one year
   B. two years
   C. three years
   D. four years

2. A salesperson may receive compensation from:
   A. his client
   B. his principal
   C. his sponsoring broker
   D. any licensed broker

3. A salesperson may draw legal documents:
   A. with permission of her sponsoring broker only
   B. under no circumstances
   C. with permission of the principal
   D. if the salesperson has a notary public license

Law of Agency Including Independent Contractor (11 hours) (11 questions)

4. If the parties to a residential real estate transaction agree to dual agency representation:
   A. all confidential information given to the agent by the seller or buyer must be disclosed to both parties
   B. both seller and buyer must pay a full commission to the agent
   C. both seller and purchaser forfeit the right to undivided loyalty by the agent
   D. DOS must be informed of the agreement

5. An illegal type of payment arrangement for brokers is a:
   A. percentage of the final sales price
   B. flat fee
   C. commission schedule set forth by the local board of REALTORS®
   D. referral fee

6. Belinda, a salesperson, works for Broker Barry and in that capacity has received informed consent from a seller to represent him in the sale of his home. What is Belinda's relationship to this seller/principal?
   A. broker's agent
   B. dual agent
   C. subagent
   D. buyer's agent

7. In a buyer agency relationship, the buyer is the:
   A. customer
   B. principal
   C. subagent
   D. third party

8. The agency disclosure form is required in which of the following circumstances?
   A. at the time that a seller enters into a listing agreement with a broker
   B. when prospects enter an open house
   C. when prospects call to inquire about a property
   D. at the closing

9. Belle Properties Brokerage and Ruby Real Estate decided that, since they were the only two companies that offered residential property for sale in a small town, they would both charge the same commission rate. These two firms are guilty of:
   A. nothing at all
   B. an illegal group boycott
   C. illegal price fixing
   D. an illegal market allocation agreement

10. In a dual agency situation within a brokerage firm, with disclosure and informed consent, one agent can represent the buyer and one the seller. Both of these agents are called:
    A. designated agents
    B. listing agents
    C. mandatory agents
    D. broker's agents

11. The sellers tell Carlos, a real estate agent, that the basement of their house floods every spring. The sellers do not wish to disclose this information. What should Carlos do?
    A. agree with his sellers
    B. inform his sellers that this information must be disclosed
    C. obtain a signed release from the sellers so that Agent Carlos is not liable should there be a lawsuit
    D. refuse to take a listing since the property has a material defect

12. What do subagents, listing agents, seller's agents, and single agents have in common?
    A. They are all dual agents.
    B. They all represent the seller.
    C. They all must belong to the multiple listing service.
    D. They are all cooperating agents.

13. If a salesperson is NOT paid according to hours worked, the salesperson is most likely classified by IRS as a(n):
    A. common law employee
    B. statutory employee
    C. independent contractor
    D. sales associate

14. Regulations governing the status of employees or independent contractors are determined by:
    A. the broker
    B. New York State Association of REALTORS®
    C. federal and state statutes
    D. Department of State

Legal Issues

Estates and Interests (3 hours) (3 questions)

15. Mike and Mindy held title to a property together with no right of survivorship. They most likely held the property:
    A. as joint tenants
    B. as tenants in common
    C. in severalty
    D. as joint tenants by the entirety

16. Water rights belong to an owner of property bordering a flowing body of water are:
    A. subsurface rights
    B. riparian rights
    C. chattel rights
    D. bundle of rights

17. Juan plans to sell some household furnishings when he sells his house. He will most likely use a document called a(n):
    A. sales contract
    B. bill of sale
    C. transfer affidavit
    D. purchase offer

Liens and Easements (2.5 hours) (3 questions)

18. Real property taxes are examples of:
    A. voluntary specific liens
    B. involuntary specific liens
    C. voluntary general liens
    D. involuntary general liens

19. A lien filed by an individual who provides labor to a property and is NOT paid is called a:
    A. *lis pendens*
    B. subordination lien
    C. mechanic's lien
    D. real property judgment

20. Goldie allows her neighbor, Mattie, to use a path on her property to access the lakefront. Which of the following is TRUE?
   A. Goldie's property is the servient tenement.
   B. This is an encroachment.
   C. This is a type of lien.
   D. This is a type of grant.

Deeds (2.5 hours) (2 questions)

21. For a deed to be eligible for recording, it must have a(n):
   A. metes and bounds description
   B. habendum clause
   C. acknowledgment
   D. covenant of warranty

22. Which of the following is NOT a judicial deed?
   A. executor's deed
   B. guardian's deed
   C. sheriff's deed
   D. installment land contract

Title Closing and Costs (2 hours) (2 questions)

23. The seller will accept a purchase money mortgage from the buyer. On the closing statement, this amount appears as a:
   A. seller debit
   B. seller credit
   C. buyer debit
   D. balancing disbursement

24. A purchaser closing cost does NOT generally include:
   A. a title insurance policy
   B. a mortgage recording tax
   C. discount points
   D. delinquent real property taxes

The Contract of Sale and Leases

Leases (1 hour) (1 question)

25. Amy transferred her lease contract to her friend, Jamie. Jamie will now have to make the lease payments to the landlord. Which of the following has taken place? A(n):
   A. assignment
   B. sublease
   C. constructive eviction
   D. holdover tenancy

Contracts (1 hour) (1 question)

26. A court ordered Nancy to pay Tessie $10,000 because she did not purchase Tessie's property even though they had a valid contract. This monetary payment is called:
   A. specific performance
   B. rescission
   C. liquidated damages
   D. novation

Contract Preparation (1 hour) (1 question)

27. In order for a real estate salesperson to prepare a fill-in-the-blanks contract of sale approved by the board of REALTORS®, the contract must:
   A. be less than three pages
   B. be clearly captioned and easy to understand
   C. have an attorney review clause
   D. be notarized

Real Estate Finance (5 hours) (5 questions)

28. Which type of mortgage loan requires, for example, monthly payments of $1,200 for 15 years and a final payment of $10,000?
    A. graduated payment mortgage
    B. flexible payment mortgage
    C. wraparound mortgage
    D. balloon mortgage

29. Up to the time a foreclosure sale is held, a borrower who has defaulted on his loan may be able to regain his property by paying the outstanding debt. This is a(n):
    A. deed in lieu of foreclosure
    B. equity of redemption
    C. deficiency judgment
    D. recovery grace period

30. The clause in a mortgage stating that a lender may declare the entire balance due if the borrower is in default is called the:
    A. prepayment penalty clause
    B. granting clause
    C. acceleration clause
    D. defeasance clause

31. In which type of mortgage are two or more parcels of real estate pledged as security for a mortgage debt?
    A. package mortgage
    B. blanket mortgage
    C. bridge loan
    D. installment land contract

32. An agency of HUD that insures loans to protect lenders against financial loss is:
    A. Fannie Mae
    B. Sonny Mae
    C. FHA
    D. Freddie Mac

Land Use Regulations (3 hours) (3 questions)

33. The New York law regulating the sale of unimproved lots across state lines is called:
    A. Interstate Land Sales Full Disclosure Act
    B. Article 9-A of the Real Property Law
    C. State Environmental Quality Review Act
    D. Uniform Fire Prevention and Building Code

34. The taking of property under the government's right of eminent domain is called:
    A. escheat
    B. estoppel
    C. *in rem*
    D. condemnation

35. Emma wishes to add another story to her home; however, the new height would not comply with the current zoning ordinance. She would need to apply for a(n):
    A. nonconforming use
    B. use variance
    C. area variance
    D. spot zone

Construction and Environmental Issues (5 hours) (5 questions)

36. The foundation walls of a property are usually composed of:
    A. concrete
    B. wood
    C. steel
    D. iron

37. The area under the roof extension is called the:
    A. frieze board
    B. fascia
    C. soffit
    D. sheathing

38. For residential one- and two-family properties in New York, and condominiums and cooperatives, which of the following is required at closing?
    A. smoke alarm and carbon monoxide detector affidavit
    B. carbon monoxide detector affidavit only
    C. agency disclosure
    D. minimum compliance affidavit

39. The New York law that requires preparation of an environmental impact statement on a property that a government body has the jurisdiction to review is the:
    A. Superfund Amendment
    B. State Environmental Quality Review Act
    C. TILA-RESPA Integrated Disclosure Rule
    D. Comprehensive Environmental Response, Compensation and Liability Act (CERCLA)

40. Sales contracts used for target properties under the Residential Lead-based Hazard Reduction Act must include:
    A. nothing different than before the law was enacted
    B. specific disclosure and acknowledgment language
    C. approval by an agent of HUD
    D. an attachment indicating the exact age of the property

Valuation Process and Pricing Properties (3 hours) (3 questions)

41. The appraisal approach most similar to a comparative market analysis is the:
    A. income approach
    B. cost approach
    C. capitalization approach
    D. sales comparison approach

42. A land utilization study that does not necessarily produce an estimate of value can be best defined as a(n):
    A. evaluation
    B. appraisal
    C. comparative market analysis
    D. value in use

43. One of the most important aspects of marketing a property is:
    A. pricing the property at the lowest possible price to make sure of a timely sale
    B. knowing the competition and adjusting pricing and marketing strategies accordingly
    C. ignoring the competition and allowing the property to sell based on its own merits
    D. effecting a sale within 18 months of the listing date

Human Rights and Fair Housing (4 hours) (4 questions)

44. Individuals who visit real estate offices posing as prospective home seekers to see if race influences the buying process are called:
    A. civil rights inspectors
    B. real estate licensees
    C. testers
    D. inspectors

45. The owner of a single-family property in Syosset on Long Island asks a salesperson to find a "nice couple without children" to purchase their home. The broker:
   A. may take this listing because the property owner has the right to specify who purchases his property
   B. may take the listing but must ask for a written statement from the owner to cover any liability problems
   C. may take the listing only with permission of her supervising broker
   D. must refuse this listing

46. The term blockbusting refers to:
   A. phone calls soliciting prospective buyers or sellers in a cease and desist zone
   B. offering property for sale only to persons of a certain race
   C. prompting homeowners to sell their properties due to the entry of certain persons of a particular race or religion into the neighborhood
   D. the government's right of eminent domain to condemn and destroy older vacant buildings in a neighborhood

47. The lending department of Money Bank decided not to make home improvement loans to residents of Lonely Heights because a survey completed by the bank showed a higher number of single-parent families living in that neighborhood. Money Bank is guilty of:
   A. redlining
   B. steering
   C. nothing at all
   D. blockbusting

Real Estate Mathematics (1 hour) (2 questions)

48. A real estate salesperson sells a property for $90,000. The commission on this sale to the real estate firm with whom the salesperson is associated is 6%. The salesperson receives 60% of the total commission paid to the real estate firm. What is the firm's share of the commission in dollars?
   A. $2,000
   B. $2,160
   C. $4,500
   D. $4,750

49. If the assessed value of a property is $217,500 and the tax value is 100% of the assessed value, what is the annual tax if the rate is $2.00 per $100?
   A. $2,450
   B. $3,500
   C. $3,475
   D. $4,350

Municipal Agencies (2 hours) (2 questions)

50. A municipal agency has the job of mapping a large parcel of land that was granted to the city. The agency that would most likely be the lead agency for this project is the:
   A. assessor's office
   B. zoning board of appeals
   C. planning board
   D. architectural review board

51. A town on Long Island does not allow any buildings higher than four stories. Francesca wants to add two more floors to her two-story building. The agency or agencies that might be involved in reviewing her construction application is/are:
    A. zoning board of appeals
    B. architectural review board
    C. conservation advisory council
    D. both A and B

Property Insurance (2 hours) (1 question)

52. The Lee family damaged their oven in a small kitchen fire and were reimbursed for the actual cost of replacing the oven. This means that their coverage was:
    A. for actual cash value
    B. for replacement cost
    C. for personal liability
    D. an umbrella policy

Taxes and Assessments (3 hours) (3 questions)

53. A type of map, drawn to scale, showing all of the property parcels with a city, town, or village, and their size, shape, and dimensions is called a(n):
    A. plat
    B. blueprint
    C. survey
    D. tax map

54. A property assessing unit may be a:
    A. city
    B. town
    C. county
    D. all of the above

55. Municipalities use residential assessment ratios:
    A. for revaluation projects
    B. if there are less than five residential sales that year
    C. for board of assessment review grievances
    D. to determine tax exemptions

Condominiums and Cooperatives (4 hours) (3 questions)

56. Which of the following is FALSE regarding a cooperative?
    A. It is a not-for-profit corporation.
    B. It is formed for the benefit of its members.
    C. It is owned by the cooperative cooperation.
    D. A unit owner receives a deed to his individual unit.

57. The owner or developer of a condominium or cooperative is called the:
    A. director
    B. sponsor
    C. trustor
    D. originator

58. The New York Attorney General's rules for testing the market for new condominium or cooperative developments are contained in:
    A. UCC-1 statement
    B. CPS1 statement
    C. Civil Practice Laws and Rules
    D. Section 443 of the Real Property Law

Commercial and Investment Properties (10 hours) (9 questions)

59. An operating statement adjusted to reflect a potential change in income and expenses based upon the investor's knowledge of the real estate market is called a(n):
    A. cash flow statement
    B. operating statement
    C. statement of net worth
    D. pro forma statement

60. The net monthly income of a seven-unit apartment building is $2,250. The capitalization rate the lender uses is 7%. What is the value of the building?
    A. $299,010
    B. $385,714
    C. $410,926
    D. $450,509

61. A process that calculates the value of an asset in the past, present, and future is called:
    A. leverage
    B. time value of money
    C. debt service
    D. net operating income

62. If a business property has an asset value of $1,000,000 with a debt of $750,000, what is the debt ratio?
    A. 50%
    B. 60 %
    C. 75%
    D. 90%

63. Which of the following is NOT a reason why investment in unimproved land has more risk than other types of real estate investments?
    A. It may be more difficult to obtain financing.
    B. There are no improvements on land.
    C. Land cannot be depreciated for tax purposes.
    D. Land always has less resale value.

64. Income received on a property without deducting expenses is called:
    A. NOI
    B. gross income
    C. net income
    D. debt service

65. The net proceeds or cash remaining after all expenses and debt services are paid is called:
    A. tax shelter
    B. gross income
    C. cash flow
    D. cash-on-cash return

66. The ratio of annual before-tax cash flow to the total amount of cash invested, expressed as a percentage is called the:
    A. capitalization rate
    B. rate of return
    C. income expense ratio
    D. cash-on-cash return

67. Investment in commercial real estate does NOT provide:
    A. deductible expenses
    B. income shelters
    C. depreciation allowances
    D. guaranteed profit over time

Income Tax Issues in Real Estate Transactions (3 hours) (3 questions)

68. Which of the following is NOT a tax bracket for federal income tax purposes?
    A. 12%
    B. 24%
    C. 32%
    D. 38%

69. Which of the following items are allowed federal tax deductions on home ownership?
    A. interest
    B. principal
    C. property taxes
    D. both A and C

70. Annie and Xavier, a married couple, bought their house five years ago for $350,000. They recently sold it for $400,000. Which of the following is TRUE?
    A. They must pay short term capital gains tax.
    B. They must pay long-term capital gains tax.
    C. They can depreciate the property for tax purposes.
    D. They do not have to pay a capital gains tax.

Mortgage Brokerage (1 hour) (2 questions)

71. If an individual holds a real estate broker's license and wants to apply for a mortgage broker registration, the document that must be submitted to the NYS Department of Financial Services with his mortgage broker application is the:
    A. dual agency affidavit
    B. estoppel certificate
    C. fee application
    D. lender certification

72. Should a real estate salesperson want a mortgage broker registration, what is the experience requirement?
    A. no further experience required
    B. one year of experience in the mortgage business
    C. two years' experience in the mortgage business
    D. one year of experience managing a real estate brokerage office

Property Management (2 hours) (2 questions)

73. Advisors to property managers who focus on long-term financial planning rather than day-to-day operations of the property are:
    A. real estate gurus
    B. resident managers
    C. financial advisors
    D. asset managers

74. A document submitted to the property owner outlining the commitment of the manager if employed is the:
    A. management agreement
    B. management proposal
    C. property projection
    D. operating expense analysis

Licensee Safety (1 hour) (1 question)

75. Dannisha is holding an open house. For her safety, she should consider:
    A. alerting her buddy
    B. having another agent accompany her
    C. having prospects enter a room first at the property
    D. all of the above

Salesperson Practice Exam 2

License Law and Regulations (3 hours) (3 questions)

1. To be licensed as a real estate broker, an individual must be at least how old?
   A. 16
   B. 18
   C. 20
   D. 21

2. Which of the following individuals is exempt from licensure?
   A. attorneys admitted to practice in the New York courts
   B. property managers who manage property for more than one individual or company
   C. individuals who only list property for sale
   D. auctioneers who only auction commercial real estate

3. To save on paperwork, Broker Bright decides to combine her office operating account with the deposits obtained from contracts of sale. Broker Bright is guilty of:
   A. nothing at all
   B. illegal commingling of funds
   C. unauthorized practice of law
   D. accepting money without authorization

Law of Agency Including Independent Contractor (11 hours) (11 questions)

4. A net listing is one:
   A. that requires the broker to have a fixed price for the property
   B. that is legal in New York
   C. that most brokers would prefer
   D. in which the seller specifies a certain amount of money to be received upon sale of the property and all monies above that amount are the broker's commission

5. A broker's agent is hired by the:
   A. principal
   B. seller
   C. customer
   D. broker

6. Which of the following is TRUE regarding dual agency relationships in New York?
   A. They are permissible with timely disclosure and informed consent.
   B. They are illegal under all circumstances.
   C. They are allowed only in commercial transactions.
   D. They are allowed only in the sale of condominium or cooperative properties.

7. A listing agreement in which the property is listed with only one broker who is entitled to a commission if he sells the property but not if the owner sells the property is called a(n):
   A. exclusive-right-to-sell agreement
   B. open listing agreement
   C. net listing agreement
   D. exclusive agency agreement

8. The first law to address antitrust violations was the:
   A. Clayton Antitrust Act
   B. TILA-RESPA Integrated Disclosure Rule
   C. Sherman Antitrust Act
   D. New York Real Property Law

9. Sell-It-Today Brokerage requires that purchasers of its listed property apply for a mortgage with EZ Money Mortgage Company. This practice is:
   A. perfectly acceptable
   B. an example of an illegal tie-in arrangement
   C. an example of an illegal group boycott
   D. an example of an illegal market allocation agreement

10. An agency relationship created by an oral or written agreement between principal and agent is a(n):
    A. implied agency
    B. express agency
    C. dual agency
    D. power of attorney

11. Martin signs an exclusive-right-to-sell listing agreement for six months with Broker Gerald. Within one month, Martin sells his house himself and refuses to pay a commission to Gerald. Martin's behavior is a possible:
    A. reformation
    B. breach of contract
    C. injunction
    D. assignment

12. Advance informed consent to dual agency is:
    A. illegal in New York
    B. for commercial transactions only
    C. used only in the marketing of condominiums and cooperatives
    D. allowable in New York with disclosure and informed consent

13. Which of the following activities is NOT an element of an independent contractor relationship?
    A. There is no compensation for specific number of hours worked.
    B. Salespersons can work any hours they choose.
    C. Commissions are paid with deductions for income taxes.
    D. The salesperson or broker may terminate the relationship at any time.

14. Real estate licensees are classified as independent contractors under:
    A. Section 3508 (a) (b) of the IRS Code
    B. common law
    C. Article 12-A of the Real Property Law
    D. Section 443 of the Real Property Law

Legal Issues

Estates and Interests (3 hours) (3 questions)

15. Which of the following is NOT one of the four unities required for joint tenancy?
    A. time
    B. interest
    C. partition
    D. possession

16. Francois and Helena purchase a property and their attorney tells them that their title offers the most complete form of ownership. Their ownership right is:
    A. fee simple on condition
    B. fee simple absolute
    C. fee simple defeasible
    D. a life estate

17. Kelly's mother deeds Kelly her beach house for Kelly's lifetime. Then the property goes to the A.S.P.C.A. in memory of her mother's favorite cat upon daughter Kelly's death. This is an example of a:
    A. fee simple absolute
    B. leasehold
    C. joint tenancy
    D. life estate

Liens and Easements (2.5 hours) (3 questions)

18. A judgment is an example of a(n):
    A. voluntary specific lien
    B. involuntary specific lien
    C. voluntary general lien
    D. involuntary general lien

19. A legal notice that a lawsuit is pending concerning title to a particular property is called a(n):
    A. injunction
    B. *lis pendens*
    C. judgment
    D. mechanic's lien

20. Lionel buys a cabin in a remote area and has no road access except through his neighbor's adjoining property. Lionel's property requires a(n):
   A. easement by condemnation
   B. negative easement
   C. easement by necessity
   D. encroachment

Deeds (2.5 hours) (2 questions)

21. A type of deed used in bankruptcy proceedings and foreclosures is a(n):
   A. sheriff's deed
   B. executor's deed
   C. referee's deed
   D. guardian's deed

22. In order to claim title by adverse possession in New York, the use must be open and notorious for how many years?
   A. 5
   B. 10
   C. 15
   D. 20

Title Closing and Costs (2 hours) (2 questions)

23. Which of the following would most likely prevent a closing from taking place?
   A. imposition of discount points by the lender
   B. hiring of an attorney by the purchaser
   C. existence of outstanding unpaid liens against the property
   D. purchase money mortgage

24. On the closing statement, a buyer credit would be the:
   A. earnest money deposit
   B. prepaid real property taxes
   C. prepaid insurance premium
   D. sale of personal property

The Contract of Sale and Leases

Leases (1 hour) (1 question)

25. A lease that automatically renews itself for another time frame at the end of the lease term unless notice is given to terminate is a(n):
   A. illegal lease
   B. periodic lease
   C. standard lease
   D. proprietary lease

Contracts (1 hour) (1 question)

26. An option is a contract that:
   A. specifies a time limit within which the optionee may choose to purchase or lease real property
   B. is a bilateral implied contract
   C. does not define a specific sales price
   D. conveys title when the optionee signs the contract

Contract Preparation (1 hour) (1 question)

27. A real estate contract of sale does NOT include a(n):
   A. contingency
   B. addenda
   C. rider
   D. codicil

Real Estate Finance (5 hours) (5 questions)

28. A HUD agency that purchases VA and FHA mortgages on the secondary mortgage market is called:
   A. RHS
   B. SONYMA
   C. Ginnie Mae
   D. FDIC

29. A mortgage clause that allows a lender to declare the balance due if the borrower sells the property is the:
    A. prepayment penalty clause
    B. alienation clause
    C. granting clause
    D. defeasance clause

30. A mortgage that provides for paying the debt by monthly payment of principal and interest and in which the interest portion of the payments decreases as the principal portion increases is a(n):
    A. balloon mortgage
    B. installment land contract
    C. swing loan
    D. amortized mortgage

31. The law that provides for accurate advertising of financial credit terms for residential mortgages is:
    A. New York Anti-Predatory Lending Law
    B. Regulation Z
    C. Community Reinvestment Act
    D. New York Mortgage Foreclosure Law

32. A type of loan in which the mortgage rate floats based on the fluctuations of a standard index is called a(n):
    A. adjustable rate mortgage
    B. straight term mortgage
    C. fixed rate mortgage
    D. fluctuating mortgage specified time

Land Use Regulations (3 hours) (3 questions)

33. Marcia has recently purchased an old barn in a rural community in upstate New York and wishes to turn it into an art studio. The administrative body she must apply to for a variance is the:
    A. town planning board
    B. zoning board of appeals
    C. local building department
    D. county clerk

34. A document that shows the boundaries and physical dimensions of a property is called a(n):
    A. feasibility study
    B. plat
    C. survey
    D. architectural rending

35. Parks and forest land could be zoned as:
    A. commercial
    B. residential
    C. public open space
    D. institutional

Construction and Environment (5 hours) (5 questions)

36. A sprayed insulation, no longer used, that caused noxious fumes is called:
    A. loose fill insulation
    B. rigid insulation
    C. UFFI
    D. batt insulation

37. The unit of measure of electrical current flowing through a wire is:
    A. voltage
    B. amperage
    C. milliGaus
    D. wattage

38. The New York statute that mandates minimum R-factors for insulation is the:
    A. Real Property Law
    B. Energy Conservation Construction Code
    C. Emergency Tenant Protection Act
    D. Sanitary Code

39. Which of the following is exempt from disclosure regulations of the Residential Lead-based Hazard Reduction Act?
   A. a duplex built before 1978
   B. a single-family residence built before 1978
   C. senior citizen housing
   D. a cooperative apartment built before 1978

40. One of the most prevalent concerns of underground storage tanks is:
   A. leakage
   B. combustion
   C. explosion
   D. fire

Valuation Process and Pricing Properties (3 hours) (3 questions)

41. One of the most important factors in selecting comparables for a comparative market analysis is to select properties:
   A. within a 50-mile radius of the subject property
   B. older than the subject property
   C. as close in location as possible to the comparable
   D. that have inferior curb appeal to the subject property

42. Surveyors' and appraisers' fees relating to the development of a property are called:
   A. hard costs
   B. indirect costs
   C. direct costs
   D. impact fees

43. An arm's length transaction means that:
   A. the parties are not related as relatives or business associates
   B. no salesperson or broker is involved in the transaction
   C. the transaction is a cash transaction and no financing is required
   D. the transaction takes place within six months of being placed on the market

Human Rights and Fair Housing (4 hours) (4 questions)

44. Hattie wants to sell her home in Kingston, New York. She decides not to use a broker so that she can sell her property to whomever she wants. Hattie:
   A. is exempt from all fair housing laws as long as she does not use a broker
   B. is exempt from fair housing laws in the sale of a single-family home
   C. can only sell her property to whomever she wants if she does not advertise
   D. is not entitled to any exemptions to fair housing laws in the sale of a single-family home in New York

45. The maximum fine for a first violation of the Federal Fair Housing Act can be up to:
   A. $10,000
   B. $25,000
   C. $75,000
   D. $150,000

46. Real estate brokers in New York must:
   A. memorize the NYS Division of Human Rights poster
   B. prominently displaying the HUD fair housing poster in their offices
   C. accept all real estate listings
   D. keep a copy of the New York Human Rights Law in the office as a reference

47. One of the differences between federal and New York human rights laws is that the federal law:
   A. does not address discrimination based on familial status and the New York law does
   B. does not address discrimination based on disability and the New York law does
   C. has fewer protected classes than the New York law
   D. does not address discrimination based on sex and the New York law does

Real Estate Mathematics (1 hour) (2 questions)

48. If Calvin buys three parcels of land for $8,000 and sells them as four separate parcels for $9,000 each, what percent profit does he make?
    A. 33%
    B. 40%
    C. 45%
    D. 50%

49. The owner of a rectangular parcel of land measuring 500 feet wide (front) by 150 feet long is offered at either $20 per front foot *or* $5,000 per acre. What is the amount of the higher offer?
    A. $3,469
    B. $6,400
    C. $10,000
    D. $12,500

Municipal Agencies (2 hours) (2 questions)

50. Which of the following is NOT a function of the building department?
    A. code compliance
    B. requiring landowners to restore or rehabilitate a historic structure
    C. inspection during construction
    D. issuing building permits

51. Dorothy wants to grant an area of undeveloped wetlands to her town. The agency that would most likely accept this grant is the:
    A. conservation advisory council
    B. planning board
    C. architectural review board
    D. building department

Property Insurance (1 hour) (1 question)

52. Which of the following is FALSE?
    A. Lenders require homeowner's insurance to obtain a mortgage.
    B. Perils are events that are always excluded from payment on the insurance policy.
    C. An endorsement is an attachment to the insurance policy.
    D. An insurance policy is a legal contract.

Taxes and Assessments (3 hours) (3 questions)

53. If the assessor determines that the market value of a property is $300,000, and the level of assessment (LOA) in the taxing unit is 75%, what is the assessment for that property?
    A. $200,000
    B. $225,000
    C. $250,000
    D. $275,000

54. Property owners are charged an extra amount on their property tax bill for the addition of three new fire trucks in the taxing unit. This charge is known as a:
    A. tax certiorari
    B. reassessment
    C. special assessment
    D. tax levy

55. A legal action brought by the taxing authority when real property taxes are not paid when due is a(n):
    A. *in rem* legal proceeding
    B. injunction
    C. Article 78 proceeding
    D. Reformation

Condominiums and Cooperatives (4 hours) (3 questions)

56. In a cooperative, the entity that is generally in charge of the approval of the prospective buyer of a cooperative unit is the:
    A. lender
    B. board of directors
    C. vote of the majority of the shareholders
    D. management company

57. In a cooperative, who owns the common areas?
    A. management company
    B. unit owner
    C. cooperative corporation
    D. all of the above

58. The terms under which a cooperative gives permission to a shareholder to make a structural change to the individual unit is called:
    A. a letter of intent
    B. house rules
    C. a subscription agreement
    D. an alteration agreement

Commercial and Investment Properties (10 hours) (9 questions)

59. An investor purchases a $2,300,000 apartment complex with a $600,000 down payment. Each month the cash flow from rentals, less expenses, is $20,000. Over a year's time, the cash-on-cash return would be:
    A. 25%
    B. 28%
    C. 32%
    D. 40%

60. The profit from income-producing property, less income tax, is known as:
    A. after tax cash flow
    B. before tax cash flow
    C. debt service
    D. the debt-to-equity ratio

61. If a property generates a $10,000 cash flow and a $2,000 tax loss that is used to offset other income, the after-tax cash flow for an investor in the 35% tax bracket is:
    A. $3,560
    B. $4,200
    C. $4,320
    D. $5,490

62. A paper income loss on investment property that is sometimes desirable to property owners is known as:
    A. gross income
    B. debt service
    C. leverage
    D. a tax shelter

63. What is the value estimate of a property (rounded) if the net operating income is $650,000 and the capitalization rate is 12%?
    A. $678,000
    B. $4,678,000
    C. $5,216,000
    D. $5,416,667

64. Generally, property owners lease commercial space according to the:
    A. rentable square footage
    B. usable square footage
    C. effective square footage
    D. carpetable area

65. Commercial lessees may view the difference between the rentable and usable area in a commercial space as the:
    A. vacancy factor
    B. loss factor
    C. unused perimeter
    D. common areas

66. One of the main differences between a loft and other types of commercial space for a lease is that a loft:
    A. is not usually divided into rooms
    B. is always more expensive per square foot than other types of space
    C. always has a private elevator
    D. is generally under rent control

67. A lease agreement for commercial property is generally:
    A. standard throughout the state
    B. customized to the particular space and tenant
    C. for ten years or more
    D. a periodic lease

Income Tax Issues in Real Estate Transactions (3 hours) (3 questions)

68. JayCee paid $400,000 for an investment property. She also has a loss of $50,000 due to a fire. She values her property at $350,000. This value is the:
    A. appraised value
    B. adjusted basis
    C. basis
    D. market value

69. Isaiah has an ownership interest in a 60-unit apartment building as a limited partner. According to IRS rules, this kind of ownership is:
    A. active income
    B. passive income
    C. portfolio income
    D. deductible income

70. In a tax-deferred exchange, the individual who accepts the funds from the sale and handles the contracts is called the:
    A. arbitrator
    B. mediator
    C. qualified intermediary
    D. coordinator

Mortgage Brokerage (1 hour) (2 questions)

71. The document that a mortgage broker uses to make certain disclosures to potential borrowers is a(n):
    A. agency disclosure form
    B. preapproval letter
    C. letter of intent
    D. preapplication disclosure and fee agreement

72. Which of the following is FALSE? A mortgage banker:
    A. may lend money
    B. may collect the loan payments
    C. closes the loan in its own name
    D. is licensed by the Federal Deposit Insurance Corporation

Property Management (2 hours) (2 questions)

73. The property manager's fee is generally:
    A. a percentage of all rental income when the rent roll exceeds a certain pre-agreed-upon amount
    B. a lump sum paid in advance on a yearly basis
    C. 25% of the rental income
    D. a base fee and a percentage of the rents collected

74. Laurel, a real estate broker, is also a property manager for an eight-unit residential property. In her role as property manager, Laurel is a:
    A. general agent
    B. fiduciary
    C. special agent
    D. both A and B

Licensee Safety (1 hour) (1 question)

75. Aileen's customers were arriving from out of town and asked Aileen to pick them up at their hotel and then view the property. What is the safest protocol for Aileen? She should:
    A. first meet the customers at the office and they should later meet at the property
    B. pick them up at the hotel
    C. first meet them at the property
    D. not conduct business with out-of-town buyers

Broker Practice Exam I

Agency Law, License Law, and Operating a Real Estate Office (16 hours total) (34 questions total)

Agency Law (9 questions)

1. A seller's broker, in his fiduciary role, may NOT:
   A. advise a seller that a listing price is too high
   B. negotiate on behalf of the seller a price below that at which the property is listed
   C. advise a buyer that the seller is anxious to sell because of a job transfer
   D. represent both the buyer and seller with disclosure and informed consent from both parties

2. The fiduciary relationship between broker and principal allows a broker to:
   A. conceal any material defects to prospective buyers
   B. follow the seller's instructions as to what classes of protected groups under the Human Rights Law should be shown the property
   C. refuse any low offers that she believes will not interest the sellers
   D. obey reasonable and lawful instructions from the principal

3. As to material defects in a property, brokers may be NOT liable because of:
   A. disclosure by the principal
   B. their skill and training
   C. inspection of the property
   D. fraudulent concealment by the principal

4. In New York, franchise firms:
   A. may engage unlicensed individuals to sell real estate to others
   B. are illegal unless they obtain special franchisee permission from the DOS
   C. may deduct a portion of the franchise fee from the final commission due to the sales associate
   D. may revoke a broker's license if the franchise fees are not paid

5. An agent's responsibility to the principal does NOT include:
   A. loyalty
   B. reasonable care
   C. confidentiality
   D. legal advice

6. Herman, a seller, lists with a brokerage firm but does not want to accept vicarious liability for any of the agents hired by his broker. The type of agent that a broker can hire to work for his principal is a:
   A. broker's agent
   B. subagent
   C. dual agent
   D. double agent

7. In New York, dual agency is:
   A. illegal under all circumstances
   B. legal with timely disclosure and informed consent
   C. legal only in firms that advertise themselves as doing business as dual agents
   D. legal only in buyer brokerage firms

8. A principal who lists a property:
   A. automatically permits subagency
   B. has the option of accepting or rejecting subagency when signing the listing agreement
   C. automatically allows subagency by allowing the agent to advertise on the internet
   D. is not liable, under any circumstances, for the acts of subagents

9. Subagents of the seller:
   A. have no duty to the buyer
   B. only have the duty to disclose whom they represent to the buyer and no other obligation
   C. must deal fairly and ethically with the buyer
   D. owe the same loyalties to the seller as the buyer

License Law (8 Questions)

10. If a broker accepts deposit money, it must be kept:
    A. with the office operating account
    B. in a separate escrow account in an insured bank
    C. in a safety deposit box
    D. in an interest-bearing stock portfolio account

11. A broker may receive compensation from more than one party in a real estate transaction:
    A. automatically, as long as the other party is an unlicensed individual
    B. automatically, as long as the other party is a licensed individual
    C. with the knowledge and consent of all parties to the transaction
    D. only if the compensation arrangement is approved by MLS

12. According to DOS regulations, which of the following is TRUE?
    A. A broker may not list his home phone number on business cards.
    B. A broker may not advertise on television.
    C. All ads must indicate that the advertiser is a real estate broker.
    D. All ads must include the type of structure, such as Cape Cod, ranch, raised ranch.

13. Property condition disclosure forms are completed by the:
    A. seller
    B. buyer
    C. listing broker
    D. cooperating broker

14. When a seller authorizes a broker to procure a specified amount for the property and then allows the broker to keep as a commission any money above this specified amount, this is known as a(n):
    A. illegal open listing
    B. illegal net listing
    C. exclusive agency agreement
    D. exclusive-right-to-sell agreement

15. Ron, a sales agent, has obtained a listing and forgotten to ask his sellers if he can put a for-sale sign on the property. Since the sellers are out of town, he asks his broker what to do. He may:
    A. put the sign on the property since he has obtained the listing
    B. not put any sign on the property without the permission of the sellers
    C. put the sign on the lawn as long as he has the permission of his broker
    D. put a sign on the lawn without permission as long as it includes the words "licensed real estate broker"

16. Broker Lately had several salespeople under her supervision, all of whom had not renewed their licenses, which had come due last month. Broker Lately:
    A. should not allow these salespeople to transact real estate
    B. may allow the salespeople to transact as it is not the broker's responsibility to make sure salespeople renew their licenses
    C. may allow the salespeople to service existing listings but not obtain new listings
    D. may allow the salespeople to discuss listings and negotiate real estate transactions in the office only but not drive buyers around or visit sellers

17. In accordance with the NYS license law, brokers have a duty to:
    A. supervise their sales associates
    B. supervise their unlicensed assistants
    C. know how to access and use *eAccessNY*
    D. all of the above

Operating a Real Estate Office (17 Questions)

18. Under the IRS code, a salesperson violates his independent contractor status if he:
    A. becomes an associate broker
    B. is paid an hourly wage
    C. works under a written contract specifying independent contractor status
    D. has no specific work hours

19. If a broker meets the terms of the listing agreement, and brings to the seller a ready, willing, and able buyer, he is entitled to his/her commission because there has been a(n):
    A. meeting of the minds
    B. validation of the listing agreement
    C. advance informed consent
    D. bilateral agreement

20. ABC Realty and Bluebird Realty agreed not to compete in their neighboring towns. ABC Realty would handle all business in the town where it was located, and Bluebird would handle all business in the town where it was located. This is an example of an illegal:
    A. market allocation agreement
    B. tie-in arrangement
    C. price-fixing arrangement
    D. group boycott

21. Redding Realty told their buyer customers that as a condition of purchasing one of the firm's listed properties they would have to obtain financing from Quick Mortgage Associates. This is an example of an illegal:
    A. group boycott
    B. price-fixing arrangement
    C. market allocation agreement
    D. tie-in arrangement

22. Broker Bleary placed a newspaper ad that did not indicate that he was a real estate broker. This is a(n):
    A. lawful advertisement
    B. acceptable ad if it is used to advertise listings only
    C. violation of DOS advertising regulations
    D. ad that is only permissible in the advertisement of commercial property

23. The TILA-RESPA Integrated Disclosure Rule (TRID) includes disclosure requirements for residential real property loans and requires which of the following forms:
    A. loan estimate form
    B. closing disclosure form
    C. HUD-1 form
    D. both A and B

24. If an appraiser wants to find the value of the parking lot of a property, he might value the parking lots of two different properties and determine adjustments to a property valuation when using the sales comparison approach. This method of analysis describes:
    A. the cost approach
    B. a comparative market analysis
    C. a paired-sales analysis
    D. a feasibility study

25. Tia works for commercial Broker Sadie in Queens, New York, but decides that she also wants to work for a residential broker. This arrangement:
   A. is allowable under DOS regulations with the consent of both brokers
   B. is not allowable under license law
   C. is permissible only for brokers and not for salespersons
   D. is permissible only if the salesperson holds the second license in a reciprocal state

26. When a salesperson or associate broker terminates their association with the broker, the broker must file a termination of association notice online to DOS with a fee in the amount of:
   A. $0
   B. $15
   C. $25
   D. $50

27. A type of corporation that pays income tax as a partnership is called a(n):
   A. subchapter S corporation
   B. C corporation
   C. general partnership
   D. limited liability company

28. A form of liability insurance required by real estate brokerage firms to protect against claims for failure to perform on a contract and/or causing financial loss is called:
   A. premises liability
   B. commercial crime bond
   C. errors and omissions
   D. fidelity policy

29. Which of the following is a federally mandated disclosure in the sale of certain real property built before 1978?
   A. agricultural district
   B. bedbug
   C. lead-based paint
   D. truth-in-heating

30. Which of the following is TRUE regarding a broker price opinion (BPO)?
   A. It is the same as an appraisal.
   B. It is a market valuation.
   C. A BPO is appropriate for every transaction.
   D. A BPO is a broker's determination of the potential selling price or estimated value of a property.

31. If online information in the real estate office is not securely protected, a compromised system can lead to:
   A. identify theft
   B. compromising the information of customers and clients
   C. compromising confidential brokerage firm documentation and data
   D. all of the above

32. Which of the following licensed or certified real estate service providers are not licensed by the NYS Department of State?
   A. home inspectors
   B. mortgage brokers
   C. appraiser assistants
   D. certified general appraisers

33. By the time Rolling Green subdivision was finally completed, two years after its first property was built, the demand for housing in the area had declined due to several large businesses leaving the community. The unsold properties were foreclosed upon. This scenario illustrates the economic theory of:
   A. growth
   B. supply and demand
   C. inflation
   D. deficit spending

34. Pablo needs a variance to develop a technology park in an area not zoned for this purpose. It would be the first of its kind in the town and is located near a wetland. What agency or agencies may be involved in the approval process?
    A. conservation advisory council
    B. zoning board of appeals
    C. planning board
    D. all of the above

Real Estate Finance (3 hours) (6 questions)

35. In New York, the borrower holds the deed to the property during the mortgage indebtedness and promises to make all payments to the lender. With regard to a mortgage, New York is a:
    A. title theory state
    B. lien theory state
    C. state that allows predatory lending
    D. none of the above

36. The importance of the prevailing loan-to-value ratio is in determining:
    A. the down payment amount
    B. whether the mortgage will be sold on the secondary market
    C. the investment quality of the property
    D. the borrower's ability to repay the debt

37. A secondary mortgage institution is known as:
    A. VA
    B. SONYMA
    C. Fannie Mae
    D. FHA

38. A type of interim financing sometimes used by developers until more permanent financing is in place after project completion is called:
    A. equity stripping
    B. mini-perm
    C. installment land contract
    D. sale leaseback

39. Melissa arranges to pay the seller of her property a certain sum of money each month. However, the sellers have also transferred title to Melissa in exchange for her promise to pay secured by a lien on the property. The sellers have taken back from Melissa which type of mortgage?
    A. bridge loan
    B. installment land contract
    C. wraparound mortgage
    D. purchase money mortgage

40. A type of transaction in which an owner can free up capital invested in a property and still retain possession and control of the property under a lease is known as a:
    A. sale leaseback
    B. ground lease
    C. wraparound mortgage
    D. purchase money mortgage

Real Property Investment (4 hours) (9 questions)

41. The greatest amount of leverage can be obtained if an investor:
    A. uses only personal funds
    B. uses an equal amount of personal funds together with borrowed funds
    C. uses solely borrowed funds
    D. invests in a property for a minimum of one year

42. Preston purchased a four-family apartment house for $300,000. He made a $100,000 down payment and financed the balance. Five years later, he sold the property for $550,000. Preston has realized a:
    A. portfolio income
    B. capital gain
    C. debt service
    D. tax loss

43. The tax deductible expenses, including depreciation of a property, are greater than the income. For tax purposes, which of the following is a result?
   A. negative amortization
   B. capital gain
   C. tax shelter
   D. boot

44. A property's cash flow refers to the:
   A. amount of activity of a certain investment account
   B. sum total of income for any given day's activity
   C. debt service
   D. net proceeds after all expenses and debt services are met

45. A provision of the tax law that permits a property owner to take a deductible allowance from the net income of property is known as:
   A. economic depreciation
   B. tax depreciation
   C. adjusted basis
   D. capital loss

46. A small residential apartment complex containing ten units rents each for $800 per month. Based on 75% occupancy, the effective gross rental income per year is:
   A. $8,000
   B. $72,000
   C. $80,000
   D. $100,000

47. If the annual net operating income for a condominium property is $480,000 and the capitalization rate is 11%, the estimated property value is:
   A. $2,290,000
   B. $2,990,000
   C. $4,363,636
   D. $5,280,000

48. An owner's office building is producing a net annual operating income of $140,000. If the owner paid $1,166,666 for the property, what rate of return is the owner receiving on the investment?
   A. 8.3%
   B. 14%
   C. 12%
   D. 16.3%

49. Rosie purchases a $2,000,000 multi-family apartment complex with a $500,000 down payment. Each month the cash from rentals, less expenses, is $15,000. Over a year's time, what is the equity dividend rate (cash-on-cash return)?
   A. 25%
   B. 36%
   C. 40%
   D. 43%

General Business Law (3 hours) (8 questions)

50. The purpose of the Foreign Investment in Real Property Tax Act (FIRPTA) is to:
   A. deter foreign investment in the U.S.
   B. encourage foreign investment in U.S. property
   C. impose a tax on capital gains derived by foreign individuals from the sale of their U.S. property
   D. surcharge the real estate broker on the sale of property to foreign investors

51. To protect consumers from unsolicited calls from service providers and others, which of the following is in place:
   A. registration on a Do Not Call list maintained by the Federal Trade Commission
   B. requirements of the CAN SPAM law regarding commercial emails
   C. NYS Department of State cease and desist lists
   D. all of the above

52. Which of the following is NOT a negotiable instrument?
    A. check
    B. promissory note
    C. CD
    D. cash

53. A requirement for negotiability would NOT include that an instrument must:
    A. be in writing
    B. be signed
    C. be worth less than $25,000
    D. contain a promise or order to pay

54. The Truth-in-Heating Law refers to the law regarding:
    A. the installation of heating and cooling in residential buildings
    B. prohibitions against landlords who unfairly charge for heating and cooling services above their costs
    C. landlords' disclosure of heating and cooling bills to prospective tenants
    D. constructive eviction if heating is not supplied to a premises during cold weather

55. Which of the following is NOT a form of personal property that may be transferred in a real estate transaction?
    A. shares of stock evidencing ownership in a cooperative
    B. bill of sale listing items sold in a property when closing
    C. heavy equipment sold at closing
    D. acreage sold with a building

56. A reorganization form of bankruptcy is known as which chapter of the Bankruptcy Code?
    A. Chapter 7
    B. Chapter 11
    C. Chapter 13
    D. Chapter 15

57. The law that imposes time limits within which litigation may be commenced is known as the:
    A. Statute of Limitations
    B. Statute of Frauds
    C. Doctrine of Laches
    D. Notice of Pendency

Construction and Development (3 hours) (8 questions)

58. What categories of building science may affect a prospective buyer's choices in deciding whether to consider traditional older properties verses newly built ones?
    A. environmental sustainability
    B. energy efficiencies
    C. technological advancements
    D. all of the above

59. In New York, all contracts of sale for new construction include a warranty for material defects in workmanship for:
    A. one year
    B. two years
    C. five years
    D. six years

60. To comply with building codes, contractors and developers file plans and specifications with which of the following agencies?
    A. local building department
    B. planning board
    C. attorney general's office
    D. both A and B

61. One of the main purposes of subdivision regulations is to:
    A. control property development within the subdivision
    B. keep out undesirable individuals
    C. raise the tax base of the community
    D. limit the developer to a certain amount of profit on the project

62. Although local codes may be more restrictive, all construction in New York must comply with which of the following laws?
   A. State Environmental Quality Review Act
   B. NYS Uniform Fire Prevention and Building Code
   C. NYS Article 9-a
   D. Interstate Land Sales Full Disclosure Act

63. Before purchasing a property, which of the following professionals might be the most helpful in assessing the quality of construction in a residential property?
   A. NYS-licensed home inspector
   B. general appraiser
   C. NYS-licensed real estate broker
   D. property developer

64. In the last 12 months in a town in New York, 8,000 residential homes at a certain price level were sold. There are now 2,000 homes on the market. What is the absorption rate for homes at this price level to sell in this area?
   A. one month
   B. two months
   C. three months
   D. four months

65. When a developer wants to construct or convert an existing building into a cooperative, what document must be filed with the NYS Attorney General?
   A. offering plan
   B. stock certificate
   C. proprietary lease
   D. alteration agreement

Conveyance of Real Property (1 hour) (3 questions)

66. The term intestate refers to:
   A. persons who die without leaving a valid will
   B. roadways that cross over two or more states
   C. transfer of possession of property from one person to another after death
   D. person who carries out the provisions of a will

67. Alienation is:
   A. land held through adverse possession
   B. a tenant at sufferance
   C. the transfer of title to property
   D. the same as alluvion

68. Title may NOT be acquired to real estate through voluntary alienation by:
   A. eminent domain
   B. sale
   C. gift
   D. dedication

Real Property Management (4 hours) (9 questions)

69. A duty of a property manager does NOT generally include:
   A. prudently investing the owner's profits
   B. maintaining the property
   C. collecting rents
   D. establishing a budget for property operation

70. An item that should NOT be included in an annual property management maintenance schedule is:
   A. window cleaning
   B. exterior painting
   C. legal fees
   D. parking lot repair

71. Which of the following should NOT be considered in selecting tenants?
   A. credit history of the tenant
   B. past landlord references
   C. marital status of the tenant
   D. employment status of the tenant

72. A typical property management agreement does NOT generally include the:
   A. scope of agent's management authority
   B. manager's fee
   C. accounting responsibilities
   D. portfolio of the owner's other investment holdings

73. If a property management office works for more than one property owner and collects rents for these owners, the license generally required is:
   A. no license
   B. an apartment information vendor's license
   C. a broker license
   D. no license, but a designation from a professional property management organization

74. The rentable square footage of most commercial space:
   A. is the square footage of the total area for which the tenant pays rent
   B. includes the usable square footage
   C. includes the tenant's pro rata share of the common areas
   D. all of the above

75. With a triple net lease:
   A. the lessee pays all expenses associated with the property in addition to the rent except for the debt service
   B. the landlord pays all of the expenses of the property
   C. the lessee pays some of the expenses of the property
   D. the lessee pays a base rent plus a percentage of the gross sales

76. An annual budget that includes income and expenses for week-to-week operations is known as the:
   A. capital reserve budget
   B. operating budget
   C. stabilized budget
   D. none of the above

77. Minus other factors, over a year's time, if the gross income of an apartment complex is $275,000, and the operating expenses (OE) are $150,000, what is the net operating income (NOI) for the year?
   A. $450,000
   B. $275,000
   C. $125,000
   D. $115,000

Taxes and Assessments (1 hour) (3 questions)

78. The accepted fair type of value for setting assessments is:
   A. market value
   B. value in use
   C. investment value
   D. book value

79. The NYS constitutional right of home rule is the authority of local governments to exercise self-government. This right of home rule is exemplified in the property tax process through:
   A. the equalization rate
   B. a grievance
   C. homestead properties
   D. a tax lien

80. A property with a market value of $80,000 is assessed at 75%. What is the tax rate per $100 if the tax bill is $900?
   A. $1.125
   B. $1.50
   C. $15.00
   D. $11.25

Advanced Fair Housing and Fair Lending (3 hours) (8 questions)

81. A protected class of individuals for housing under the New York Human Rights Law but NOT under the Federal Fair Housing Act is:
    A. family status
    B. physical disabilities
    C. military status
    D. national origin

82. Although there are some exemptions in the federal and NYS laws regarding the sale and rental of housing, there is no exemption based on:
    A. rental of an apartment in an owner-occupied two-family house
    B. rental of a room by the occupant of a house or an apartment
    C. race
    D. a private club that does not operate for commercial purposes but exempt as long as it provides lodging for the benefit of its members only

83. The Americans with Disabilities Act covers:
    A. existing commercial buildings
    B. public buildings such as museums and theatres
    C. multi-family housing
    D. all of the above

84. Gentrification in a neighborhood can cause:
    A. displacement of current residents
    B. higher property values
    C. influx of new business establishments
    D. all of the above

85. When lending institutions refuse to make loans to purchase, construct, or repair dwellings by discriminating against those in protected classes under human rights law, this illegal practice is known as:
    A. redlining
    B. blockbusting
    C. steering
    D. predatory lending

86. The Community Reinvestment Act has to do with:
    A. a developer's willingness to build new housing in declining neighborhoods
    B. municipalities investing in declining neighborhoods
    C. lenders making loans available to lower-income purchasers
    D. real estate brokers marketing properties in lower income neighborhoods

87. Elena, a gay Latina, single working mother, wants to rent a three-bedroom apartment in a four-family apartment complex in Brooklyn, New York. She is refused a rental and not given an explanation. Possible violations for the refusal may include illegal discrimination because of:
    A. marital status
    B. sexual orientation
    C. race
    D. all of the above

88. Housing discrimination can be deterred by:
    A. laws to protect discrimination
    B. stringent legal penalties for fair housing discrimination
    C. changing negative, false, and harmful belief systems of certain individuals
    D. all of the above

Achieving Agreements through Transaction Analysis (6 hours) (12 questions)

89. When an agent represents a client in a transactional agreement, what is the most essential ingredient of the agreement?
    A. wants of the transaction party
    B. needs of the transaction party
    C. needs and wants of the agent
    D. none of the above

90. If BJ signs an exclusive right-to sell listing agreement, then BJ is the broker's:
 A. client
 B. customer
 C. partner
 D. fiduciary

91. The overall objective for any real estate transaction is to reach an agreement:
 A. on fair terms
 B. within a reasonable period of time
 C. that is beneficial to all parties
 D. all of the above

92. In any agency agreement, the agent must represent the best interests of the:
 A. brokerage firm
 B. customer
 C. client
 D. all parties to the transaction

93. The primary objective of the agent in a real estate transactional agreement should be to reach an agreement:
 A. at all costs
 B. without sacrificing the best interests of the client in order to reach an agreement
 C. that equally represents the interests of the customer and client
 D. none of the above

94. What viable factor is usually the most important to the parties in negotiating a real estate agreement?
 A. interest rate deadlines
 B. timing considerations
 C. price of the property
 D. maintenance issues with a particular property

95. In reaching a transactional agreement, a real estate agent, in working for a client, can and should do which of the following?
 A. locate qualified buyers for a seller
 B. locate suitable properties for a buyer
 C. work with other brokers to reach an agreement acceptable to all of the parties to the transaction
 D. all of the above

96. The commission for a real estate broker is:
 A. negotiable between the broker and client
 B. always paid entirely by the seller
 C. always a percentage of the selling price of the property
 D. generally a flat fee

97. The services to be performed by the real estate broker for a client should best be:
 A. implied
 B. agreed to with a handshake
 C. specifically stated in the listing agreement or buyer agency representation agreement
 D. decided as the transaction goes forth

98. Which of the following is an important driving force in the formation of the transactional agreement?
 A. motivations of the individual parties to the transaction as to why they want to sell and purchase
 B. family dynamics
 C. buyer moving into the "right" neighborhood
 D. all of the above

99. Once a transactional agreement is reached that is acceptable to all parties, there has been:
 A. a meeting of the minds
 B. an offer and acceptance
 C. a commission earned by the broker
 D. all of the above

100. In a transactional agreement, the broker must always represent the best interests of:
 A. all parties to the transaction
 B. the client
 C. the brokerage firm
 D. all of the above

Broker Practice Exam 2

Agency Law, License Law, and Operating a Real Estate Office (16 hours) (34 questions total)

Agency Law (9 questions)

1. When hiring a broker's agent, who may have vicarious liability for the acts of the broker's agent?
   A. listing agent
   B. buyer's agent
   C. tenant's agent
   D. all of the above

2. The compensation paid to a broker is negotiable between the:
   A. broker and the multiple listing service
   B. broker and the principal
   C. broker and the real estate board
   D. office policy together with the decision of the listing agent

3. Which of the following is TRUE?
   A. A buyer or seller can agree to dual agency in advance of it occurring.
   B. Dual agency can only be agreed to when it occurs.
   C. Dual agency is illegal in New York under all conditions.
   D. All real estate agents are dual agents.

4. The required use of the agency disclosure form for property sales or rental refers to:
   A. one- to four-unit residential properties only
   B. all properties for sale or rent in New York
   C. one- to four-unit residential properties together with land to be used for residential subdivisions
   D. one- to four-unit residential properties as well as condominiums and cooperatives in any size building

5. The overall purpose of the agency disclosure law is to:
   A. protect the commissions earned by real estate agents
   B. ensure that buyers realize that a seller's agent does not represent their best interests
   C. make consumers aware of the agency relationship of a real estate agent and the choices available to them
   D. protect the broker from being liable for the acts of principals who have listed with them

6. If a prospective purchaser refuses to sign the agency disclosure form:
   A. the agent cannot legally show the property
   B. the agent may show the property but must complete and keep on file a declaration form stating the facts of the refusal
   C. the broker may show the property only after obtaining special permission from DOS
   D. the agent may show the property if he has the buyers sign a statement saying they were shown the disclosure form

7. An exclusive single agency relationship:
   A. is not allowable under DOS regulations
   B. only occurs when there is a buyer agency relationship
   C. is not a fiduciary relationship
   D. occurs if a broker represents either the buyer or the seller but not both

8. The IRS form that must be prepared yearly by the broker for salespersons who are independent contractors is:
   A. W-2
   B. 941
   C. FICA
   D. 1099-MISC

9. In a brokerage firm, the listing contracts are typically owned by the:
   A. brokerage firm
   B. salesperson who listed the property
   C. multiple listing service together with the brokerage firm
   D. principals who engaged the firm to market their properties

License Law (8 questions)

10. Broker Lawless advised some buyers that he was working with a full covenant and warranty deed that was preferable to a quitclaim deed. Which of the following is TRUE?
    A. Broker Lawless may give this advice as long as he discloses to the sellers that he is not an attorney.
    B. He can give this advice as long as there are witnesses present.
    C. Broker Lawless should not give out legal advice of any kind.
    D. He should consult guidelines furnished by the local board of REALTORS® before giving legal advice.

11. How many years of experience as a salesperson is required for a broker license?
    A. one
    B. two
    C. three
    D. five

12. The maximum fine that can be imposed by the DOS for violation of the license law is:
    A. $500
    B. $1,000
    C. $2,500
    D. no specific penalty under the law

13. Applicants for whom English is a second language:
    A. may not obtain licensure in New York
    B. must demonstrate a fair knowledge of English by passing the NYS exam without assistance
    C. may qualify under the statute to use a dictionary while taking the state exam
    D. must complete an extra 15 hours of study in English before taking the state exam

14. Applicants for the broker license must be at least how old?
    A. 18
    B. 20
    C. 21
    D. 25

15. The continuing education requirement for brokers who have been licensed for 15 or more continuous years before July 1, 2008, is:
    A. 45 hours upon license renewal
    B. 22.5 hours upon license renewal
    C. 45 hours every four years
    D. exemption from any continuing education requirements

16. George owns more than 50 apartment buildings that he has managed over the past 25 years. Now George wants to obtain a broker license. Which of the following is TRUE?
    A. George's experience as an apartment manager should give him the qualifying experience to obtain a broker license.
    B. George must obtain a salesperson license before applying for broker licensure.
    C. George's experience in managing apartments does not count toward the experience requirement for broker licensure.
    D. George does not need to become a salesperson first, but he must pass the salesperson state exam before applying for broker licensure.

17. Who of the following are exempt from licensure as long as they have no sales agents working for them?
   A. brokers who have 15 or more years' experience
   B. attorneys admitted to practice in New York
   C. brokers, associate brokers, or sales agents who have 15 or more years' experience
   D. property managers working for more than one owner

Operating a Real Estate Office (17 questions)

18. A trade name broker is:
   A. a corporation
   B. a form of business organization that uses a name already used by another brokerage firm in New York
   C. generally a sole proprietorship using a name other than the personal name of the broker
   D. a brokerage firm which does not belong to the board of REALTORS®

19. An allowable activity under the law for multiple listing services is:
   A. fixing commission rates
   B. adopting rules prohibiting a member from doing business with another
   C. admitting part-time brokers to MLS
   D. suggesting a commission rate in an educational course

20. According to antitrust law, which of the following is TRUE?
   A. Boards of REALTORS® may fix commission rates.
   B. Boards of REALTORS® may suggest commission rates in education courses.
   C. MLS services may refuse a listing if it does not find the commission rate acceptable.
   D. Commission rates are negotiable between agent and principal.

21. Which of the following is NOT a category of real estate agent licensure?
   A. salesperson
   B. broker
   C. associate broker
   D. mortgage loan originator

22. A mortgage loan servicer is licensed by which of the following New York agencies?
   A. Department of Financial Services
   B. Department of State, Division of Licensing Services
   C. Department of State, Division of Corporations
   D. Department of Law

23. What is one of the differences between a C and an S corporation?
   A. An S corporation is taxed as a partnership.
   B. An S corporation can only do business in New York.
   C. A brokerage firm cannot be set up as an S corporation.
   D. The S corporation pays a greater franchise tax.

24. One of the advantages of a limited liability company is that it:
   A. pays a lower corporation franchise tax
   B. is taxed as a partnership
   C. cannot be dissolved by judicial decree
   D. is the only form of corporation allowed for a real estate brokerage firm

25. Lenny, an associate broker, created an ad for a listing and published it with the local paper. Lenny:
   A. had every right to do so because he is a licensee
   B. should have let the marketing department of the firm write the ad
   C. should have had the ad approved by the broker before having it published
   D. would have had to ask permission of the MLS before publishing the ad

26. Justine posted an ad on the brokerage firm website which read in part: Justine Dupree, "real estate licensee." What is wrong with this part of the ad?
    A. There is nothing wrong at all.
    B. She excluded her middle name.
    C. She must include the type of license she has next to her name.
    D. Licensees in the brokerage firm should not post their names; only the name of the broker or brokerage firm.

27. The TILA-RESPA Disclosure Rule applies to which one of the following mortgages?
    A. residential property
    B. home equity lines of credit
    C. business loans
    D. reverse mortgages

28. Many brokerage firms use behavioral assessment tests during the interview process for new agents. These tests are mainly to find out:
    A. personality traits
    B. emotional stability
    C. any prior criminal activity
    D. levels of reading, writing, and math skills

29. The party to a real estate listing who should ultimately decide where the property should be advertised online is the:
    A. brokerage firm
    B. listing broker
    C. seller
    D. multiple listing service

30. According to the National Association of REALTORS®' policies, once a property is posted online through a multiple listing service, a listing can be transferred for posting to another party:
    A. without the listing broker's consent
    B. with the consent of the multiple listing service
    C. only with the listing broker's consent
    D. none of the above

31. The difference between the duties of the home inspector and the appraiser is that the home inspector:
    A. does not give a value estimate of the property but the appraiser does
    B. examines the property; the appraiser never does
    C. makes repairs to a property when called for; the appraiser does not
    D. is not licensed in New York but all appraisers are

32. The cost approach to value:
    A. is never used to value residential property
    B. computes the market price of the property by considering the cost of the land plus the cost of construction, less depreciation
    C. is similar to the comparative market analysis
    D. is similar to the income capitalization approach to value

33. In managing a real estate office, the broker must:
    A. implement a financial plan
    B. implement a data security system
    C. make available a policies and procedures manual
    D. all of the above

34. Generally, the day before a real estate closing, what is one of the tasks of the sales agent handling the closing?
    A. The agent has done her job when there is a meeting of the minds.
    B. The agent accompanies the buyers on a final walk-through of the property.
    C. She reviews the abstract of title with the buyers.
    D. She has the sellers complete the property condition disclosure form.

Real Estate Finance (2 hours) (6 questions)

35. The function of the FHA is to:
    A. make mortgage loans
    B. buy mortgages on the secondary market
    C. insure loans to protect lenders against financial loss
    D. make loans for targeted low-income housing

36. The loss of funds available to lending institutions for making mortgage loans caused by the withdrawal of funds by depositors is known as:
    A. disintegration
    B. stagflation
    C. disintermediation
    D. illiquidity

37. A capital short market occurs when:
    A. funds for underwriting are plentiful
    B. lenders do not have available funds for underwriting mortgages
    C. lenders are selling mortgages to the secondary mortgage market
    D. mortgages are assignable and are sold to the secondary mortgage market before the borrower repays the debt

38. A moderate and temporary decline in economic activity that occurs during a period of otherwise increasing prosperity is known as:
    A. recession
    B. depression
    C. stagflation
    D. marginal regression

39. An economic condition in which economic growth is at a standstill but inflation still exists is known as:
    A. inflation
    B. depression
    C. recession
    D. stagflation

40. The type of mortgage in which two or more parcels of real estate are pledged as security for repayment of the mortgage debt is known as a(n):
    A. shared appreciation mortgage
    B. bridge loan
    C. installment land contract
    D. blanket mortgage

Real Property Investment (4 hours) (9 questions)

41. A risk in real estate investment does NOT include:
    A. a downturn in the real estate market
    B. illiquidity of the investment
    C. environmental problems associated with a proposed development
    D. lender participation in the financing

42. Which of the following is NOT a fixed expense in the investment of income property?
    A. vacancy
    B. insurance
    C. property taxes
    D. water/sewer

43. Eugene is considering the purchase of a 10-year-old office building and is analyzing the project to determine the price he wants to pay. What factor is NOT important in determining the price?
    A. the initial cost to construct the building
    B. his desired rate of return
    C. the vacancy level of the building
    D. how long he wishes to hold the property

44. In the sale of a capital asset held for more than twelve months, the seller realizes a gain of $242,000. The amount of taxable gain is:
    A. $193,600
    B. $96,800
    C. $145,200
    D. $242,000

45. In estimating the value of an office building containing 22,400 square feet, an appraiser established the annual rental income to be $400,000. The appraiser also learned that monthly expenses averaged $16,700. If an investor in this property was realizing a net return of 13.5%, what would be the appraiser's estimate of the property's value (rounded)?
   A. $2,962,962
   B. $1,484,444
   C. $1,478,518
   D. $2,964,600

46. If the asking price of a property is $300,000 and the property has gross rents of $50,000, what is the gross rent multiplier?
   A. 3
   B. 4
   C. 5
   D. 6

47. If the gross rent multiplier is 7 and the gross rent per year for the property is 30,000, what is the estimated investment value of the property based on this calculation?
   A. $210,000
   B. $233,000
   C. $235,000
   D. $273,000

48. If a property valued at $600,000 produces total income in the amount of $100,000, what is the gross income multiplier?
   A. 2
   B. 3
   C. 5
   D. 6

49. If the net operating income of a property is $275,000 and the debt service is $110,000, what is the debt service coverage ratio?
   A. 1.5
   B. 2.0
   C. 2.5
   D. 3.0

General Business Law (3 hours) (8 questions)

50. Brokers many become involved in the sale of marital property when there is a divorce action because:
   A. the property of the spouses must be sold should there be a divorce
   B. brokers are also licensed to serve as counselors as to how to rid the parties of their properties
   C. there may be a court order to sell the family residence and other properties
   D. properties automatically devalue when there is a divorce action

51. A signature on the back of a promissory note by someone other than a maker, drawer, or acceptor is known as a(n):
   A. assignment
   B. endorsement
   C. bearer's signature
   D. acknowledgment

52. In New York, a mechanic's lien must be filed with the county clerk or other government entity within how many months of completion of the contract?
   A. 3
   B. 4
   C. 5
   D. 6

53. Which of the following is TRUE?
   A. The NYS Agricultural Districts Law promotes and protects availability of land for farming purposes.
   B. There may be restrictions as to the access of water and sewer services in an Agricultural District.
   C. Real estate agents must present to a prospective purchaser an Agricultural District Disclosure Form and Notice when marketing property in a certified Agricultural District.
   D. All of the above are true.

54. According to NYS and IRS regulations, which of the following is TRUE?
    A. Most gifts of money are subject to the federal gift tax.
    B. Most estates are subject to estate tax.
    C. Gifts to spouses are taxable gifts.
    D. The gift tax does not apply to the first $15,000 given to another in each year.

55. A mechanic's lien is:
    A. the same as any other lien
    B. specific only to personal property
    C. filed by a person who provides labor to a property
    D. allowed in New York only for work performed on commercial properties

56. In New York, if a landlord owns six or more units, the security deposit:
    A. must be placed in an interest-earning checking account
    B. must be invested in safe securities
    C. must be returned to the tenant if a new owner purchases the property
    D. can be renegotiated during the lease term

57. A main difference between mediation and arbitration is that:
    A. arbitration is the same as litigation
    B. the arbitrator makes a decision, while a mediator does not
    C. mediation does not have a neutral third party
    D. mediation is not a form of dispute resolution

Construction and Development (3 hours) (8 questions)

58. Under New York law, when a developer files an offering plan with the attorney general to convert an existing building to a condo or co-op, how much time do the tenants have for an exclusive right to buy their apartment?
    A. 30 days
    B. 60 days
    C. 90 days
    D. 120 days

59. Laura, a developer, wants to ensure that homeowners in her subdivision do not park RVs on the front lawn. Laura can accomplish this through:
    A. deed restrictions
    B. special use permits
    C. amendments to the building code
    D. carefully screening purchasers who want to buy a house in the subdivision

60. What is the effect that the NYS constitutional amendment of home rule has on subdivision development?
    A. It gives local municipal agencies decision making power over subdivision approval.
    B. It allows a developer to forego planning board approval.
    C. It makes it easier in all cases for a development to obtain municipal approval for a subdivision.
    D. It allows a developer to participate in the lifting of a moratorium on development if there is one.

61. Building specifications are:
    A. the same as blueprints
    B. similar to a survey of the property
    C. written narratives that explain the building plan
    D. explanations of the demographics of the property

62. The reason why home inspections of new home construction may be different under the home inspector license law is that:
    A. new home construction has many components unfamiliar to the home inspector
    B. the definition of residential housing in the home inspector license law does not include new construction
    C. home inspectors never inspect new construction
    D. home inspectors cannot give advice or opinions regarding new construction

63. In New York, which of the following bodies have the statutory authority to review site plans?
   A. mayor's office
   B. local court system
   C. local building department
   D. local planning board

64. The NYS Truth-in-Heating Law refers to:
   A. landlords furnishing prospective tenants with heating and cooling bills
   B. landlords disclosing the dates of installation or repairs to heating and cooling equipment
   C. landlords and tenants deciding who will pay the electric bill for the unit
   D. landlords providing warranty information for the heating and cooling equipment for the building

65. The NYS rules for how a condominium or cooperative may be advertised is set forth in the:
   A. condominium bylaws
   B. CPS1 statement
   C. alteration agreement
   D. NYSDOS advertising regulations

Conveyance of Real Property (1 hour) (3 questions)

66. A testatrix is:
   A. a witness who appears at a bankruptcy hearing
   B. a woman who makes a valid will
   C. a person who is unlawfully in possession of another's property
   D. a man who has died and who has not left a valid will

67. The loss of land when a sudden or violent change in a watercourse washes it away is:
   A. accretion
   B. avulsion
   C. erosion
   D. annexation

68. In a mortgage foreclosure, the property owner may satisfy the lien up to the foreclosure sale through:
   A. the law of eminent domain
   B. a partition proceeding
   C. the right of redemption
   D. fulfilling the requirements of the adverse possession statute in New York

Real Property Management (4 hours) (9 questions)

69. A type of insurance that covers the risks that an owner assumes when the public enters a property is:
   A. public liability insurance
   B. error and omissions insurance
   C. fidelity policy
   D. commercial crime bond insurance

70. A skill NOT required for a property manager is to:
   A. understand building systems
   B. supervise others
   C. handle landlord–tenant relations
   D. draw contracts

71. In the property management business, the individual who oversees the day-to-day operation of the property or properties is known as the:
   A. asset manager
   B. site manager
   C. portfolio manager
   D. grounds manager

72. The necessary steps to increase the net operating income for a property is to:
   A. increase the potential gross income
   B. reduce operating expenses
   C. reduce vacancy and collection loss
   D. all of the above

73. Which of the following is NOT a fixed expense in property management and/or ownership of income property?
    A. debt service
    B. property taxes
    C. maintenance and repairs
    D. insurance

74. Amir, the property manager, offered prospective tenants a 25% reduction in the first two months and last two months of rent if they signed a two-year lease. This arrangement is known as a(n):
    A. landlord concession
    B. bad business practice
    C. percentage lease
    D. index lease

75. Clauses in a lease that call for increased costs to the tenant for different reasons and at specified times during the lease term are called:
    A. index clauses
    B. escalation clauses
    C. favorability clauses
    D. occupancy clauses

76. The concept of modified gross rent refers to a:
    A. reduction in rent after a specified time
    B. lease escalation clause
    C. type of apportionment of expenses between a landlord and tenant
    D. none of the above

77. A property manager's fee usually consists of a base fee plus a percentage of the:
    A. effective gross income
    B. potential yearly income
    C. value of the property
    D. stabilized budget

Taxes and Assessments (1 hour) (3 questions)

78. The amount that a municipality must raise through taxes on real property is known as the:
    A. stabilized budget
    B. tax levy
    C. special assessment
    D. assessment roll

79. The Mores have been unable to pay their property taxes for the past two years. Recently, they discovered that their property was encumbered. Based on these facts only, which of the following has most likely encumbered the property?
    A. mechanic's lien
    B. grievance
    C. tax lien
    D. homestead misclassification

80. To take advantage of tax exemptions allowed to the Industrial Development Agency (IDA), private owners transfer title temporarily to the IDA and make certain payments to the IDA for the temporary tax exemption. These payments are known as:
    A. development incentives
    B. deed in lieu of foreclosure
    C. PILOTS
    D. REITS

Advanced Fair Housing and Fair Lending (3 hours) (8 questions)

81. Under the federal Fair Housing Act, discriminatory behavior that has a disproportionate adverse impact on any of the protected classes is known as:
    A. disparate impact
    B. redlining
    C. steering
    D. blockbusting

82. Lenders in a certain community consistently refuse to make loans to qualified Latino purchasers. The behavior of the lenders in this community are an example of:
    A. blockbusting
    B. steering
    C. redlining
    D. institutionalized discrimination

83. Federal laws that address fair lending include the:
    A. Equal Credit Opportunity Act
    B. Fair Lending Act
    C. Fair Housing Act
    D. all of the above

84. According to a number of studies, affordable housing may or may not affect property values depending on which of the following factors?
    A. design and management of affordable housing
    B. compatibility between affordable housing and the host neighborhood
    C. concentration of affordable housing
    D. all of the above

85. The NYS Human Rights Law is broader in scope than the federal Fair Housing Act in that it covers discrimination as to:
    A. age
    B. credit transactions
    C. employment
    D. all of the above

86. A locally protected class in NYC, and possibly other municipalities in New York, that is not included in the NYS Human Rights Law for housing discrimination is:
    A. alienage or citizenship status
    B. sexual orientation (including same-sex marriage)
    C. marital status
    D. military status

87. In New York, to comply with fair housing laws, the real estate office should:
    A. offer ongoing training and education
    B. report fair housing misconduct
    C. comply with fair housing advertising regulations
    D. all of the above

88. Lucinda and Marco are a married couple with two teenage children. Lucinda works part time as a waitress and Marco is a taxicab driver. They have ample savings and are legally permanent residents originally from Haiti. They are denied a rental in a four-unit apartment building in Queens, New York, and are given no reason for the denial. Per the federal, NYS, and NYC human rights laws, they are protected under which of the following classes?
    A. family status
    B. citizenship status
    C. lawful occupation
    D. all of the above

Achieving Agreements through Transaction Analysis (6 hours) (12 questions)

89. A real estate agent negotiating a transactional agreement CANNOT do which of the following tasks?
    A. assist a seller in deciding what price to ask for a property
    B. assist a seller-client in gathering documents for a closing
    C. assist a buyer to prepare an offer to purchase
    D. draw up the contract of sale

90. Obligations that an agent must offer to a client include:
    A. competency
    B. skill
    C. care and diligence
    D. all of the above

91. Factors that an agent must consider in forming a transactional agreement include:
    A. seller concessions
    B. contract contingencies
    C. multiple offers
    D. all of the above

92. Which of the following is TRUE?
    A. The process of transaction analysis does not always culminate in a successful transactional agreement.
    B. The law of agency need not be adhered to in the making of a transactional agreement.
    C. A transactional agreement does not involve the principles of negotiation.
    D. The motivation of the parties is not an important consideration in the formation of a transactional agreement.

93. A successful transactional agreement can be negotiated if:
    A. the broker does not always negotiate in only the best interest his or her client
    B. there is no confidentiality agreement between the broker and client
    C. the dual objectives of both parties are prudently addressed by their brokers
    D. none of the above

94. In a transaction analysis, some of the duties that an agent must perform at the outset include:
    A. estimating a range of value for the property
    B. deciding how the financial climate can contribute or not contribute to a successful transaction
    C. inquiring as to the financial limitations of the parties to the transaction
    D. all of the above

95. Michael had a rather nonproductive year and was looking to make a quick sale. He was representing a client to buy a two-family income property and was pushing the client very hard to close the deal even though the client was wanting to further negotiate with the seller to get the price down. Is there anything wrong with Michael's behavior?
    A. Agents can advise their clients as they please
    B. Michael is violating the fiduciary duties of obedience, loyalty, and care
    C. Michael should not sacrifice the interests of the client just to achieve the agreement
    D. B and C

96. Arne, a seller, is dissatisfied with the terms of the transactional agreement that his broker has negotiated because he believes he is being pushed to close before he has located another property. Arne wants to refuse the offer. The buyer, however, has no place to live and is anxious to close immediately. What, if anything, is wrong with this agreement?
    A. Nothing at all is wrong.
    B. The transactional agreement should be mutually beneficial to both parties and it is not.
    C. Arne has little or nothing to say; the broker or brokers decide when the parties are to close.
    D. The broker should explain to Arne that his commission is due because he has achieved a meeting of the minds.

97. Howie has recently obtained his real estate license and is negotiating his first transactional agreement. Howie is not really sure about how to negotiate the agreement and what his role is going to be. Which of the following obligations of a real estate agent is Howie violating should he negotiate an agreement for his seller?
    A. competency
    B. skill
    C. care
    D. all of the above

98. The principles of transaction analysis apply to which of the following real property transactions?
    A. sale
    B. purchase
    C. lease
    D. all of the above

99. In his role as an agent, Joshua has negotiated with his client, the seller, and also the broker who represents the buyer to the transaction. What, if anything, is wrong with Joshua's behavior as agent of the seller?
    A. Nothing is wrong—he is doing his job.
    B. He is in violation of New York license law.
    C. He is in violation of the law of agency.
    D. He is guilty of illegal self-dealing.

100. Donna, in her role as agent for the seller, has received multiple offers on a property she has listed for the seller. Donna must:
    A. sort out only the best offers and present them to her client
    B. present all offers to the client
    C. tell the customers who are making the offers the offering price of the best offer so they should act accordingly
    D. insist that her seller accept the offer that she feels is in the client-seller's best interest

Answer Key

All answers are explained in this Answer Key. For further explanation, refer to *New York Real Estate for Salespersons, 6th e* Revised and *New York Real Estate for Brokers, 6th e.*

Answer Key for Review Questions

License Law and Regulations/Operating a Real Estate Office

1. D: A licensee must only accept a commission from his or her sponsoring broker so this is not a violation of the license law.

2. D: Auctioneers who sell real property must have a real estate license. Building superintendents working for one owner, public officers, and attorneys who do not employ salespersons do not require a license.

3. B: A licensee who deposits an earnest money check in his personal checking account instead of in the broker's trust account is guilty of commingling. Conversion is the illegal use of another's money. Escheat is the state's right to a decedent's property if no heirs are found.

4. C: A major purpose of the license law is to protect the public.

5. C: A broker must complete 120 hours of qualifying education.

6. B: The regulatory agency that oversees the licensure process in New York is the NYS Department of State.

7. B: The minimum age for a salesperson licensure is 18.

8. C: Individuals do not need U.S. citizenship to obtain a salesperson license in New York.

9. C: When transacting real estate business, a licensee must carry his or her photo ID card.

10. A: Licensees must complete continuing education requirements every two years upon license renewal unless exempt.

11. D: Jamie is an unlicensed assistant and does not require a real estate license.

12. B: To open a real estate brokerage firm, Bill must decide the type of business organization for the brokerage. He must indicate this on the broker application with supporting documentation.

13. C: A legal requirement for operation of a broker's office does NOT include submission of all contract forms for DOS approval.

14. B: The NYS Department of State's Occupational Licensing Management System is called *eAccessNY*. TRID is short for the TILA-RESPA Integrated Disclosure Rule. The NYS Department of Financial Services uses the Mortgage Nationwide Licensing System to process mortgage-related registrations and licenses in New York. TILA is short for the Truth-in-Lending Act.

15. A: If a broker moves a principal or branch office, DOS must be notified online within five days. The broker may indicate a change of address to the DOS using his or her account online through *eAccessNY*.

16. C: To obtain exam results from the salesperson or broker NYS licensure exam, applicants should view exam results through their accounts in *eAccessNY*.

17. C: Andy, the broker, is entitled to the full commission as originally agreed upon, as he has brought about a meeting of the minds. His commission is not legally dependent upon the closing going through; however, he may have to litigate to collect his commission.

18. D: A seller broker or buyer broker cannot write or rewrite any form of contract. This act constitutes the illegal practice of law. In New York, only attorneys can draw real estate contracts.

19. A: This ad violates DOS regulations because it does not mention the name of the geographical area in which the property is located.

20. B: To coordinate market activities and other activities in the real estate firm, the real estate office should have available a written policies and procedures manual.

Law of Agency

21. B: A broker's commission is determined by agreement between the broker and principal. There are no set fee schedules for broker commissions.

22. D: In the sale of one- to four-unit residential real estate, and residential condominiums and cooperatives in any size building, a listing agent must first disclose his or her status to a prospective buyer at the first substantive contact, such as when the listing contract is signed.

23. B: When recruiting licensees to work in a real estate office, the broker should first administer a personality and critical thinking skills test. Inquiry into family status violates anti-discrimination laws in New York as to employment.

24. C: In this example, Danielle must have signed an exclusive right-to-sell agreement that states that she must pay Robert his commission no matter who sells the property.

25. A: A buyer broker, who represents the buyer as a client, can never be a subagent of the seller. Subagency would indicate seller representation.

26. D: An agency relationship is always consensual. There has to be an agreement between the parties.

27. A: The most common agency relationship that brokers have with their principals is as a special agent. A general agent manages various affairs pertaining to the property. A power of attorney is permission to handle the limited affairs of another. A universal agency is an all-encompassing power of attorney.

28. D: If there is no specific contact with an agent and no substantive contact, then the agency disclosure form is not required.

29. B: Price fixing occurs when competitors in a certain group charge the same or similar price. A group boycott is a conspiracy in which a person or group is coerced into not doing business with another person or group. An illegal market allocation agreement occurs when competing companies agree to split a territory among them. A tie-in arrangement occurs when a party selling a service to a buyer, as a condition of sale, has the buyer purchase another product from the seller.

30. D: A tie-in arrangement occurs when a party selling a service to a buyer, as a condition of sale, has the buyer purchase another product from the seller. A group boycott is a conspiracy in which a person or group is coerced into not doing business with another person or group. Price fixing occurs when competitors in a certain group charge the same or similar price. An illegal market allocation agreement occurs when competing companies agree to split a territory among them.

31. A: In general, most real estate licensees, through an agreement with the broker, and allowable under IRS law, are independent contractors.

32. D: An associate broker/independent contractor can be an office manager.

33. D: There is no law that says a broker must accompany a sales agent/independent contractor when showing a property. However, the seller may request this.

34. A: IRS regulations require that the sales agent enter into a written independent contractor agreement with the broker.

35. B: In order to qualify under IRS regulations for independent contractor status, the sales agent must be licensed.

36. C: The IRS requires the filing of Form 1099-MISC for all independent contractors who earn $600 or more in the calendar tax year.

37. D: Independent contractors must file yearly federal and state tax returns just as employees do.

38. C: In New York, brokers must keep records as to the sale or mortgage of one- to four-unit properties for at least three years.

39. B: Under IRS regulations, although a salesperson is an independent contractor, the broker supervises the sales agent.

40. D: The salesperson/independent contractor is responsible for all withholding and other tax obligations.

41. C: A real estate agent is a special agent who has narrow authorization to act on behalf of the principal. A general agent has more authority to act on behalf of a principal, for example, as a property manager.

42. D: An exclusive agency listing is only listed with one broker although other brokers can market the property as subagents.

43. A: In the rental of one- to four-unit residential properties and condominium and cooperatives in any size building, at the first substantive contact, an agent must present the agency disclosure form.

44. A: By disclosing the divorce action to the buyer, Broker Beth has violated her fiduciary duty of loyalty to her client.

45. B: A broker's agent works through another broker to assist in the marketing of a property. A principal is not vicariously liable for acts of the broker's agent.

46. C: In New York, dual agency is legal with timely disclosure and informed consent.

47. D: Subagents, listing agents, seller agents, and single agents are all cooperating agents.

48. C: In an exclusive right-to-sell contract, the listing broker is entitled to a commission when anyone including the broker, owner, or other brokers sell the property.

49. C: Vacant land is not covered under Section 443 of the Real Property Law that requires the use of the agency disclosure form.

50. D: Sellers, buyers, landlords, and tenants may consent to dual agency in advance of it occurring and may indicate consent on the agency disclosure form. This consent applies to the sale or rental of one- to four-unit residential property and residential condos and coops in any size building. Dual agency is legal in New York with disclosure and informed consent.

Legal Issues

Part I Estates and Interests

51. D: The term *pur autre vie* means for another life. Therefore, the term refers to a life estate measured by the life of someone other than the life tenant.

52. C: Real property is in a fixed place and has the characteristic of immobility.

53. B: Tenants by the entirety refer to a married couple.

54. D: Public parks and historical monuments are examples of special purpose real estate.

55. A: A life estate is ownership or possession for someone's lifetime. A leasehold estate is a rental estate with possession, not ownership.

56. B: Fee simple absolute, fee simple defeasible, and fee simple on condition all imply some form of ownership. A leasehold estate implies possession, not ownership.

57. A: Because the condition states that the daughter cannot use the property for commercial purposes, the example is a fee simple on condition.

58. A: Ownership in severalty refers to ownership by one owner. Think of the concept as the owner being "severed" from others.

59. B: Chattel is another term for personal property.

60. A: An estate for years can be for any fixed time as short as one day. Joint tenancy is a type of ownership. Usury is a practice that charges more interest than is lawfully allowed.

Part II Liens and Easements

61. C: A lien is a claim that one person has against the property of another for a debt.

62. B: An easement is a nonpossessory use of land by another.

63. A: The meaning of the term *lis pendens* is that a legal notice has been filed that a lawsuit is pending.

64. C: Mortgages are voluntary specific liens because a mortgagor contracts for the mortgage and creates a specific lien against a specific real property.

65. D: A mechanic's lien is involuntary because it is against an individual who owes a debt. A mechanic's lien creates a specific lien against the real property.

66. B: Although certain types of liens have priority over other types, the factor that determines the priority is the time and date of filing.

67. A: Utility companies obtain an easement in gross. Easement appurtenant, easement by prescription, and easement by grant are other types of easements.

68. C: The dominant tenement is the property that benefits from the easements. The servient tenement is the property that allows the easement and is where the easement is located.

69. D: Items that extend into another's property are called encroachments. Easements are nonpossessory interests in another's property.

70. C: A license is a temporary privilege.

Part III Deeds/Conveyance of Real Property

71. C: The deed is the document that conveys title to real property.

72. C: In Latin, *habendum* means "to have," so the *habendum* clause means "to have to and to hold." The defeasance clause appears in a mortgage.

73. D: A quitclaim deed has no guarantee of title. A full covenant and warranty deed has the broadest guarantee of title.

74. C: To execute a deed or any other legal document means to sign it. Deeds are signed by the grantor.

75. B: The party that conveys title to real property is the grantor. The grantee receives title and is the party of the second part on the deed.

76. A: The legal term for the transfer of property is called alienation. *Lis pendens* is type of notice indicating that a legal action is pending.

77. B: A binder is a written document for the purchase and sale of real property. It is a not a deed.

78. C: A type of property description used in a deed that starts with a point or place of beginning is called a metes and bounds description. Description by monument may refer to a large rock or other landmark and is not commonly used in New York. Description by lot and block, also found on a deed, refers to the location of the property. Description by reference links the description to another document such as a plat or tax map.

79. A: When a landowner donates a parcel of land for public use, this is called dedication. Adverse possession is a method of acquiring title to real property by conforming to certain statutory requirements.

80. D: A male appointed in a will to carry out its provisions is the executor. The legatee receives something from the will. A testator or devisor is a male party who makes a will, while a testatrix is a woman.

81. B: Alienation after death is through a will.

82. B: Dedication is a voluntary type of alienation. Adverse possession, a lien foreclosure sale, or a bankruptcy are all examples of involuntary alienation.

83. A: The Statute of Frauds requires all documents that create an interest in real estate to be in writing. The Statute of Limitations has to do with the statutory time limit to bring a legal action against a party.

84. D: A person may receive title under adverse possession in New York if the possession has been open and notorious for at least ten years and a court has ruled in favor of the adverse possessor.

85. C: If a person dies and leaves a valid will, he is said to die testate. A person who does not leave a valid will is said to die intestate. A devise is a gift of real property though a will. An estate in New York is processed through Surrogate's Court and this process is called probate.

86. A: A gift of real property in a will is called a devise.

87. C: The gradual buildup of land in a watercourse over time by deposits of silt, sand, and gravel is called accretion.

88. D: A quitclaim deed contains no warranties whatsoever. The grantor makes no statement or even implies ownership of the property being quitclaimed to the grantee.

89. B: Tenancy in common, the correct answer, is an estate characterized by two or more people who hold title to a property at the same time with no rights of survivorship. A tenancy in common requires that each tenant hold an undivided interest in the entire property.

90. B: Evidence that something of value is present in a deed is known as consideration. Earnest money is the deposit money in a real estate contract of sale. Chattel is another name for personal property. A devise is a gift of real property through a will.

Part IV Title Closing and Costs

91. C: Title to real estate is transferred upon execution and delivery of a valid deed.

92. A: Generally, in the closing process, attorneys for a lender represent the best interests of the lending institution. The purchasers' attorney, if the purchasers hire one, represents their best interests.

93. D: A federal statute that regulates disclosure and closing requirements for mortgage loans on residential property is the TILA-RESPA Integrated Disclosure Rule. The Fair Housing Act prohibits discrimination in housing on the basis of race, color, religion, or national origin. The Interstate Land Sales Disclosure Act is a federal law that regulates the sale of subdivided lands across state lines. The Mortgage Forgiveness Debt Relief Act offers several important tax breaks when mortgage debt is forgiven.

94. C: The successive conveyances of title, starting with the current deed and going back an appropriate time (typically 40 to 60 years) is the chain of title; title must be unbroken to be good and, therefore, marketable.

95. B: The document that illustrates the measurement, boundaries, and area of a property is called a survey. A feasibility study determines a project's usefulness and projected success in the community. A plat is subdivision map.

96. A: A condensed history pertaining to the title of a property is called an abstract of title. A chain of title is the successive conveyances of title to a property. Title insurance insures the policy owner against loss if the title is not good.

97. D: One of the most important roles of a licensee just before closing is to arrange and accompany a prospective purchaser through a final inspection of the property. Attorneys examine the deed, prepare the abstract of title, and prepare the closing statement.

98. B: A New York tax on the conveyance of title to real property is called the real estate transfer tax. The capital gains tax is a federal tax on profits from the sale of real estate. The mortgage recording fee is the charge for recording a mortgage.

99. A: Unpaid utility bills are the responsibility of the seller at closing.

100. C: The seller will not require mortgage insurance as his mortgage will generally be paid off at closing.

101. B: When all interested parties to a title closing meet, their main purpose is to transfer title to real property from seller to buyer.

102. B: The January 20xx takes priority over the June 20xx deed because the June 20xx deed is not recorded.

103. C: The Commission Escrow Act applies to one- to four-unit residential properties as well as individual condominiums and cooperatives sold by real estate brokers and sales agents. The law protects the broker's real estate commission when a seller does not pay the full commission upon closing.

104. A: Although the property was granted to C, Grantor D then transferred the title to E. There was no transfer from Grantor C to Grantor D. Therefore, there is a break in the chain of title.

105. A: A title insurance policy is required by the lender and is not issued without an acceptable abstract or title opinion. An abstract of title is a history of the title showing the transfers of property over the years. The NYS Department of Financial Services is not involved with this process.

106. B: The TILA-RESPA Integrated Disclosure Rule regulates activities of lending institutions in making mortgage loans for housing. The Act applies only to most residential federally financed or refinanced properties.

107. D: The earnest money deposit is a credit to the buyer on the closing statement. The purchase price, loan origination fee, and discount points are buyer debits on the closing statement.

108. C: The purchase price is a seller credit on the closing statement. Delinquent property taxes, a purchase money mortgage, and the broker commission are all seller debits.

109. A: FIRPTA stands for the Foreign Investment in Real Property Tax Act. The purpose of the federal law is to impose a tax on capital gains derived by foreign people from the sale of their U.S. property. A flip tax is sometimes imposed on the transfer of cooperatives.

110. C: A cooperative is a type of property ownership in which the owner receives shares of stock in a cooperative corporation. All of the other choices in the question may be transferred with a deed.

Part I Leases

111. A: A periodic lease automatically renews itself at the end of the term unless notice is given.

112. B: A leasehold estate implies possession, not ownership. Therefore, it is never conveyed by a deed.

113. C: A month-to-month tenancy can be for any timeframe. A periodic estate automatically renews itself unless notice is given. A freehold estate is an ownership estate.

114. B: A tenant who was originally in lawful possession of the premises but does not leave after the right to possession ends is a holdover tenant. A trespasser was never in lawful possession in the first place.

115. C: A lease is a type of contract. A deed is not a contract. An option and a promissory note are contracts.

116. D: There are no statutory requirements for the term of a lease in New York. It can be for one day and for any specified duration. The term is negotiated between the landlord and the tenant.

117. D: According to New York law, leases must be in clear language and appropriately captioned.

118. C: Should there be an emergency, the landlord has a right to enter a premises without specific permission in the lease.

119. A: If a tenant is forced to leave the premises because of lack of basic services, it may be a constructive eviction. Actual eviction occurs when a landlord physically forces tenants to leave the premises. A *lis pendens* is a notice that a lawsuit is pending regarding a property.

120. D: A new owner of a leased property must abide by all of the terms of the leases that are in place at the time and may not make changes until lease expiration.

Part II Contracts

121. B: Consideration is the giving of something of value as an inducement to contract. Quiet enjoyment has to do with possession of one's property. A power of attorney gives a person authority to act for another in legal matters.

122. C: A meeting of the minds indicates that a buyer and seller have agreed to the contract terms and the sale of the property can move forward. Offer and acceptance have been achieved.

123. A: The Statute of Limitations addresses time limits to sue. The TILA-RESPA Integrated Disclosure Rule addresses lender disclosures for closings. The law that requires real estate contracts must be written to be valid in court is called the Statute of Frauds. The Uniform Commercial Code regulates commercial paper such as notes, drafts, and checks.

124. B: A contract between two parties who have definitely agreed to the contract terms is called an express bilateral contract.

125. A: Under an installment land contract, the purchaser does not have legal title to the property. Legal title is conveyed when the contract terms have been fulfilled.

126. B: Novation is the substitution of a new contract for a prior contract. There is no contract substitution with a sublet. Rescission means to annul the contract.

127. D: The listing contract between the seller and agent is executory because a buyer has not been found and the contract is not complete. An implied contract arises through the actions of the parties. Void and unenforceable contracts are not valid.

128. C: A contract stating "time is of the essence" means that the contract must be performed on or before the date stipulated in the contract.

129. B: An earnest money deposit is not legally required for an offer to purchase.

130. D: A contract with a minor can generally go forward but is voidable by the minor.

Part III Contract Preparation

131. D: A purchase money mortgage is a type of seller financing. Assumable, home equity line of credit (HELOC), and FHA are types of mortgages.

132. B: A portion of a property purchase price that is paid in cash and not a part of the mortgage is the down payment. A binder is a type of agreement to purchase. An assumable mortgage is a type of mortgage. A mortgage commitment is a lender's promise to loan a certain amount of funds.

133. A: The purchaser is generally the first to sign the contract of sale because he or she is making the contract offer to the seller.

134. D: Raphael's advice regarding the "as is" clause in the contract constitutes the illegal practice of law.

135. B: An attorney holds an IOLA account (Interest on Lawyer's Account).

136. A: The Lawyer's Fund for Client Protection has to do with the protection of escrow accounts that attorneys hold for client monies.

137. C: The accepted practice in many upstate areas is for the broker to hold a purchaser's deposit in escrow until closing. Should a salesperson receive a deposit check, he or she must turn it over to his broker.

138. C: A customary deposit is 10% of the purchase price, so Keri would put down a deposit of $45,000. This percentage can vary from deal to deal.

139. C: A contract of sale is binding when the attorney for each party approves the contract.

140. D: A census statement is not used for a closing. Attorneys and others may require a survey, certificate of occupancy, and prior deed to prepare for a closing.

Real Estate Finance

141. C: The mortgagor is the borrower. The mortgagee is the lender.

142. A: The mortgagee is the lender. The mortgagor is the borrower.

143. B: A mortgage is a written document pledging a property as security for the repayment of a loan.

144. D: The VA loans up to a certain amount and does not always require a down payment.

145. B: A balloon mortgage is best described as having a larger payment due at the end of its term.

146. A: When a lender is willing to lower the interest rate at the time the loan is made in return for extra payments of points up front, this is called a buydown. Usury is the charging of a higher interest rate than allowed by law. A satisfaction of mortgage is a document stating that the mortgage debt is fully paid.

147. D: An amortized mortgage loan is one that is paid in monthly payments of principal and interest.

148. C: A wraparound mortgage is a subordinate mortgage that includes the same principal obligation secured by a first mortgage against the same property. It is a type of seller financing.

149. B: A satisfaction of mortgage is a document from the lender stating that the loan is paid in full. The closing disclosure form, required by TRID, is used by lenders to itemize closing costs. A certificate of title sets forth the title examiner's opinion of the title.

150. B: The New York agency that raises money from tax-free bonds and applies the money to mortgage loans is called SONYMA (State of New York Mortgage Association). Fannie Mae (short for Federal National Mortgage Association) is part of the secondary mortgage market. FDIC is a federal agency that protects bank deposits. The RHS (Rural Housing Service) is a federal agency that makes loans for rural housing.

151. C: A conventional loan involves no participation of a federal government agency such as FHA and is not always amortized.

152. C: A blanket mortgage is one in which two or more parcels are pledged as security for the mortgage debt.

153. B: One of the most difficult loans for a lender to underwrite because it asks for funds to create a project that does not exist is a construction loan. A home equity line of credit uses the residence as collateral for a loan. A purchase money mortgage is a form of seller financing.

154. A: Negative amortization occurs when the monthly payment is less than full interest and does not pay any principal. A nonconforming loan is a loan that does not follow the guidelines set forth by the Federal Reserve Bank. A deficiency is the amount of funds that may still be owed to a lender after the property was foreclosed upon and the foreclosure did not bring in the amount owed to the lender. A default occurs when an obligation is not performed such as failure to make a mortgage payment.

155. A: A mortgage given by a purchaser to the seller to cover part of the purchase price is known as a purchase money mortgage. A swing loan is a type of interim loan in which a borrower uses the equity in one property to obtain the funds necessary to buy another property. With an installment land contract, title is not transferred to the buyer until the mortgage is paid.

156. B: The mortgage alienation clause allows the lender to declare the balance due if the mortgagor sells the property during the mortgage term. The defeasance clause protects the borrower in having the lien released upon full payoff of the debt. Because the balance is being paid off early, the lender may be entitled to or is exercising its right to a prepayment penalty. Not all lenders charge this penalty should the loan be paid off early.

157. B: Loan underwriting is the process that analyzes the financial data and credit history of a prospective borrower.

158. C: A short-term loan that may provide funds over and above an already existing loan until permanent financing is in place is known as gap financing.

159. B: A type of mortgage that gives the lender the option to convert the outstanding balance into an agreed-upon percentage of ownership in the property is known as a convertible mortgage. A subordinate mortgage is one that is second in priority to another. A bridge loan is a short-term loan used to obtain interim financing.

160. D: A sale-leaseback is a transaction in which a property owner sells a property to an investor who immediately leases back the property to the seller as agreed to in the sales contract. Release land subdivision financing occurs when a lender releases a portion of the indebtedness on a mortgage when a certain portion of land is developed and paid for. A ground lease is a lease on unimproved land. There is no such thing as conversion mortgaging.

Land Use Regulations/Development

161. D: Eminent domain allows government to take property for public use only if it is for the use and benefit of the public. Escheat allows property to revert to the state only if heirs cannot be found. Zoning ordinances are public land use controls and deed restrictions are private land use controls.

162. A: The doctrine of laches refers to a loss of legal rights because of failure to assert them.

163. B: The New York law that protects residents in the purchase of vacant subdivided land sold on the installment plan is Article 9-A of the Real Property Law. Article 12-A is a New York law pertaining to salespersons and brokers. The Statute of Frauds states that contracts that create an interest in real estate must be in writing.

164. C: When property reverts to the state due to the lack of heirs, it is called escheat. Eminent domain is the government's right to take property for the use and benefit of the public with just compensation.

165. C: The agency that coordinates information relevant to an environmental impact statement is called the lead agency. The zoning board of appeals oversees variance requests.

166. A: Zoning ordinances are an example of a government's police power.

167. D: Local building departments oversee building code compliance. The zoning board of appeals oversees variance requests. HUD is a federal agency that oversees housing issues. The Department of Environmental Conservation oversees water-related and other environmental issues.

168. B: An in-law apartment that is connected to a residential home is called an accessory use.

169. A: Hospitals, schools, and courthouses are examples of institutional zoning. Public open space includes parks.

170. B: The imposition of a delay in developing property in a given area is a moratorium. Transfer of development rights involve the exchange of zoning privileges from areas with low population needs, such as farmland, to areas of high population needs, such as downtown areas. Demography is a study of the social and economic statistics of a community. Infrastructure refers to the support systems of a community.

171. C: A subdivision plat in New York is generally recorded with the local county clerk's office.

172. A: Topography is defined as the physical features and contours of land. The services of a community such as roads, hospitals, police, and fire departments are known as the infrastructure. The study of the social and economic statistics of a community is called demography. Geology is the science of the history of the earth through the study of rocks, soil, and land formation.

173. A: The purpose of planning is to provide for the orderly growth of a community.

174. B: The agency that has the statutory authority to review and approve plans for subdivision development is the local planning board or commission. Building permits allow construction to take place. A building department issues a certificate of occupancy (CO) if the structure meets code requirements. The Department of Environmental Conservation is a New York agency. The county assessor's office oversees the real property tax assessment process.

175. B: The New York law that requires local government to assess the environmental significance of actions that it must approve is the State Environmental Quality Review Act. Under the Superfund Amendment to CERCLA, innocent landowners who purchase property not knowing about contamination have a defense against liability for cleanup and fines. The Federal Clean Air Act regulates air quality standards. The Environmental Protection Agency (EPA) oversees a variety of environmental concerns.

176. C: If a property owner is denied a request for a variance, he or she may petition the New York Supreme Court through an Article 78 proceeding. An Article 78 proceeding is a lawsuit brought against an administrative agency.

177. A: Vincent needs a use variance. A use variance allows an owner to use the property for a certain purpose.

178. A: One of the differences between a request for a variance and a special use permit is that special use permits do not require that the applicant demonstrate undue hardship. A special use permit is not permitted in the zone except with the special permission of the planning board or other legislative body. An Article 78 proceeding is a lawsuit brought against an administrative agency.

179. D: The New York agency that oversees wetland protection is the NYS Department of Environmental Conservation.

180. B: A type of loan that provides interim financing for subdivision development is called a mini-perm loan. A sale leaseback is a transaction in which a property owner sells a property to an investor who immediately leases back the property to the seller as agreed in the sales contract. In a package mortgage, personal property, in addition to real property, is pledged to secure payment of the mortgage loan. A junior mortgage is any mortgage that is junior or lower in priority to a first mortgage on a property.

Construction

181. D: The NYS Department of Health furnishes guidelines for minimum separation distances between a well and a septic system and other sanitary guidelines.

182. C: Insulation has to do with the interior of the structure, not the exterior or site.

183. B: The concrete base below the frost line that supports the foundation of a structure is the footing. The foundation wall rests upon the footing. A slab on grade is a type of foundation. A girder is a support beam.

184. A: The wooden skeleton of a residential structure of a residential property is called the frame. It is composed of wooden framing members.

185. C: Openings for doors and windows in a residential property are supported by headers. Lally columns are support columns. Rafters are framing members for the roof. The sill plate is the base for the framing.

186. B: The greater the degree of insulation, the greater the R-factor. The R-factor is a measure of heat transfer through the walls of a structure.

187. D: A type of heating system that heats water in a boiler and then uses one or more circulator pumps to allow the heated water to travel to convectors or radiators is called a hot water system. Forced warm air systems include a duct system that blows warm air. A heat pump produces cool and warm air.

188. A: The water supply and wastewater systems are always separated with two separate piping systems. The supply pipes bring clean water into the structure and the wastewater systems carry used water from the structure.

189. B: The minimum electrical service installed in a residential home must be 100 amps but new construction generally has 150 to 200 amp service.

190. A: A device that melts and opens a circuit to stop electrical power when overheating occurs is called a fuse. The distribution panel is where the fuses or circuit breakers are located. The service drop is the electrical service coming into the property.

191. B: The first wooden member of the house used as the nailing surface for the floor system is the sill plate. The foundation wall rests upon the footing. The fascia is a board that is perpendicular to the soffit. The ridge beam is part of the roof structure.

192. B: The Act administered by the federal Consumer Financial Protection Bureau that regulates the sale of unimproved lots across state lines is called the Interstate Land Sales Full Disclosure Act. The Superfund Amendment addresses environmental liability upon transfer of title.

193. C: The National Electric Code offers minimum guidelines and standards for electrical installations. The Code is a national standard for electrical installation and service written to safeguard people and property from hazards arising from the use of electricity.

194. C: The law that is the guideline for New York's drinking water regulations is the Safe Drinking Water Act. The Superfund Amendment addresses environmental liability upon transfer of title. The Residential Lead-based Paint Hazard Reduction Act of 1992 sets forth the procedures in disclosing the presence of lead-based paint for sales of target properties built before 1978.

195. D: The New York law that provides minimum standards for construction materials and safety is the NYS Fire Prevention and Building Code. The New York General Business Law provides for a one-year builder's warranty against construction defects and a six-year warranty against material defects. The New York law that protects residents in the purchase of vacant subdivided land sold on the installment plan is Article 9-A of the Real Property Law.

196. A: According to the New York General Business Law, a builder must warrant new construction against defects in construction for one year.

197. B: According to New York law, after signing a home improvement contract, an owner has three business days after the contract is signed to cancel it.

198. D: The NYS Department of Health regulates the water supply system in New York. The federal organization that oversees navigation, flood control, and dredging projects is the U.S. Army Corps of Engineers.

199. B: The New York law that sets minimum efficiency requirements for the design of new buildings and renovations and additions to existing buildings is the Energy Conservation Construction Code (ECCCNYS). Article 9-A protects New York residents in the purchase of vacant subdivided land sold within and without New York on the installment plan.

200. B: A seller must sign an affidavit indicating the presence of a smoke alarm and carbon monoxide detector in the sale of one- and two-family residential properties, residential condominiums and cooperatives, and residential dwellings that have appliances or systems that may emit carbon monoxide or that have an attached garage.

Environmental Issues

201. D: The Superfund Amendments and Reauthorization Act imposed stringent cleanup standards and expanded the definition of those responsible for cleanup. The National Environmental Policy Act and Clean Air Act are other federal environmental laws. The State Environmental Quality Review is a New York law.

202. B: Local drinking water problems are remediated by local departments of health.

203. C: One of the biggest dangers in highly corrosive water is that it may contain large amounts of lead. Although radon may enter a house through the water supply systems (for example, a well), it is a gas and not corrosive. PCBs are a byproduct of electrical transformers. CFCs are a gas and are not corrosive.

204. A: The NYS Department of Environmental Conservation licenses pest inspectors in New York.

205. B: Asbestos is a fibrous mineral that was used in many construction applications in the past but is no longer used.

206. D: The Residential Lead-based Hazard Reduction Act calls for a mutually agreeable ten-day period for a lead paint assessment before a purchaser becomes obligated under a contract. The Act applies to target properties built before 1978.

207. D: Radon most generally enters the home through small cracks in the foundation wall. This is because radon comes from the ground.

208. A: No level of radon is considered safe. If a property has more than four picocuries of radon, remediation is generally necessary.

209. B: If the indoor air quality of a commercial building causes large numbers of people to fall ill, the building is said to have sick building syndrome.

210. D: A toxic liquid organic compound used as an insulating medium for electrical transformers and has polluted the soil and waterways are called PCBs. Radon is a radioactive gas. UFFI is an insulation that contains formaldehyde. Chlorofluorocarbons are in a class of gasses that is dangerous to our ozone layer and is no longer used.

Valuation Process and Pricing Properties

211. C: An analysis of the competition in the marketplace that a property will face upon sale attempts is called a comparative market analysis. An appraisal employs at least one of the approaches to value such as the cost approach. An evaluation is not necessarily used to find market value.

212. D: The comparative market analysis is not an appraisal approach to value. The income, sales, and cost approaches are all appraisal approaches to value.

213. C: An owner who uses a residential property for vacation purposes only may attribute value in use to this property. Assessed value is applied by an assessor; insurance value is replacement value; and investment value is the return expected by an investor.

214. A: Feasibility studies, highest and best use studies, and land utilization studies are all forms of evaluation studies. An appraisal of a single-family home is an estimate of market value.

215. C: A property will probably not sell for market value if the buyer and seller are related to each other. An arm's length transaction means that buyer and seller do not know each other.

216. D: Price is not always equivalent to the market value of the property. It may be more or less.

217. B: If there are construction problems and time constraints, the cost of the property may exceed the market value. One reason is that time is money.

218. D: Indirect costs are the costs of architecture, engineering, licensing, permits, and other expenses. Hard or direct costs are for labor and materials.

219. A: Comparables used in the creation of a comparative market analysis should be as similar as possible to the subject property.

220. C: Properties yet to be built are not an appropriate comparable for a comparative market analysis because market conditions may be different when these properties are placed on the market.

Human Rights and Fair Housing/Advanced Fair Housing and Fair Lending

221. C: Redlining is an illegal practice by lenders that excludes people from culturally diverse neighborhoods from receiving housing loans. Steering is a violation of the Federal Fair Housing Act and is a practice by real estate brokers that encourages culturally diverse people toward or away from certain areas.

222. A: The Civil Rights Act of 1866 prohibits all discrimination based on race in the buying, selling, and leasing of property—no exceptions.

223. B: For a violation of the Federal Fair Housing Act, there can be a civil penalty of up to $75,000 for a first-time offense and a civil penalty of $150,000 for subsequent violations.

224. D: Blockbusting occurs when real estate salespeople tell homeowners that a member of a protected class is moving into their neighborhood causing them to panic and place their homes for sale.

225. A: Steering occurs when real estate agents lead prospective homeowners toward or away from certain areas.

226. C: One of the differences between the federal Fair Housing Law and the New York Human Rights Law is that the New York law covers commercial property as well as residential. There are other differences such as New York has more protected classes than the federal law.

227. D: The Americans with Disabilities Act covers buildings open to the public as well as multi-family dwellings.

228. B: In addition to federal law, protected classes under the New York Human Rights Law include age and marital status. Other protected classes in New York, not covered by federal law, include sexual orientation, gender identity, and military status.

229. B: Nancy cannot discriminate because of race in the renting of her apartment. The Civil Rights Act of 1866 prohibits all racial discrimination. There are no exceptions.

230. A: An area designated by the NYS Department of State where salesperson and brokers may not solicit listings is in a cease and desist zone. Homeowners may request that the DOS place them on a cease and desist list.

Real Estate Mathematics

231. B: $12,500 ÷ 0.07 = $178,571

232. D: $8,250 ÷ 0.075 = $110,000

233. C: $475,000 × 0.02 = $9,500
$475,000 + $9,500 = $484,500
$484,500 × 0.02 = $9,690
$484,500 + $9,690 = $494,190

234. A: 52 × 162 = 8,424 square feet
$75,000 ÷ 8,424 = $8.90

235. C: 43,560 ÷ 425 = 102.5 feet (rounded)

236. D: $175,000 × 0.90 = $157,500

237. B: $2,500 ÷2 = $208.33
$208.33 ÷ 2 = $104.17
$208.33 + $104.17 = $312.50

238. C: $120,000 × 0.80 = $96,000
$96,000 × 0.03 = $2,880

239. A: $50,000 × 0.095 = $4,750

240. B: $2,304 ÷ 0.024 = $96,000
$96,000 ÷ 0.80 = $120,000

Municipal Agencies

241. B: The legislative power of a city is vested in its city council. The legislative power of towns is vested in the town council; in villages, it is in the village board of trustees.

242. D: The main function of a city or town planning board is to advise on land use matters.

243. C: In most cities and towns, the zoning boards of appeals or other similar agencies hear variance requests. The town board deals with policy and laws and the planning board addresses land use issues.

244. A: In many municipalities, the conservation advisory council advises on wetland regulations. The architectural review board oversees building design. The zoning board of appeals hears various requests.

245. D: Building departments do not rule on variance applications. This is performed by another agency, usually the zoning board of appeals.

246. C: The document containing each property's assessment in a municipality is the assessment roll. The tax map shows the boundaries and measurements of lots in the taxing jurisdiction.

247. B: In some cities and towns, the official or agency that collects fees for water usage and other permits is the receiver of taxes. The tax assessor performs assessments.

248. A: The New York agency that oversees wetland regulations is the NYS Department of Environmental Conservation. The NYS Department of Health oversees water-related issues, disease control, and licensing of physicians and other health professionals.

249. B: A town or village planning board consists of five to seven members who are appointed.

250. D: The conservation advisory council usually addresses environmental issues. The historic preservation commission, zoning board of appeals, and building department would most likely deal with renovating historic property.

Property Insurance

251. A: A clause in an insurance policy that changes or modifies the policy is called an endorsement. A peril is a type of known hazard. A deductible is the amount the insured must pay towards a claim before receiving any policy benefits. An umbrella policy is an excess liability policy, providing additional coverage above that offered by primary policies.

252. B: Insurance obtained through the New York Property Insurance Underwriting Association can be undesirable because the premiums are higher than those obtained through the voluntary market.

253. B: FEMA (Federal Emergency Management Agency) administers the National Flood Insurance Program. Local programs work with FEMA.

254. D: In New York, a windstorm deductible must be disclosed to the insured.

255. C: As long as the insurance company states the reason for the cancellation, an insurance policy may be cancelled within 60 days. Other insurance department regulations apply to cancellations.

256. D: The cost of a homeowner's policy is directly related to the policyholder and the property. There are no statewide fee schedules.

257. C: The insured must pay a deductible before receiving policy benefits from a claim. A premium is the money the property owner must pay for insurance coverage. Perils are events that do damage. An endorsement is a document attached to the policy that modifies or changes the original policy in some way.

258. B: An umbrella policy is an excess liability policy providing additional coverage above that offered by primary policies. A homeowner's special form policy is a type of homeowner's insurance.

259. A: The declarations page of the policy outlines the basic coverage contained in the policy.

260. D: Functional obsolescence is flawed or faulty property rendered inferior because of advances and change. This is not specifically covered in the insurance policy.

Taxes and Assessments

261. C: Gas stations are private and not tax exempt. Government buildings such as a VA hospital and state office buildings are property tax exempt, as well as religious organizations such as synagogues.

262. C: The tax rate is determined by the amount of the tax levy. The assessor values property for tax purposes.

263. B: The percentage at which properties are assessed in a locality is called the level of assessment. The tax levy is the amount that a municipality must raise to meet budgetary requirements. The residential assessment ratio (RAR) is the assessed value divided by the sales price of the property. The tax rate is the amount of money needed by a municipality to meet budgetary requirements divided by the taxable assessed and nonexempt value of all the real property within that jurisdiction.

264. D: Reassessments can be performed on properties when improvements are made and on a regular prescribed basis.

265. D: The state does not collect property taxes. Cities, towns, and villages may be taxing jurisdictions.

266. B: Property owners under 25 are not exempt from paying property taxes if the only reason is their age. People with disabilities, seniors, and veterans can be partially exempt from paying real property taxes.

267. D: The purpose of the board of assessment review is to hear grievances. Taxes are levied by the taxing jurisdiction, and uniform percentages are determined by the taxing jurisdiction. The NYS Office of Real Property Tax Services computes the equalization rate.

268. B: If a property owner believes that his property's assessed value is greater than the property's full value, he may claim that he has been subject to excessive assessment. Unequal assessment occurs when a property is assessed at a higher percentage of value than the average of all other properties on the same assessment roll. Unlawful assessment includes properties that under law are fully exempt from real property taxation. Misclassification occurs when a property is wrongfully classified on the assessment roll, such as if a property is classified as a homestead property when it is a nonhomestead property.

269. A: A judicial review of a tax protest in the New York Supreme Court is called a tax certiorari proceeding. A grievance is a property tax complaint brought before the board of assessment review. An Article 78 proceeding is a lawsuit brought against an administrative agency.

270. C: The first task in determining the assessment for tax purposes is to establish the market value of each parcel of land within the taxing unit.

271. C: Government-owned property is generally completely exempt from the payment of property taxes.

272. A: Local governments in New York have the option of offering a reduction of property taxes to senior citizens. The other choices in the question do not have property tax exempt status.

273. B: An *in rem* legal proceeding takes place against the real property directly and not the individual.

274. C: Tax maps for the assessing unit are maintained by the local assessor.

275. C: The RAR is an indication of the level of assessment for residential real property in a municipality. The residential assessment ratio (RAR) is not used by municipalities conducting revaluation review projects.

276. B: An appraisal for tax purposes and an appraisal for mortgage purposes are different in that a tax assessment takes the market value from the appraisal and applies a uniform percentage.

277. D: The New York agency that certifies residential assessment ratios is the State Board of Real Property Tax Services.

278. B: A factory is not a homestead property. A farm dwelling, condominium, or duplex would be classified as a type of residential or homestead property.

279. C: A written complaint filed with the board of assessment review to protest an assessment is known as a grievance. An *in rem* legal proceeding occurs when an action is brought against the real property directly and not against an individual and his personal property.

280. A: The NYS Office of Real Property Tax Services oversees property tax laws and regulations. It is within the NYS Department of Taxation and Finance. The NYS Department of State oversees the licensure process for salespersons and brokers, among other duties. The NYS Department of Financial Services oversees insurance and banking laws and regulations. The Department of Law includes the NYS Attorney General's office.

Condominiums and Cooperatives

281. A: Ownership in a cooperative is evidenced by shares of stock, not a deed. A recognition agreement is an agreement between the cooperative and other entities. An alteration agreement is an agreement for improvements to the unit between the cooperative corporation and the unit owner.

282. B: A cooperative owner has a leasehold interest in the unit that is evidenced by a proprietary lease. Freehold and fee simple absolute indicate ownership in real property.

283. D: The proprietary lease is given to a cooperative shareholder upon purchase of the unit. The declaration, prospectus, and initial price of the units are included in the condominium offering plan.

284. B: House rules govern daily behavior in the cooperative. The alteration agreement is an agreement between a shareholder and the cooperative corporation to make improvements to the unit. A recognition agreement is an agreement between the cooperative and other entities. A letter of intent is an agreement to purchase a condominium that may or may not be binding.

285. C: Although a board package addresses a number of issues, some of them personal, it mainly consists of financial data.

286. D: An agreement that outlines the responsibilities between the cooperative corporation and the lender is called a recognition agreement. The CPS1 statement defines how a condominium or cooperative must be advertised and rules for testing the market before the offering plan is approved by the Attorney General. The alteration agreement is an agreement between a cooperative owner and the cooperative corporation regarding an owner's improvements to the unit.

287. B: A condop is a building that has both condominium and cooperative ownership.

288. A: Pet restrictions and repair obligations are disclosed in the condominium's by-laws. A letter of intent is an agreement to purchase a condominium. A CPS1 statement contains the Attorney General's regulations to advertise and market the condominium before the offering plan is approved.

289. D: During the CPS1 phase, the Attorney General will not allow the condominium or cooperative developer to set a definite price for the units.

290. C: The mansion tax is statewide and applies to one-, two-, and three-unit properties as well as condominiums and cooperatives that sell for $1 million or more.

Commercial and Investment Real Estate/Real Property Investment

291. B: Depreciation is a tax-deductible paper loss that allows investors to show less income or a deduction for tax purposes.

292. C: The mortgage principal is not tax deductible.

293. C: $15,000 × 12 = $180,000; $180,000 ÷ $500,000 = 36%

294. D: $850,000 × 0.12 = $102,000

295. B: Property owners generally charge for the rentable square footage that includes elevators, hallways, and other common areas, not the usable square footage which is the specific office space.

296. D: The natural breakeven point describes when an investor will generate a positive return. Attornment refers to a transfer of a right usually in a lease. Expense stop is a type of lease payment arrangement.

297. D: A lease clause that states that future owners cannot terminate a lease if the owner fulfills his obligations is a nondisturbance clause. An escalation clause allows for increments in the lease payment. An estoppel clause confirms the lease terms. A subordination clause subordinates a lease to any mortgages on the property.

298. A: A type of lease escalation clause is the porter's wage formula that allows lease increments according to the porter's hourly wage. Estoppel, use, and subordination clauses are other types of lease clauses.

299. A: Generally, the more dollars the investor risks or puts up for an investment, the greater his or her return.

300. C: Leverage, or borrowed funds, describes the use of other people's money. The more leverage an investor has, the less of his own funds he needs to put into the investment.

301. D: Real estate investment is not a liquid investment as are investments in the stock or bond market. Real estate investment is not characterized by instant or short-term turnover.

302. C: A real estate investor may defer capital gains taxes by exchanging like kind properties. This type of investment is made according to a 1031 exchange allowable under IRS regulations.

303. B: A feasibility study is a detailed economic analysis that considers the cost of site development, construction, financing, tax considerations, rates of return on similar investments, and the benefit to the community. An operating statement is a report of rental property receipts and disbursements, resulting in net income. The potential gross income is a projection of the gross income for a property. A proforma statement reflects a potential change in income and expenses.

304. C: A short sale is a transaction in which the sale proceeds fall short of the balance owed on the property.

305. B: Foreclosed properties are generally sold at an auction. A short sale is a transaction in which the sale proceeds fall short of the balance owed on the property. A lender forecloses on a property.

306. B: In a short sale, the borrower sells the mortgaged property for less than the outstanding balance on the loan, and turns over the proceeds of the sale to the lender. The lender incurs the financial loss but avoids the cost and uncertainty of a foreclosure or continued nonpayment of the mortgage.

307. D: A proforma schedule reflects a potential change in income and expenses. A feasibility study is a detailed economic analysis that considers the cost of site development, construction, financing, tax considerations, rates of return on similar investments, and the benefit to the community.

308. D: Foreclosed properties are usually offered "as is," by a lender, and when the borrower is in default on the mortgage.

309. B: The rate of return is the percentage of income that the investor receives back on an investment. The loan-to-value ratio compares a lender's loan amount to the property value. Leverage, or borrowed funds, describes the use of other people's money. The time value of money calculates the value of an asset in the past, present, or future.

310. C: The study of how a change in one factor affecting a real estate investment can affect the income to the property is known as sensitivity analysis. A feasibility study is a detailed economic analysis that considers the cost of site development, construction, financing, tax considerations, rates of return on similar investments, and the benefit to the community.

Income Tax Issues in Real Estate

311. D: According to IRS rules, property taxes are deductible for a personal residence including a second home, and a condominium that is a personal residence. Real property taxes are deductible for commercial real estate as well.

312. C: Gains held on assets that are held for less than 12 months are known as short-term capital gains. Long-term capital gains are gains held on assets for 12 months or more.

313. D: Petros's personal misfortune with investing in the stock market and having a loss is not tax deductible.

314. C: According to regulations for a 1031 exchange, a personal residence is not eligible for a tax-deferred exchange.

315. B: Points, under certain conditions, are tax deductible. Appraisal fees, notary fees, and a mortgage preparation fee do not qualify for a tax deduction.

316. A: The main housing credit agency in New York is the NYS Division of Housing and Community Renewal (DHCR). HUD is a federal housing agency. FEMA is a federal agency that addresses various disasters. The NYS Division of Human Rights addresses civil rights issues.

317. D: According to IRS regulations, nonresidential property may be depreciated over 39 years.

318. B: A tax bracket of 25% for federal income does not exist. Federal income tax brackets are 10%, 12%, 22%, 24%, 32%, 35%, and 37%.

319. C: According to IRS regulations for a tax-deferred exchange, a real estate exchangor has 45 days from the closing to contract for another (replacement) property.

320. D: In a tax-deferred exchange, any cash in the exchange is called the boot.

Mortgage Brokerage

321. A: The New York agency that registers mortgage brokers and licenses mortgage bankers is the NYS Department of Financial Services.

322. C: A NYS-licensed real estate broker can use his or her experience as a real estate broker to obtain a mortgage broker's registration. A salesperson requires two years' experience in the mortgage business.

323. A: A mortgage broker who represents a purchase in negotiating a mortgage loan has a fiduciary relationship with the client and is the client's agent.

324. C: A mortgage broker who represents the purchasers in negotiating a mortgage while also representing the sellers as a real estate broker in the same transaction is acting as a dual agent.

325. C: According to the banking law, a minimum line of credit to be licensed in New York as a mortgage banker is $1 million.

326. C: A lender's preapproval letter verifies the applicant's credit and employment history. This letter shows the capability of the purchaser to obtain a mortgage commitment although the letter is not a commitment. An appraisal is an estimate of value.

327. A: A request by a purchaser to reserve a certain loan interest rate for a specified time is called a rate lock. A commitment is a promise by a lender to make a mortgage loan. A rate cap is a limit on an interest rate.

328. D: Loan underwriting is the process in which the financial data and credit history for a prospective borrower is analyzed by the lender. Preapproval requires that a lender validate a borrower's credit and employment history. This evaluation precedes the underwriting process and is not as involved.

329. D: A lender's rebate is a form of payment to a mortgage broker for negotiating a loan from the lender.

330. C: A loan that does not meet the Federal Bank loan criteria for funding is called a nonconforming loan. A straight term loan is one that may have interest only payments in the early stages of the loan.

Property Management

331. C: According to New York law, if a property manager works for one owner, he does not need a license.

332. A: The management agreement, which is a contract between the owner and the manager, creates an agency relationship between the two. The management proposal outlines what the property manager will do for the owner. A listing agreement is an agreement to market a property. A letter of intent is an agreement to purchase a property.

333. B: In managing a property, risk management has to do with the liability of the owner when the public enters a property. This risk is covered by liability insurance.

334. D: If a building is 98% occupied, the property manager may feel justified in raising the rents. This is because the building is already generating a positive cash flow and there is less risk due to competition.

335. D: Property income and expenses for week-to-week operations are computed in an operating budget. Cash flow is the profit after income and expenses are deducted. Capital reserve is a budget for repairs and improvements to the property. The stabilized budget is an income and expense projection over a number of years.

336. A: $750 × 6 = $4,500 × 12 = $54,000; 7 × $1,050 = $7,350 × 12 = $88,200; $88,200 + $54,000 =$142,200 × 0.05 = $7,110; $142,200 – $7,110 = $135,090.

337. B: The property management report relates expense items to the operating budget for a certain period. The property management agreement is the terms for management of the property agreed to between the manager and the owner. The rent roll is the total annual rents for the property. The stabilized budget is a projection of income and expenses over time.

338. C: Lydia's assessment of items that may need repair is an example of preventative maintenance. Actually repairing an item when needed is corrective maintenance.

339. A: If a property manager works for more than one owner, a broker or salesperson license is required. BOMI affiliations and IREM designations are available from these professional organizations if certain requirements are met.

340. D: Alexa, as fiduciary, must disclose to the owner all monies received, and place these monies into the property management account.

341. D: A resident manager who is a salaried employee of the owner and only manages the property where she lives does not need a real estate license.

342. C: The management agreement automatically creates a general agency relationship between the owner and the manager. The property manager becomes a fiduciary; a position of trust. A special agency covers one specific transaction.

343. A: Providing the greatest net return possible for the owner is the primary function of the property manager. Most other functions serve to produce this net maximum return. Collecting rents, residing on the property, and screening and locating tenants are possible functions of a property manager, but not required.

344. C: To save payroll and other employee costs, the property manager may subcontract individuals and companies. With regard to maintenance, a property manager must supervise physical property maintenance and routinely inspect the building.

345. C: The stabilized budget is a forecast of income and expenses as may be reasonably projected over a short term, typically five years. The operating budget is an annual budget and includes income and expenses for week-to-week operation. The capital reserve budget, also called a replacement reserve, is a projected budget over the economic life of the property. It includes variable expenses such as repairs, decorating, remodeling, and capital improvements.

346. B: It is a violation of federal and state fair housing laws for a property manager to maintain records on the racial composition of the neighborhood. A property manager's function is to solicit tenants, hire, train, and supervise employees and maintain adequate insurance for the owner.

347. D: Although not always involved with leasing or renting, a manager for a condominium, cooperative, or homeowners association is very involved in the physical management of the property. Tasks may include coordinating common facility maintenance, landscaping, security, and enforcement of the association's or board of directors' regulations.

348. C: The Certified Property Manager (CPM) designation is a National Association of REALTORS® designation offered through the Institute of Real Estate Management (IREM), a NAR affiliate.

349. A: Setting higher rates for families with children violates fair housing laws. However, the property manager must consider supply and demand and present vacancy rates.

350. B: In managing a property, risk management has to do with the liability of the owner when the public enters a property. This risk is covered by property insurance. Corrective and preventative maintenance are other functions overseen by the property manager.

Licensee Safety

351. C: There are many reasons why safety measures are extremely important to the practice of real estate. But one of the main reasons is that agents often work alone in the office, and elsewhere, and are also alone in unfamiliar surroundings.

352. D: Visitors to a real estate office should sign into a visitor log at the reception area. It is best that at least one other staff member be available to meet and identify the visitor should there be problems later. A more complete investigation of a prospect should take place at the first meeting to more fully identify the prospect.

353. B: The initial meeting with prospects should always take place at the real estate office. In this way, the agent can find out more information regarding the prospect in a location where the agent has more control and safety.

354. A: An intake sheet, published by the National Association of REALTORS®, that helps the agent to profile a prospect for identity purposes is called a prospect information form. The agency disclosure form assists consumers to understand available agency relationships with a real estate agent. A needs and wants checklist helps to identify the desires for housing. A binder is a form that does not have all the essential elements of a contract but that serves to outline the scope of the transaction.

355. A: A prearranged schedule of checking in with a buddy should be formulated when the agent is alone in the office, at a listing presentation, at an open house, or showing a property. The buddy should know where the agent is at all times particularly when in the office alone or when showing a property.

356. D: Conducting an open house without the assistance of at least one other agent, walking into a room at a showing first and having the prospects follow the agent in, and showing abandoned or foreclosed property without the assistance of at least one other agent are activities that are not conducive to the safe showing of a property.

357. B: The most efficient method of protecting documents while sending them online is to encrypt the document. Encryption is the process of converting information or data into a code often used to prevent unauthorized access.

358. D: An insurance policy that helps protect a real estate office against claims that focus on failure to perform on a contract is called errors and omissions insurance. An umbrella policy is an excess liability policy that provides additional coverage above that provided by primary policies. A fidelity policy, also known as a commercial crime bond, protects a company against its claims of fraudulent behavior by employees. A package policy contains several different types of policies that may include liability and property insurance.

359. C: In New York, a person may legally use physical force in self-defense under the NYS Penal Code, Article 35. Article 12-A of the Real Property Law pertains to salespersons and brokers. Article 15 of the New York Real Property Action and Proceedings Law is the adverse possession statute. Article 9-A of the Real Property Law addresses subdivided lands within and without New York only when sold through an installment land contract.

360. A: A method of risk reduction that a real estate office can employ to induce safety is to create a written policies and procedures manual.

General Business Law

361. B: Negotiable instruments are a substitute for money.

362. A: Brokers must explain and have sellers read the explanation and acknowledge that they have read the explanation of the exclusive right-to-sell and the exclusive agency agreement in the listing of one-to-three-unit properties. This requirement does not apply to condos and coops. The binder and contract of sale are used for the offer and purchase of the property. An open listing contract is one in which more than one broker lists the property for sale.

363. A: The signer of a check is known as the drawer. A drawee is a person ordered in a draft to make payment. The payee is the recipient of money.

364. D: When renting a property with six or more units in New York, with regard to the security deposit, a landlord can pay the interest annually to the tenant, apply interest to the tenant's rent, or pay the interest to the tenant when the lease term ends.

365. B: A homestead exemption refers to an exemption, up to a certain amount, from the bankruptcy, of the primary residence of the person filing bankruptcy. An *in rem* legal proceeding occurs when an action is brought against the real property directly and not against an individual and his personal property.

366. A: A legal method for dividing marital property in some actions for divorce is through a court partition proceeding. Escheat occurs upon the death of someone when no heirs can be found and the property reverts to the state. Eminent domain is the government's right to take private property for public use with just compensation to the owner. Adverse possession is a legal proceeding in which a person can claim a right to a property after using the property for at least ten years, certain conditions are met, and a court proceeding awards title to the property.

367. C: According to the Statute of Limitations in New York, the timeframe to bring legal action in a contract dispute is six years.

368. B: In New York, judgments against a debtor are enforced by a court order instructing the sheriff to attach and seize the debtor's property. An Article 78 proceeding is a legal proceeding brought forth regarding a claim against a government agency.

369. D: Stagnation is an economic cycle and is not a method through which a lawsuit can be resolved. Legal disputes may be resolved through either litigation, arbitration, or mediation.

370. C: The type of bankruptcy in which the debtor's nonexempt property is sold for cash, the proceeds distributed to creditors, and unpaid debts discharged is called a Chapter 7 bankruptcy. Chapter 13, consumer debt adjustment, is a rehabilitation form of bankruptcy for individuals. Chapter 11, reorganization bankruptcy, provides a method for reorganizing the debtor's financial affairs under the supervision of the bankruptcy court.

Achieving Agreements through Transaction Analysis

371. B: Dual agency occurs when a real estate broker represents the buyer and seller in the same transaction.

372. C: A transaction agreement to sell and purchase real property should be mutually beneficial to all parties to the transaction. A unilateral agreement is a type of contract in which one party makes an express promise, or undertakes to perform on a contract without a reciprocal agreement from the other party.

373. C: A transactional agreement should be formulated to be in the best interests of the client, not the broker. It should be the end result of a transaction analysis, be mutually beneficial to the parties, and should be entered into without sacrificing the interests of the client simply to reach an agreement.

374. D: With a dual agency arrangement, an agent cannot offer the fiduciary duty of undivided loyalty to a client.

375. A: A power of attorney is a legal arrangement in which one has the legal right to manage some or all of the affairs of another. Loyalty, obedience, and accountability are all fiduciary duties that agents owe their principals.

376. A: For a real estate transactional agreement, a real estate broker can be best described an agent with fiduciary duties. The principal is the client. The broker should also assume the role of a negotiator to assist in reaching a transactional agreement beneficial to the parties.

377. B: The first step in transaction analysis is to identify the needs and wants of the parties to the transaction. Although a seller should complete a property condition disclosure form, this is not the first step in the transaction analysis process.

378. B: A user-friendly confidentiality agreement is either a listing agreement with a seller or a buyer-agency representation agreement with a buyer. The NYS agency disclosure form defines choices for consumers in choosing their desired agency relationship with a real estate agent.

379. C: The services to be performed by the agent who represents a seller are documented in the listing agreement.

380. D: The role of the real estate agent in transaction analysis includes good listening skills, creating discussion and dialogue between the parties, and communicating an attitude of agreement.

Answer Key for Practice Exams

Salesperson Practice Exam 1

License Law and Regulations

1. B: The salesperson and broker licensure terms are for two years.

2. C: A salesperson may receive compensation only from his sponsoring broker.

3. B: It is unlawful for a salesperson or broker to draw legal documents.

Law of Agency Including Independent Contractor

4. C: A dual agent cannot give the fiduciary duty of undivided loyalty.

5. C: A local board of REALTORS® cannot set a commission schedule. The commission is negotiated between the broker and the principal.

6. C: Belinda, because of her relationship with her broker, is a subagent of the principal. The broker is the agent of the principal.

7. B: In buyer agency, the buyer is the principal.

8. A: From the choices in the question, the only circumstance where the disclosure form is required is when the listing agreement is signed.

9. C: When two real estate firms conspire to charge the same commission rate, they are guilty of illegal price fixing. An illegal group boycott occurs when one group or person is persuaded or coerced to not do business with another group or person. An illegal market allocation agreement occurs when competing companies agree to split a territory among them.

10. A: Designated agents are agents in the same brokerage firm where one agent represents the buyer and the other represents the seller. Designated agency is used when a dual agency situation arises. A broker's agent is hired by another agent to assist the agent.

11. B: Although many properties listed for sale have material defects, the agent has a duty to disclose the defects to all interested parties.

12. D: All types of agents that work together to bring about the real estate transaction are cooperating agents. There is no requirement that all agents be dual agents, represent the seller, or belong to the multiple listing service.

13. C: A real estate salesperson who is an independent contractor, under IRS rules, is one who is not paid according to hours worked but according to an independent contractor agreement between the agent and the broker.

14. C: The federal IRS code and conforming New York statutes govern independent contractors.

Legal Issues

Estates and Interests

15. B: Tenancy in common occurs when two or more people hold title to a property at the same time. Joint tenancy and tenants by the entirety (a married couple) are ownerships attained with the unities of time, title, interest, and possession. Ownership in severalty implies sole ownership.

16. B: Riparian rights belong to an owner of property bordering a flowing body of water. Chattel refers to personal property. Subsurface rights are rights to property below the surface of the earth. The bundle of rights is all of the rights inherent in real property ownership.

17. B: Juan will most likely use a bill of sale. Sales contracts and purchase offers are used in the sale of real property.

Liens and Easements

18. B: Real property taxes are involuntary because they are imposed by the taxing jurisdiction. They are specific to the real property.

19. C: A mechanic's lien is a claim by someone who has performed work on a property and has not been paid. A *lis pendens* is a notice that a lawsuit is pending.

20. A: Goldie's property allows the easement so it is the servient tenement. An encroachment is the intrusion of an object on another's property. A lien is a charge against another's property.

Deeds

21. C: A deed must have an acknowledgment to be recorded. Not all deeds have a metes and bounds description, a *habendum* clause, or a covenant of warranty.

22. D: An executor's deed, guardian's deed, and sheriff's deed are all forms of judicial deeds. An installment land contract is not a deed but rather a contract for a deed.

Title Closing and Costs

23. A: The purchase money mortgage is a form of seller financing. The seller is giving a mortgage rather than receiving money so it is a debit to the seller.

24. D: Delinquent real property taxes generally must be paid before a closing can take place. Most often, the seller pays his back taxes before closing.

The Contract of Sale and Leases

Leases

25. A: Because the lease contract has been transferred to Jamie, an assignment has taken place. Under a sublease, the original tenant, Amy, would be responsible for the lease payments. Constructive eviction occurs when the tenant is forced to move out of a leased premise because of unlivable conditions. A holdover tenancy occurs when a tenant remains in a leased premise after lease expiration.

Contracts

26. C: Nancy had to pay Tessie liquidated damages. Had there been specific performance, Nancy may have had to pay the purchase price of the property. Rescission is a withdrawal of the contract. Novation is the substitution of new contract for an old contract.

Contract Preparation

27. C: In order for a real estate salesperson to prepare a fill-in-the-blanks contract of sale approved by the Board of REALTORS®, it must contain an attorney review clause.

Real Estate Finance

28. D: A balloon mortgage is not fully amortized and a larger payment, called a balloon, is due at the end of the mortgage term. A graduated payment is a type of mortgage in which payment is lower in the early years and increases on a scheduled basis. A wraparound mortgage is a subordinate mortgage that includes the same principal obligation secured by a first mortgage against the same property. It is a type of seller financing.

29. B: Equity of redemption occurs when a borrower who has defaulted on his loan may be able to regain his property by paying the outstanding debt. A deficiency judgment is a charge by a lender to parties who default on their loan and when a foreclosure proceeding does not cover the full debt on the property. A deed in lieu of foreclosure is a document transferring a property to the lender to avoid foreclosure proceedings.

30. C: The acceleration clause allows the lender to declare the entire balance due if the borrower defaults. The prepayment penalty clause is a fine imposed by the lender if the mortgage is paid off before it is due. The granting clause is part of a deed. The defeasance clause gives the borrower the right to pay off the loan.

31. B: A blanket mortgage allows two or more parcels to be pledged as security for the loan. A package mortgage allows personal property, in addition to real property, to be pledged to secure payment of the mortgage loan. A bridge loan is a short-term loan. An installment contract allows title to pass to the borrower once the mortgage obligations are fulfilled.

32. C: FHA, the Federal Housing Authority, is an agency of HUD. Fannie Mae, Sonny Mae, and Freddie Mac are not affiliated with HUD.

Land Use Regulations

33. B: Article 9-A is the New York law that regulates the sale of unimproved lots across state lines. The Interstate Land Sales Full Disclosure Act is a similar federal law. The State Environmental Quality Review Act is a New York law regulating environmental issues when land is improved. The Uniform Fire Prevention and Building Code is a New York construction code.

34. D: Condemnation is the act of taking a property because of an eminent domain action. Escheat occurs when the government takes property of the deceased if no heirs are found. Estoppel is generally a court order to stop an act. *In rem* is a type of legal proceeding against real property and not the individual's personal property.

35. C: Emma would need an area variance. A use variance allows a property to be used for a certain purpose. A nonconforming use is one that already existed before the zoning was changed. Illegal spot zoning occurs when property does not conform to the surroundings.

Construction and Environmental Issues

36. A: Foundations are poured concrete or concrete block.

37. C: The soffit is the area under the roof extension. The fascia is a board that is perpendicular to the soffit. The third component of the roof overhang is the frieze board. This is a wooden framing member fastened directly under the soffit, against the top of the wall. Sheathing is a plywood material that covers the roof rafters.

38. A: In New York, in the sale of one- and two-family residential properties, as well as condominiums and cooperatives, the seller must present a signed smoke alarm and carbon monoxide detector affidavit at closing.

39. B: The New York law that requires preparation of an environmental impact statement on properties that a government body has the jurisdiction to review is the State Environmental Quality Review Act. The Superfund Amendment and CERCLA address liability upon transfer of title. The TILA-RESPA Integrated Disclosure Rule is a federal law requiring disclosure by lenders in making residential mortgage loans.

40. B: Disclosure of knowledge of the existence of lead-based paint must be made in the sale or lease of pre-1978 target residential properties.

Valuation Process and Pricing Properties

41. D: Because both the comparative market analysis and the sales comparison approach compare properties that are similar to the subject, the CMA is most similar to the sales comparison approach. The income (capitalization) approach and cost approach are other appraisal approaches to value.

42. A: Evaluations do not necessarily produce an estimate of value, as does an appraisal or CMA. Value in use is not a land utilization study but defines the usefulness of a property to the owner.

43. B: A real estate agent must be able to adjust the listing price according to the market.

Human Rights and Fair Housing

44. C: Testers are volunteers who visit real estate firms and other businesses to assess equal treatment for all.

45. D: Real estate agents cannot violate human rights laws in taking listings or any other real estate activity.

46. C: Illegal blockbusting includes prompting homeowners to sell their properties due to the entry of certain persons of a particular race or religion into the neighborhood.

47. A: The lender is guilty of illegal redlining; that is, denying or restricting loans in a certain area by a lending institution. Steering is a practice by real estate brokers that encourages culturally diverse people toward or away from certain areas. Blockbusting occurs when real estate salespeople tell homeowners that a member of a protected class is moving into their neighborhood causing them to panic and place their homes for sale. These activities are all violations of the Federal Fair Housing Act and New York laws.

Real Estate Mathematics

48. B: $90,000 × .06 = $5,400
$5,400 × .60 = $3,240; $5,400 - $3,240 = $2,160

49. D: $217,500 × .02 = $4,350

Municipal Agencies

50. C: The planning board would most likely have the task of mapping a large parcel of land that was granted to the city. The assessor's office values property for tax purposes. The zoning board of appeals hears variance requests. The architectural review board oversees building design.

51. D: Francesca will have to apply for a variance so she will need to go before the zoning board of appeals. But she probably also has to gain approval for the project from the architectural review board. It is possible that the board will not allow the project and then she will not need to apply for the variance. The conservation advisory council oversees environmental issues including wetlands.

Property Insurance

52. B: The coverage that the Lees have is for replacement cost. Replacement cost means that the insured is covered and reimbursed for the actual cost of replacing the damaged property. Actual cash value means that the insured is reimbursed for the replacement cost minus the physical depreciation of the lost or damaged property. An umbrella policy is an excess liability policy providing additional coverage above that offered by primary policies.

Taxes and Assessments

53. D: The map referred to in the question is a tax map. A plat is a property map such as a subdivision map. A blueprint is an architect's rendering of a structure. A survey is a detailed rendering of the physical boundaries, elevations, and other details of a property.

54. D: An assessing unit that levies real property taxes can be a city, town, or county.

55. C: A residential assessment ratio (RAR) is used for board of assessments review grievances and small claims hearings. RARs are not used if there are less than five residential sales that year in the taxing unit, for revaluation projects, or determining tax exemptions.

Condominiums and Cooperatives

56. D: A cooperative shareholder receives a proprietary lease to the cooperative unit, not a deed.

57. B: The owner or developer of a condominium or cooperative is called the sponsor. A trustor transfers a trust fund or other account to a trustee.

58. B: The CPS1 statement contains the Attorney General rules for testing the market for a new condominium or cooperative development. The UCC-1 statement is filed with the county clerk when a condominium is transferred. The Civil Practice Laws and Rules (CPLR) addresses legal procedures in New York. Section 443 of the Real Property law addresses agency disclosure.

Commercial and Investment Properties

59. D: The pro forma statement reflects a potential change in income and expenses. The cash flow statement, operating statement, and statement of net worth are other types of financial statements.

60. B: $2,250 × 12 = $27,000; $27,000 ÷ 0.07 = $385,714 (rounded)

61. B: A process that calculates the value of an asset in the past, present, and future is called the time value of money. Leverage is the use of other people's money. Debt service is the payment of principal and interest. Net operating income is property expenses deducted from gross income.

62. C: $750,000 ÷ $1,000,000 = 75%

63. D: Land does not necessarily have less resale value than other types of investment property.

64. B: Income received on a property without deducting expenses is gross income. Once expenses are deducted, the remaining monies are net income. NOI stands for net operating income. The net operating income is the operating income minus operating expenses and debt service or the cash flow. Debt service is the annual amount to be paid to pay off or reduce a loan.

65. C: Once all expenses and debt service are paid, the monies remaining are called cash flow. A tax shelter is a method of protecting income from taxation. Gross income is income received without subtracting expenses. The cash-on-cash return is a value measurement for a property that considers the equity in the property measured against the cash flow.

66. D: The cash-on-cash return considers the equity in the property against the cash flow. The capitalization rate is the annual return that an investor expects to receive. The rate of return is the percentage amount that an investor receives back on the investment.

67. D: Just as other types of investments, like the stock market, for example, profit is never guaranteed for any type of investment.

Income Tax Issues in Real Estate Transactions

68. D: There is no 38% federal tax bracket for income tax purposes. The highest tax bracket is 37%.

69. D: According to the IRS, mortgage interest and property taxes are all federal tax deductions for property ownership.

70. D: Annie and Xavier do not have to pay a capital gains tax on the sale of their property. They have lived in their house for five years and the profit on the sale of $50,000 is less than their $500,000 married couple exemption.

Mortgage Brokerage

71. A: If an applicant for a mortgage broker's registration also holds a real estate broker's license, he must submit a dual agency affidavit to the NYS Department of Financial Services. An estoppel certificate may be included in a commercial lease.

72. C: A real estate salesperson needs two years of experience in the mortgage brokerage business to apply for a mortgage broker registration. A licensed real estate broker can use this license as the experience for the mortgage broker registration.

Property Management

73. D: Advisors to property managers who focus on long-term financing planning rather than day-to-day operations of the property are asset managers.

74. A: A document submitted to the property owner outlining the commitment of the property manager once he is employed is the management agreement. The management proposal is submitted before the agreement and outlines what the property manager plans to accomplish.

Licensee Safety

75. D: To safely conduct an open house, Dannisha should alert her buddy, have another agent accompany her, and allow the prospects to enter a room at the property first.

Salesperson Practice Exam 2

License Law and Regulations

1. C: A person must be at least 20 years old to be licensed as a real estate broker in New York.

2. A: Attorneys who are admitted to practice in the New York courts are exempt from obtaining a license as long as they do not employ salespeople.

3. B: According to New York law, brokers must maintain a separate escrow account for client monies including deposits. The office operating account must be separate.

Law of Agency Including Independent Contractor

4. D: An illegal net listing contract allows the broker to keep as a commission any money obtained from the sale above a sale price specified by the seller.

5. D: A broker's agent is one who is hired by a broker to assist the broker in selling or finding a property for the principal.

6. A: Under New York law, dual agency is permissible with disclosure and informed consent of buyer and seller.

7. D: With an exclusive agency arrangement, the broker is legally entitled to the commission if the exclusive broker or another broker effects sale of the property, but not if the owner sells the property without the assistance of any broker. An exclusive-right-to-sell agreement allows the broker to receive a commission no matter who sells the property. An open listing arrangement allows the property to be listed with a number of brokers who receive a commission only if they sell the property. An illegal net listing contract allows the broker to keep as a commission any money obtained from the sale above a sale price specified by the seller.

8. C: The first law to address antitrust violations was the Sherman Antitrust Act. The Clayton Antitrust Act is another antitrust law. The TILA-RESPA Integrated Disclosure Rule is a federal law that regulates lender disclosures in making residential mortgage loans.

9. B: This example illustrates an illegal tie-in arrangement because as a condition of sale, the buyer must obtain financing from a specified company. An illegal group boycott occurs when one group or person is persuaded or coerced to not do business with another group or person. An illegal market allocation agreement occurs when competing companies agree to split a territory among them.

10. B: An agency relationship created by an oral or written agreement between a principal and agent is an express agency. Implied agency can be created through the acts of the parties. Dual agency occurs when one broker represents the buyer and seller in the same transaction. A power of attorney allows a person to legally manage the affairs of another.

11. B: Under an exclusive right-to-sell contract, Martin owes a commission to Broker Gerald even though Martin sells the house himself. This is a possible breach of contract. Reformation permits a court to rewrite a contract perhaps in case of a typographical or other mistake. Injunction is a court order to stop an act. Assignment is the giving over of the contract to another.

12. D: Under an amendment to Section 443 of the New York Real Property Law, buyers or sellers may give advance informed consent to dual agency by indicating consent on the Agency Disclosure Form.

13. C: In the independent contract relationship, there are no deductions taken for income taxes. Paying income tax is the responsibility of the licensee.

14. A: Real estate licensees are classified as independent contractors under Section 3508 (a) (b) of the IRS Code. Article 12-A applies to the New York salesperson and broker license law. Section 443 of the New York Real Property Law applies to agency disclosure.

Legal Issues

Estates and Interests

15. C: Partition is a court action to divide a property owned by tenants in common. The unities that make up a joint tenancy are the unities of time, title, interest, and possession.

16. B: The most complete form of real property ownership is fee simple absolute. Fee simple defeasible estates have conditions for ownership. A fee simple defeasible ownership is recognized by the words "but if" in the transfer. A life estate is ownership for a person's life or another's life.

17. D: This question is an example of a life estate (with a remainder interest). The property will go to another party after the life tenant. A fee simple absolute estate is complete title to a property. A leasehold estate is not ownership but rental. A joint tenancy is a type of ownership with the right of survivorship.

Liens and Easements

18. D: A judgment is an involuntary general lien because it is without the permission of the property holder and can apply to all of his property.

19. B: A *lis pendens* is a notice that a lawsuit is pending affecting title or possession of a property. An injunction is a court order to stop an act. A judgment is a lien against all property of the debtor. A mechanic's lien is a lien for unpaid labor or materials.

20. C: Lionel's property requires an easement by necessity because it is landlocked and Lionel cannot exit the property any other way. An easement by condemnation is created by eminent domain. A negative easement is an easement not to do something such as block a view. An encroachment is the intrusion of an object across a boundary line.

Deeds

21. C: A type of deed used in bankruptcy proceedings and foreclosures is a referee's deed. A sheriff's deed, executor's deed, and guardian's deed are other types of judicial deeds.

22. B: In order to claim title by adverse possession in New York, the use must be open and notorious for ten years.

Title Closing and Costs

23. C: Outstanding liens would generally delay a closing because the title would not be clear. Discount points, the hiring of an attorney by the purchaser, and a purchase money mortgage are all common closing events.

24. A: On the closing statement, the earnest money deposit appears a buyer credit. Prepaid real property taxes, a prepaid insurance premium, and the sale of personal property are all seller credits.

The Contract of Sale and Leases

Leases

25. B: A periodic lease automatically renews itself at the end of the term unless notice is given. A proprietary lease is given to cooperative unit owners along with shares of stock as evidence of their ownership share.

Contracts

26. A: The option specifies a time limit in which the optionee can choose to purchase. An option is a unilateral contract because only one party, the optionor, makes a promise. It is not a contract to convey title.

Contract Preparation

27. D: A codicil is an addition to a will. Contingency clauses, addenda, and riders are all possible additions to the contract.

Real Estate Finance

28. C: A HUD agency (Department of Housing and Urban Development) that purchases VA (Department of Veterans Affairs) and FHA (Federal Housing Administration) mortgages on the secondary market is Ginnie Mae (Government National Mortgage Association). RHS is the Rural Housing Service that makes loans and grants to rural properties. SONYMA is the State of New York Mortgage Agency that loans money for target properties. FDIC (Federal Deposit Insurance Corporation) insures bank deposits.

29. B: A mortgage clause that allows a lender to declare the balance due if the borrower sells the property is the alienation clause. The prepayment penalty clause is a fine imposed by the lender if the mortgage is paid off before it is due. The granting clause is part of a deed. The defeasance clause gives the borrower the right to pay off the loan.

30. D: A mortgage that provides for paying the debt by monthly payment of principal and interest and in which the interest portion of the payments decreases as the principal portion increases is an amortized loan. A balloon mortgage does not fully retire the debt. An installment land contract calls for a transfer of title after all payments are made. A swing loan is a type of short-term loan.

31. B: Regulation Z of the Truth-in-Lending Act addresses the accurate advertising of credit terms. The Community Reinvestment Act encourages lenders to meet the credit needs of communities. The Anti-Predatory Lending Law is a New York law that places many restrictions on high-cost (subprime) loans that are first or junior mortgages. The New York Mortgage Foreclosure law enhances the subprime lending law.

32. A: An adjustable rate mortgage rate floats based on a standard index as opposed to a fixed rate that stays the same throughout the mortgage term. A straight term mortgage allows interest only payments for a specified time.

Land Use Regulations

33. B: In New York, variance requests are brought to the zoning board of appeals.

34. C: The boundaries and physical dimensions of a property are shown in a survey. A feasibility study determines a project's usefulness and projected success in the community. A plat is a subdivision map.

35. C: Parks and forests could be zoned as public open space. Institutional properties include hospitals and schools.

Construction and Environment

36. C: UFFI (urea formaldehyde foam insulation) is a type of spray-inside-the-wall insulation that is no longer allowed. This is because it contained irritating and unhealthful levels of formaldehyde. Loose fill, rigid, and batt are other types of insulation.

37. B: The amount of electrical current flowing through a wire is the amperage. Voltage is the force or push of the current. A milliGauss is a measurement of electromagnetic field strength.

38. B: The Energy Conservation Construction Code of New York State mandates minimum R-factors for insulation. The Real Property Law addresses real estate license law and other property issues. The Emergency Tenant Protection Act governs rent control and rent regulations. The Sanitary Code is overseen by the NYS Health Department and addresses health and sanitation issues.

39. C: Senior citizen housing is generally exempt from disclosure under the Residential Lead-based Hazard Reduction Act. The Act is aimed at children who might eat lead from paint chips and dirt.

40. A: One of the most prevalent concerns for underground storage tank is leakage caused over time by erosion, wear, and tear of the tank material.

Valuation Process and Pricing Properties

41. C: The goal of an accurate CMA is to find properties in as close proximity as possible to the subject property.

42. B: Surveyors and appraiser's fees relating to property development are indirect costs. Hard or direct costs are costs for labor and materials. Impact fees are made to the municipality by a developer for infrastructure and other requirements.

43. A: An arm's length transaction means that the parties are not related as relatives or business associates.

Human Rights and Fair Housing

44. D: In New York, in the sale of a single-family home, there are no exemptions in the New York Human Rights Law whether or not Hattie uses the services of a real estate broker. She also cannot discriminate against a person's race in any real property sale as this violates the federal Civil Rights Act of 1868, in which there are no exemptions for racial discrimination.

45. C: The civil monetary penalties for violations of the Fair Housing Act is a maximum civil penalty for a first violation of $75,000, and $150,000 for subsequent violations.

46. B: According to the New York Human Rights law, brokerage offices must display the HUD fair housing poster.

47. C: Federal law has fewer protected classes than New York. The New York Human Rights Law adds to the federal law the protected classes of marital status, age, sexual orientation, gender identity, and military status.

Real Estate Mathematics

48. D: 3 × $8,000 = $24,000; $9,000 × 4 = $36,000; $36,000 – $24,000 = $12,000 = 50%

49. C: 150 × 500 = 75,000 sq. ft.; 75,000 ÷ 43,560 sq. ft./acres = 1.72 acres
1.72 acres × $5,000 = $8,600 acreage basis; $20 × 500 = $10,000 front foot basis

Municipal Agencies

50. B: Government agencies in New York cannot require property owners to restore or rehabilitate a historic structure. The building department oversees compliance with the building code, inspects properties during and after construction, and issues building permits.

51. A: The conservation advisory council accepts grants made to the municipality for lands under its jurisdiction such as wetlands. The planning board oversees land use issues. The architectural review board oversees building design. The building department oversees the building code.

Property Insurance

52. B: Perils are events that cause damage and are included on the insurance policy. Some perils are excluded from basic policies but may be added to the policy or obtained in a separate policy (for example, flood insurance). Lenders require homeowner's insurance to obtain a mortgage, an endorsement is an attachment to the insurance policy, and an insurance policy is a legal contract.

Taxes and Assessments

53. B: The level of assessment is the percentage of market value at which properties are assessed. $300,000 × .75 = $225,000.

54. C: The purpose of a special assessment is to collect payment for a share of improvements made to the area. A judicial review of a tax protest in the New York Supreme Court is called a tax certiorari proceeding. Reassessments can be performed on properties when improvements are made, and on a regular prescribed basis. The tax levy is the amount that a municipality must raise to meet budgetary requirements by taxing real property.

55. A: An *in rem* legal proceeding is a legal action brought against the real property and not against an individual and his personal property. An injunction is a court order to stop a specific action. A judicial review of a tax protest in the New York Supreme Court is called a tax certiorari proceeding. A reformation is a court order that permits the parties to rewrite a contract when a mistake such as a clerical error is made.

Condominiums and Cooperatives

56. B: With a cooperative apartment purchase, the board of directors must approve a prospective buyer.

57. C: In a cooperative, the cooperative corporation owns the common areas.

58. D: The alteration agreement is a contract between the shareholder and the cooperative to make structural changes to the unit. A letter of intent is an agreement to purchase a condominium that may or may not be binding. House rules govern daily behavior in the cooperative. Subscription agreements are the contracts that the sponsor possesses to purchase shares of stock in the cooperative units.

Commercial and Investment Properties

59. D: $20,000 × 12 = $240,000; $240,000 ÷ $600,000 = 40%.

60. A: The profit from income producing properties, less income taxes, is the after tax cash flow. The before cash tax flow is profit before income taxes. Debt service is the payment of principal and interest. Debt is what the investor owes. Equity is the investor's interest in the property. The debt-to-equity ratio describes the percentage of the capital that is invested.

61. B: $10,000 + $2,000 = $12,000; $12,000 × 0.35 = $4,200

62. D: A paper income loss on investment property is called a tax shelter. Gross income is income received without deducting operating expenses. Debt service is the payment of principal and interest. Leverage is the use of other people's money.

63. D: $650,000 ÷ 0.12 = $5,416,667 (rounded)

64. A: Property owners lease commercial space according to the rentable square footage that is the entire space. The usable square footage does not include elevators and hallways, for example.

65. B: The loss factor is the area that is part of the rented space that is not specifically usable to the tenant.

66. A: A loft is a type of commercial space that is not generally divided into rooms.

67. B: Unlike many residential leases, a commercial lease is generally customized. This is because most spaces are unique and there are different needs for each tenant. A periodic lease automatically renews itself for another period at the end of each period unless one party gives notice to the other at the prescribed time.

Income Tax Issues in Real Estate Transactions

68. B: The adjusted basis includes other costs such as the fire that devalued the property. The basis is the cost of the property.

69. B: A limited partner does not materially participate in the managing and operation of the investment. Therefore, under the IRS code, Isaiah's income from the investment is classified as a passive activity. Active income includes salaries or income from a business in which the taxpayer materially participates. Portfolio income is interest, annuities, dividends, royalties, and profits from the sale of portfolio assets.

70. C: In a tax-deferred exchange, the individual who accepts the funds from the sale and handles the contract is called the qualified intermediary (QI).

Mortgage Brokerage

71. D: The pre-application disclosure and fee agreement is used by mortgage brokers to make certain disclosures regarding the mortgage fee and other matters. The agency disclosure form discloses whom the real estate agent represents in the sale of rental of one- to four-unit residential properties and condominiums and cooperatives in any size building. A preapproval letter is a document from a lender stating that a purchaser is preapproved for a loan. A letter of intent is an agreement to purchase a property such as a condominium.

72. D: The NYS Department of Financial Services licenses mortgage bankers.

Property Management

73. D: There are various fee arrangements between a property manager and owner. One of them is a base fee and a percentage of the rents collected.

74. D: Because they perform a variety of duties, property managers are general agents. Because of their role as agents, a fiduciary relationship, a position of trust, exists between the manager and the owner. A special agent generally performs one duty such as marketing the real estate.

Licensee Safety

75. A: Aileen should first meet the customers at the real estate office and they should later meet at the property. Many customers come into an area from other places and Aileen should welcome the opportunity to do business with them.

Broker Practice Exam I

Agency Law, License Law, and Operating a Real Estate Office

Agency Law

1. C: A seller's broker, in his fiduciary role, may not advise a buyer that the seller is anxious to sell because of a job transfer. Because of the fiduciary relationship, the principal is owed loyalty, faith, trust, and confidentiality by the agent hired.

2. D: A broker must obey reasonable and lawful instructions from the principal. The broker must disclose material defects to the buyer even though the buyer is a third party outside of the fiduciary relationship between the broker and the principal. The broker must obey all human rights laws and present all offers to the sellers.

3. D: The principal must disclose all information to the agent bearing on the agency relationship. If the agent is found liable to third parties for the principal's misrepresentation, the agent is entitled to repayment from the principal. The repayment is indemnification to the agent and makes the agent financially whole.

4. C: A franchise is an umbrella organization that lends its name and expertise to member firms that carry the franchise name. In New York, with some franchise firms, the franchise fee portion is deducted from the final commission due the sales associate.

5. D: Giving legal advice to principals or customers may constitute the unauthorized practice of law by real estate agents. Agents should refer legal questions to an attorney. Loyalty, reasonable care, and confidentiality are all common law fiduciary duties of an agent to the principal.

6. A: A broker's agent is an agent who cooperates or is engaged by a listing agent, buyer's agent, or tenant's agent. In this relationship, the principal is not vicariously liable for acts of the broker's agent. The broker who engaged the broker's agent agents accepts this liability.

7. B: In New York, dual agency is legal with timely disclosure and informed consent.

8. B: Subagency can be created when a seller and broker agree, usually by means of an MLS, that other agents will also work for the seller. The principal can agree to accept or reject the option of subagency when signing the listing agreement.

9. C: Subagents of the seller must also deal honestly and ethically with the buyer or customer and disclose any pertinent information that may affect the value of the specific property.

License Law

10. B: Once a broker receives a deposit, he or she must immediately deposit it in an escrow account until the money is needed such as at closing. At closing, sometimes the deposit money comprises some or all of the broker's commission. In certain areas, brokers turn over deposit money to the seller's attorney who places it in his or her escrow account.

11. C: Generally, if a real estate broker receives compensation from more than one party in the transaction, the broker must disclose the fact and receive the consent of all parties to the transaction.

12. C: All ads placed by a broker must indicate that the advertiser is a real estate broker and give the broker's name or the brokerage firm name and either the phone number or address of the brokerage firm. Ads that do not contain this information are called blind ads.

13. A: A property condition disclosure form, used in the sale of one- to four-unit residential properties and completed by the seller, assists in disclosing property defects and other issues to prospective buyers.

14. B: An illegal net listing is one in which a broker sets a sales price for a property and uses any amount that the property sells above that amount for his or her commission.

15. B: The sales agent must obtain permission from the sellers to post a for sale sign on their property. Offering a property for sale or lease without the authorization of the owner is a violation of the license law.

16. A: Broker Lately must not allow unlicensed salespeople to transact real estate. This is a violation of the license law.

17. D: Real estate brokers have a duty to supervise their sales associates and also their unlicensed assistants in accordance with the New York license law. They must also be able to perform duties required of them through the use of *eAccessNY*, the NYS DOS secure password-protected occupational management licensing system.

Operating a Real Estate Office

18. B: Under the IRS code, real estate licensees are independent contractors. As such, work hours for an independent contractor cannot be mandated by a broker. Independent contractors are not paid an hourly wage or weekly salary and are compensated for work product.

19. A: If a broker meets the terms of the listing agreement, and has brought to the seller a ready, willing and able buyer, he or she is entitled to the commission even if the property does not close. Advance informed consent refers to a consumer's consent to dual agency before it occurs.

20. A: An illegal market allocation agreement is one in which competitors divide or allocate a market area for sales and agree not to compete in those areas. A tie-in arrangement is between a party selling a service to a buyer, that, as a condition of sale, the buyer will buy another product from the seller or not do business with another. Price fixing occurs when competitors in a certain group

conspire to charge the same or similar price. A group boycott is a conspiracy in which a person or group is coerced into not doing business with another person or group.

21. D: A tie-in arrangement is between a party selling a service to a buyer, that, as a condition of sale, the buyer will buy another product from the seller. A group boycott is a conspiracy in which a person or group is coerced into not doing business with another person or group. Price fixing occurs when competitors in a certain group conspire to charge the same or similar price. A market allocation agreement is an agreement between competitors who are dividing or assigning a certain area or territory for sales.

22. C: All ads placed by a broker must indicate that the advertiser is a real estate broker and give the either the broker's name or the brokerage firm name and either the phone number or address of the brokerage firm. Ads that do not contain this information are called blind ads.

23. D: The TILA-RESPA Integrated Disclosure Rule (TRID) includes disclosure requirements for residential real property loans and requires the use of the loan estimate form and the closing disclosure form. The HUD-1 form was a closing disclosure form formerly used in residential mortgage transactions and is still used when the property does not conform under the TRID regulations.

24. C: If an appraiser wants to find the value of a parking lot of a property, he might value the parking lots of two different properties, and determine adjustments to a property valuation when using the sales comparison approach. This method of analysis describes paired sales analysis. The cost approach to value is an appraisal valuation that theoretically rebuilds the structure as new and then adjusts to its present condition. A feasibility study analyzes a project before inception and compares the data with similar projects to determine if the project will succeed. A comparative market analysis (CMA) is an analysis of the competition in the marketplace that a property encounters upon sale attempts.

25. A: Associate brokers and salespersons who want additional licenses must obtain permission from each sponsoring broker and submit a statement to DOS from each sponsoring broker indicating acknowledgment of each licensure.

26. A: When a salesperson or associate broker terminates their association with the broker, the broker must file a termination of association notice online to the DOS but there is no fee. However, there is a $20 fee paid to the DOS for a new association.

27. A: A subchapter S corporation is a type of corporation that is permitted to function as a corporation but is taxed as a partnership. An advantage of a subchapter S corporation is that since it is taxed as a partnership, it does not have to pay corporate income tax. It avoids the double tax that a C corporation pays. A C corporation must pay corporate income tax to the IRS. With general partnerships, the partners are personally liable for partnership debts exceeding partnership assets. Owners of a limited liability company LLC (called members) are not personally liable for the obligations of the LLC. An LLC is taxed as a partnership.

28. C: A form of liability insurance required by real estate brokerage firms to protect against claims for failure to perform on a contract and/or causing financial loss is called errors and omissions

insurance. Premises liability insurance protects an owner from claims that an individual was hurt on their property. A commercial crime bond is a type of insurance that protects a company from loss by the dishonesty or fraudulent acts of its covered employees. It is also known as a fidelity policy. This type of insurance is sometimes purchased by a property management company.

29. C: The federal Residential Lead-based Paint Hazard Reduction Act sets forth procedures to be followed in disclosing the presence of lead-based paint for the sale of properties built prior to 1978. There are also local laws addressing lead-based paint disclosure. Agricultural District disclosure and the Truth-in-Heating law are New York State laws that require disclosure. The Bedbug Act is a New York City law.

30. D: A broker price opinion is a process used by a hired sales agent to determine the potential selling price or estimated value of a property. It is not an appraisal or market valuation, which is performed by an appraiser. Many lenders require, and other real estate transactions dictate, that an appraisal must be performed.

31. D: If online information in the real estate office is not securely protected, a compromised system can lead to identify theft, and the compromise of client and customer information and confidential broker documentation and data.

32. B: Home inspectors, appraiser assistants, and certified general appraisers are all licensed by the NYS Department of State. Mortgage brokers are registered by the NYS Department of Financial Services.

33. B: If properties are not selling because there is an overabundance of housing compared to the demand, this illustrates the economic theory of supply and demand. Inflation is an increase in money and credit relative to available goods that results in higher prices. Deficit spending occurs when the government spends money in excess of the revenue and uses borrowed money rather than money from taxation.

34. D: The zoning board of appeals would have to grant a variance for the project. The planning board would have to decide if a technology park is viable for the town. Because of the proximity of the project to a wetland, the conservation advisory council that advises on the protection of natural resources would be involved as well.

Real Estate Finance

35. B: As to mortgages, New York is a lien theory state. The borrower holds the deed to the property during the mortgage term. The borrower promises to make all payments to the lender and the mortgage becomes a lien on the property, but title remains with the borrower. In a title theory state, a mortgage transfers title to a property to the mortgagee (lender), who holds title until the mortgage has been paid off, at which time title passes to the mortgagor (borrower and then owner). Some lenders and mortgage brokers may be guilty of illegal predatory lending practices that take advantage of the consumer. Among other illegal practices, a lender will make unaffordable loans based on borrower assets rather than on the ability to repay an obligation ("asset-based lending").

36. A: The loan-to-value ratio establishes how much the borrower will pay from his or her personal funds toward the purchase of the property. This is the down payment.

37. C: Fannie Mae (short for Federal National Mortgage Association) is part of the secondary mortgage market where mortgage loans are purchased from the primary mortgage market. The VA (Department of Veterans Affairs) and FHA (Federal Housing Authority) are government-backed agencies and are part of the primary mortgage market. SONYMA (State of New York Mortgage Agency) makes mortgage loans to target areas in New York.

38. B: Mini-perm financing is a type of interim financing sometimes used by developers until more permanent financing is in place upon completion of a project. Equity stripping, the process of reducing the equity value of a real estate asset, is a type of asset protection strategy. It encumbers the property with debt to the extent that there is little or no equity for creditors to acquire. With an installment land contract, title is not transferred to the buyer until the mortgage is paid. A sale leaseback is a transaction in which a property owner sells a property to an investor who immediately leases back the property to the seller as agreed to in the sales contract.

39. D: A purchase money mortgage is a type of seller financing in which the seller holds some or all of the mortgage on the property. A bridge loan is a legal short-term loan used to obtain interim financing for projects before a long-term loan is in place. With an installment land contract, title is not transferred to the buyer until the mortgage is paid. A wraparound mortgage is a subordinate mortgage that includes the same principal obligation secured by a superior mortgage against the same property.

40. A: A sale leaseback is a transaction in which a property owner sells a property to an investor who immediately leases back the property to the seller. A ground lease is a long-term lease of unimproved land, usually for construction purposes. A wraparound mortgage is a subordinate mortgage that includes the same principal obligation secured by a superior mortgage against the same property. A purchase money mortgage is a type of seller financing in which the seller holds some or all of the mortgage on the property.

Real Property Investment

41. C: By using other people's money (OPM), the investor's buying power is increased. The use of borrowed funds is called leverage.

42. B: Capital gain is the profit realized from the sale of a real estate investment. Portfolio income includes interest, annuities, dividends, and royalties. Debt service includes mortgage principal and interest payments.

43. C: A tax shelter is best defined as a paper loss; it is a phrase used to describe some of the advantages of real estate investments. Negative amortization occurs when the monthly payment is less than full interest and does not pay any principal. The interest that is unpaid accrues and the principal balance owed increases. Capital gain is the profit realized from the sale of a real estate investment. Boot is the cash received in a tax-deferred exchange.

44. D: The cash flow represents the net proceeds after all expenses are met and may be measured before or after taxes are considered. Debt service is the annual amount needed to pay off or reduce a loan.

45. B: Tax depreciation is a provision of the tax law, applicable to certain types of assets, that permits a property owner to take a business deduction for annual depreciation. Depreciation due to physical deterioration is economic depreciation. The adjusted basis consists of the price paid for the property, plus expenses incurred in acquiring the property, and the cost of any capital improvements (less depreciation if applicable). Capital loss occurs when investment is sold at a loss.

46. B: 10 × $800 = $8,000 rental income per month; $8,000 × 12 months = possible $96,000 rental income per year; reduced by .75 × $96,000 = $72,000 effective gross rental income.

47. C: Divide the annual net operating income by the capitalization rate. $480,000 ÷ 0.011 = $4,363,636 (the estimated property value).

48. C: Divide the net annual operating income by the purchase price. $140,000 ÷ $1,166,666 = 12% rate of return.

49. B: Over a year's time, the before-tax income would be $15,000 × 12 = $180,000; so the equity dividend rate or cash-on-cash return would be: $180,000 ÷ $500,000 = 36%.

General Business Law

50. C: The purpose of the Foreign Investment in Real Property Tax Act (FIRPTA) is to impose a tax on capital gains derived by foreign individuals from the sale of their U.S. property.

51. D: To protect consumers from unsolicited calls from service providers and others, consumers may place themselves on a Do Not Call list maintained by the Federal Trade Commission. Consumers are also protected by the CAN SPAM laws that protect consumers from receiving unwanted commercial emails. If the NYS Department of State designates certain areas of the state as cease and desist zones, then homeowners can be placed on a cease and desist list to deter unwanted solicitations from real estate brokers.

52. D: Negotiable instruments are a substitute for money so cash is not a negotiable instrument. Negotiable instruments include drafts, checks, promissory notes, and certificates of deposit.

53. C: Requirements of negotiability must be in writing, be signed, contain a promise or order to pay, be payable at definite time or on demand, and must be a specific or fixed sum of money (any denomination).

54. C: The NYS Truth-in-Heating Law requires that landlords furnish prospective tenants with heating and cooling statements in the lease of residential property.

55. D: Acreage (land) sold along with a building is real property. Shares of stock evidencing ownership in a cooperative, bills of sale of personal property sold at a closing of real property, and heavy equipment are all personal property.

56. B: Chapter 11, a reorganization form of bankruptcy, provides a method for reorganizing the debtor's financial affairs under the supervision of the bankruptcy court. With Chapter 7, a liquidation form of bankruptcy, the debtor's nonexempt property is sold for cash. Chapter 13, a consumer debt adjustment, is a rehabilitation form of bankruptcy for individuals.

57. A: The Statute of Limitations imposes time limits within which litigation may be commenced. The Doctrine of Laches can bar an action even though the specified period has not yet run out if there has been an unreasonable delay. The Statute of Frauds requires that contracts that create an interest in real estate be in writing. A notice of pendency is legal notice that a lawsuit is pending.

Construction and Development

58. D: Advancements in building science including environmental sustainable design, energy efficiencies, and advancements in technology might be a more desirable property for some buyers. Other buyers may want more traditional older properties that might cost less money in the short term and with which they are more familiar. Advancements in building science, however, may be more cost effective going forward.

59. D: According to Article 36-B of the NYS General Business Law, implied in all contracts of sale for new housing is a one-year builder's warranty against defects in construction; a two-year warranty for all plumbing, electrical, heating, and air conditioning systems; and a six-year warranty covering material defects.

60. D: To comply with building codes, contractors and developers must file plans with the building department and/or the town or county planning board. Other state and local agencies may be involved with the approval process for the project.

61. A: New York empowers local government, cities, and counties, through subdivision regulations or ordinances, to protect purchasers and control property development within the subdivisions.

62. B: The NYS Uniform Fire Prevention and Building Code provides minimum standards for fire prevention and construction for all buildings in every municipality in New York except for New York City that has its own code. Local municipalities may have more restrictive standards. The State Environmental Quality Review (SEQR) is a process that requires all levels of state and local government to assess the environmental significance of actions for which they have discretion to review, approve, fund, or undertake. Article 9-A of the Real Property Law addresses the sale of vacant subdivided land in New York and outside of New York when sold on the installment plan. The Interstate Land Sales Full Disclosure Act regulates sale of unimproved lots across state lines.

63. A: A NYS-licensed home inspector would be able to offer a valid opinion as to the quality of the construction in a residential property. Although not required to know *letter and verse* of the building codes, a trained and experienced home inspector is familiar with codes and construction standards. An appraiser is one who estimates the value of real property. Although real estate brokers may know about construction standards and offer very valid opinions, most likely their greater expertise

and goal is in marketing the property. The developer may or may not be versed in construction standards and his goal is also to market the property.

64. C: In the last 12 months, 8,000 homes sold ÷ 2,000 currently on the market = 4.0. The amount of houses turned over four times in the past year: 12 months ÷ 4 (the turnover rate) = 3 months which is the absorption rate. This indicates that there is a 3-month inventory of housing at that price level currently on the market.

65. A: When a developer wants to construct or convert a building into a cooperative, he or she must submit an offering plan to the NYS Attorney General. A purchaser who buys a cooperative apartment receives a stock certificate indicating the amount of shares the cooperative is worth. There may be one certificate stating the total amount of shares or one certificate for each share. A proprietary lease is an occupancy agreement to the cooperative apartment that defines the conditions to occupy the apartment. The alteration agreement describes the terms under which a cooperative shareholder may make changes to the apartment.

Conveyance of Real Property

66. A: If no valid will exists, a person is said to have died intestate.

67. C: Transfer of title to real property is described in law as alienation. Adverse possession is a method of acquiring a title after compliance with certain statutory regulations over a long period. A tenant at sufferance is a tenant that had rightful possession to a property through a lease, but no longer has the permission of the owner to continue to possess the property. Alluvion is increased soil, gravel, or sand to a land mass resulting from the current of the water.

68. A: The sale, gift, or dedications of a property are all voluntary transfers and alienation of property. Eminent domain and adverse possession are types of involuntary alienations of title.

Real Property Management

69. A: Duties of a property manager include maintaining the property, collecting rents, and establishing a budget for property operation. The property manager's duties do not generally include investing an owner's profits.

70. C: Legal fees are not included in an annual property management maintenance schedule.

71. C: The concerns of a property manager when selecting tenants for residential properties include the credit history of the tenants, past landlord references, and employment status. Consideration of marital status for apartment rental is illegal under the NYS Human Rights Law.

72. D: A property management agreement includes the scope of agent's management authority, a manager's fee, and accounting responsibilities. It does not generally include a portfolio of the owner's other investment holdings.

73. C: If a property management office works for more than one property owner and collects rents for these owners, the license generally required is a broker license.

74. D: Rentable square footage equals the entire leased space including the usable square footage and the tenant's pro rata share of the building's common areas, such as the lobby, hallways, and restrooms.

75. A: A lessee who contracts for a triple net lease pays all expenses associated with the property in addition to the rent, except for the debt service. With a gross lease, the landlord pays all of the expenses of the property. With a net lease, the tenant pays some of the expenses of the property. With a percentage lease, the lessee has a base rent plus an additional monthly rent that is a percentage of the lessee's gross sales.

76. B: An annual budget that includes income and expenses for week-to-week operations is known as the operating budget. The capital reserve budget, also called a replacement reserve, is a projected budget over the property's economic life. The stabilized budget is a forecast of income and expenses as may be reasonably projected over a short term, typically over five years.

77. C: \$275,000 gross income – \$150,000 operating expenses (OE) = \$125,000 net operating income (NOI) for the year.

Taxes and Assessments

78. A: Market value is an accepted type of value for setting assessments. Value in use is based on the property's usefulness to an investor and not necessarily for its market value. Investment value is the amount of return on a certain dollar investment a property will produce.

79. A: The NYS constitutional right of home rule is the authority of local governments to exercise self-government. There are many reasons for the equalization rate including allocation of costs—such as for jointly operated hospitals among participating localities or an injury to a volunteer firefighter, among others—determination of the level of STAR exemptions, and apportionment of sales tax revenues and joint indebtedness. All of these items allow local government to apportion funds across municipalities as needed because in New York, the level of assessment is unequal. Property owners may file grievances if they believe their assessment is wrong. A homestead is residential property. When a taxpayer is delinquent in paying property taxes, a tax lien attaches against the property.

80. B: 0.75 × \$80,000 = \$60,000;
900 ÷ \$60,000 = .015 × 100 = \$1.50

Advanced Fair Housing and Fair Lending

81. C: A protected class under the New York Human Rights Law for housing but not under the federal Fair Housing Act is military status. Family status, physical disabilities, and national original are protected classes under the federal Fair Housing Act and its amendments.

82. C: Although there are some exemptions in the federal and NYS law regarding the sale and rental of housing, there is no exemption based on race. The NYS Human Rights Law exempts the rental of an apartment in an owner-occupied two-family house, and the rental of a room by the occupant of a house or an apartment. The federal Fair Housing Act exempts a private club that does not operate for commercial purposes as long as it provides lodging for the benefit of its members only and not to the general public.

83. D: The American with Disabilities Act covers existing commercial buildings, public buildings, and multi-family housing with at least four units.

84. D: A process of renovation and revival of deteriorated urban neighborhoods by the influx of more affluent residents is known as gentrification. The result is increased property values and displacement of lower-income families and small businesses. However, property values can increase and newer business can offer more jobs and better services to the current population as many people do not leave a gentrified neighborhood.

85. A: When lending institutions refuse to make loans to purchase, construct, or repair dwellings by discriminating on the basis of federal or state protected classes, this illegal practice is known as redlining. Steering is a violation of the federal Fair Housing Act and is a practice by real estate brokers that encourages culturally diverse people toward or away from certain areas. Blockbusting occurs when real estate salespeople tell homeowners that a member of a protected class is moving into their neighborhood, causing them to panic and place their homes for sale. Some lenders and mortgage brokers may be guilty of illegal predatory lending practices that take advantage of the consumer. Among other illegal practices, a lender will make unaffordable loans based on borrower assets rather than on the ability to repay an obligation ("asset-based lending").

86. C: The Community Reinvestment Act has to do with lenders making loans available to lower-income purchasers.

87. D: It seems that Elena may have been discriminated against because of marital status and race, protected by the federal Fair Housing Act and NYS Human Rights Law, and sexual orientation protected by the NYS Human Rights Law.

88. D: Housing discrimination can be deterred by laws to protect against discrimination, stringent legal penalties for those who violate discrimination laws in housing and lending, and people understanding the moral and ethical responsibilities to accept and support all individuals in attaining equal opportunity and human rights.

Achieving Agreements through Transaction Analysis

89. B: When an agent represents a client in a transactional agreement, the essential ingredients of a transactional agreement are the needs of the transaction party. The wants are secondary and are best described as the un-tempered (or un-moderated or lessened) desires of the party.

90. A: If BJ signs an exclusive right-to-sell agreement, then BJ is the broker's client.

91. D: The overall objective of a transactional agreement is to reach an agreement on fair terms within a reasonable period of time, which is beneficial to all of the parties to the transaction.

92. C: In an agency agreement, the broker must represent the best interests of the client.

93. B: The primary objective of the broker in a real estate transactional agreement is to reach an agreement without sacrificing the interests of the client simply to achieve an agreement.

94. C: Although not true in every case, and there are many other considerations; the price of a property is generally the most important viable factor in the purchase and sale of real property.

95. D: An agent can locate qualified buyers for a seller or suitable properties for a buyer, and can work with other brokers to reach a transactional agreement that is beneficial to all parties to the transaction.

96. A: Many commission arrangements are possible but a commission is negotiable between a broker and his or her client as stated in the seller listing agreement or buyer agency representation agreement. A commission can be a percentage of the selling price, a flat fee, or a combination of both.

97. C: The services to be provided by the broker should be specifically stated in the listing agreement or the buyer agency agreement.

98. A: An important driving force in the formation of the transactional agreement is for the agent to know the motivations of the individual parties to the transaction as to why they want to sell and purchase. Family dynamics and moving into the "right" neighborhood are indicators of discriminatory behavior and practice that violates fair housing laws and is morally and ethically offensive.

99. D: As in other real estate agreements, once an agreement has been reached for the purchase and sale of real property, there has been a meeting of the minds, and offer and acceptance, so the broker's commission has been earned.

100. B: In a transactional agreement, the broker must always represent the best interests of the client.

Broker Practice Exam 2

Agency Law, License Law, and Operating a Real Estate Office

Agency Law

1. D: The listing agent, buyer's agent, or tenant's agent hires the broker's agent. Therefore, these agents will have vicarious liability for the acts of the broker's agent.

2. B: The fee or rate of commission paid to a real estate broker is strictly negotiable between the broker and the principal or client. Brokers are typically paid by a percentage commission of the final sales price or less often by a flat fee for services rendered.

3. A: According to Section 443 of the New York Real Property Law, buyers and sellers can select and allow a dual agency relationship in advance of it actually occurring. This concept is called advance informed consent to dual agency.

4. D: The agency disclosure form details consumer choices about representation at the first substantive contact with a prospective seller, and applies to all one- to four-unit residential properties, and residential condominium and cooperative properties in any size building.

5. C: The overall purpose of the agency disclosure form is to protect the public in making informed choices regarding real estate agent representation.

6. B: If a buyer or seller refuses to sign the disclosure form, the agent can show the property but must complete a declaration form, have it acknowledged, and provide a copy to the broker to be kept on file for a period of three years.

7. D: An exclusive single agency is a relationship in which the agent or agents in the transaction represent the interests of either the buyer or the seller.

8. D: If the worker earns more than $600, the employer must only file a Form 1099-MISC with the IRS to report the worker's earnings for the year. The W-2, 941, and FICA forms are responsibilities of employers who hire employees, not independent contractors.

9. A: The brokerage firm owns the listing contracts.

License Law

10. C: A broker who discusses types of deed with a customer is giving legal advice. This act violates New York license law and regulations.

11. B: A salesperson must be licensed for two years full time in order to apply for a broker license in New York.

12. B: Violation of the license law is a misdemeanor and is punishable by a $1,000 fine and/or a maximum sentence of one year's imprisonment.

13. B: Article 12-A of the New York license law states that applicants must demonstrate a fair knowledge of the English language.

14. B: A broker applicant must be at least 20 years old; a salesperson applicant must be at least 18 years old.

15. D: Individuals exempt from continuing education are brokers licensed before July 1, 2008, who are engaged in the real estate business full time and licensed with no lapse in licensure for 15 years.

16. A: George can probably use his equivalent real estate experience as a property manager to become a licensed broker in New York.

17. B: Attorneys admitted to practice in New York can act as real estate brokers and are exempt from licensure as long as they do not have sales agents working for them.

Operating a Real Estate Office

18. C: Trade name brokers conduct business as a sole proprietorship, using a name other than their personal name.

19. C: Admitting part-time brokers to MLS is an allowable activity under the federal antitrust laws for multiple listing services.

20. D: Commission rates are negotiable between agent and principal. Under federal and New York antitrust law, brokerage firms, franchises, real estate boards, and multiple listing services cannot combine to fix commission rates.

21. D: A mortgage loan originator (MLO) is registered with the NYS Department of Financial Services. The MLO's duty is to find mortgage money.

22. A: A mortgage loan servicer (MLS) is one who receives scheduled periodic payments from a borrower for a mortgage and is licensed by the NYS Department of Financial Services.

23. A: Corporations that are not subchapter S are known as C corporations. A subchapter S corporation is a type of corporate organization that is permitted to function as a corporation but is taxed as a partnership. A C corporation must pay corporate income tax to the Internal Revenue Service (IRS), and the shareholders are also taxed on their dividends that are profits of the corporation. Therefore, a double tax is paid at the corporate level and the shareholder level.

24. B: A limited liability company (LLC) may be formed by one or more persons. This form of business combines the most favorable attributes of both partnerships and corporations. Owners of an LLC (called members) are not personally liable for the obligations of the LLC; however, an LLC is taxed as a partnership.

25. C: Under the DOS advertising regulations, ads published by an associate broker, a salesperson, or a team must be listed with, represented by, and approved by the broker.

26. C: Ads must accurately state the type of license held by the broker, associate broker, or salesperson named in the ad. Under the NYS advertising regulations, the use of the titles "sales associate," "licensed sales agent," or simply "broker" is prohibited.

27. A: The TILA-RESPA Integrated Disclosure Rule applies to mortgage for residential property. It does not cover home equity lines of credit, business loans, or reverse mortgages.

28. A: Behavioral assessment tests administered by the brokerage firm to screen prospective agents are to evaluate personality traits of the licensee that will work in their particular firm.

29. C: The party to a real estate listing who should ultimately decide where the property should be advertised online is the seller.

30. C: According to the National Association of REALTORS ®' policies, once a property is posted online through a multiple listing service, a listing can be transferred for posting to another party only with the listing broker's consent.

31. A: A home inspector does not make a value estimate of the property, but an appraiser does. Home inspectors do not make repairs to the property during a home inspection and both the home inspector and the appraiser are licensed by the NYS Department of State.

32. B: Depending on the property and other circumstances, the appraiser uses one or more approaches to estimate the value of real property. In the cost approach to value, the appraiser computes the market value of a property by considering the cost of land plus cost of construction, less depreciation. The sales comparison approach has similarities to the comparative market analysis. The income capitalization approach is used by appraisers to value commercial or income properties.

33. D: In managing a real estate office, the broker must implement a financial plan, install a date security system, and make available a policies and procedures manual.

34. B: Generally, the day before closing, a real estate agent accompanies the buyers on a final walk-through of the property. Reviewing an abstract of title constitutes the illegal practice of law on the part of the real estate agent. The seller property condition disclosure form is generally completed by the seller and shown to the buyers when the buyers show an interest in purchasing the property.

Real Estate Finance

35. C: The function of the FHA (Federal Housing Authority) is to insure loans to protect lenders against financial loss.

36. C: Disintermediation is the loss of funds available to lending institutions for making mortgage loans. It is caused by the withdrawal of funds by depositors for investment in higher yield securities

in times of higher interest rates. Stagflation is an economic condition in which economic growth is at a standstill (stagnant) but inflation still exists.

37. B: A capital-short market occurs when lenders do not have funds for underwriting mortgages.

38. A: Recession is a moderate and temporary decline in economic activity that occurs during a period of otherwise increasing prosperity. Depression is the lowest possible point in the economic cycle. Stagflation is an economic condition in which economic growth is at a standstill (stagnant) but inflation still exists.

39. D: Stagflation is an economic condition in which economic growth is at a standstill (stagnant) but inflation still exists. Inflation is an increase in money and credit relative to available goods, resulting in higher prices. Depression is the lowest possible point in the economic cycle. Recession is a moderate and temporary decline in economic activity that occurs during a period of otherwise increasing prosperity.

40. D: In a blanket mortgage, two or more parcels of real estate are pledged as security for payment of the mortgage debt. The shared appreciation mortgage (SAM) allows the lender to benefit from the appreciation of property value in exchange for a lower rate of interest to the borrower. A bridge loan is a short-term loan used to obtain interim financing for projects before a long-term loan is in place. An installment land contract is a form of seller financing and is sometimes called a "contract for deed."

Real Property Investment

41. D: Lender participation in financing is not a risk in considering a real estate investment. A downturn in the real estate market, illiquidity of the investment, and environmental problems associated with a proposed development are investment risks.

42. A: Vacancy loss of income is variable and often unpredictable and dependent on market conditions. Insurance premiums, property taxes, and water/sewer fees are fixed expenses.

43. A: The initial cost to construct the building is not of importance because the building has already been built. The price will be more relevant to his desired rate of return, the vacancy level of the building, and how long he decides to hold the property.

44. D: A gain or loss realized from a sale or exchange of property usually is a recognized gain or loss for tax purposes. Recognized gain means that the taxpayer must pay taxes on the gain or profit. The taxpayer's income and filing status determines the percentage of capital gains tax to be paid.

46. C: \$400,000 – (\$16,700 × 12) = \$199,600
\$199,600 ÷ .135 = \$1,478,518 (rounded)

47. D: \$300,000 ÷ \$50,000 = 6 (GRM)

47. A: 7 x $30,000 = $210,000 (Estimated value of the property)

48. D: $600,000 ÷ $100,000 = 6 (GIM)

49. C: $275,000 ÷ $110,000 = 2.5 (DSCR)

General Business Law

50. C: Brokers may become involved in the sale of marital property when there is a divorce action because there may be a court order to sell the marital residence and other properties.

51. B: An endorsement is a signature by someone other than a maker, a drawer, or an acceptor that is placed on an instrument to negotiate (or transfer) it to another person. Endorsements may be written on the back of the instrument. An assignment is the transfer of rights under a contract.

52. B: In New York, a mechanic's lien must be filed with the county clerk or other government entity within four months of completion of the contract.

53. D: The NYS Agricultural Districts Law promotes and protects availability of land for farming purposes. There may be restrictions as to the access to water and sewer services in an Agricultural District and real estate agents must present to a purchaser an Agricultural Form and Notice when purchasing property in an NYS designated agricultural district.

54. D: If a person receives money or property from another, the donor may be subject to a federal gift tax. If an individual makes a gift to someone else, the gift tax does not apply to the first $15,000 given to that person each year.

55. C: A mechanic's lien is a specific lien filed by a person who provides labor to a property.

56. A: In New York, if a landlord owns six or more units, he must deposit the security deposit in an interest-earning checking account.

57. B: Although arbitration and mediation are both forms of dispute resolution involving a neutral third party, the arbitrator makes a decision and the mediator does not. However, the mediator will make suggestions to resolve the dispute.

Construction and Development

58. C: Under New York law, when a developer files an offering plan with the Attorney General to convert an existing building to a condo or co-op, the tenants have a 90-day exclusive right to buy their apartment. During this period, the sponsor cannot negotiate separate prices.

59. A: The purpose of a deed restriction is to limit the use or appearance of a given property. A special-use permit is a permit for a use that is not allowed in the zone without the approval of the planning board or other legislative body.

60. A: The effect that the NYS constitutional amendment of home rule has on subdivision development is it gives local municipal agencies decision making power over subdivision approval.

61. C: Building specifications are written narratives that explain the building plan. The specifications may include the materials used and any design features not visible in the plan.

62. B: The reason why home inspection of newly built property may be different under the home inspection license law is that the definition of residential housing in the home inspector law does not include new construction. This does not mean that the home inspector cannot advise and counsel clients as to the structure and any problems that he or she observes with the new construction. Problems observed may be covered under the builder's new home warranty and under New York warranty laws.

63. D: In New York, local planning boards have the statutory authority to review site plans. The review of the site plan allows the planning board to evaluate the proposal's physical, social, and economic effects on the community.

64. A: The NYS Truth-in-Heating Law requires sellers and landlords of residential property to furnish prospective buyers and tenants with a complete set of heating and cooling bills, or summary of the bills for the life of the structure or the preceding two years.

65. B: The rules for the CPS1 apply to cooperatives, condominiums, and properties offered by homeowners associations. It sets out the New York Attorney General's rules governing how a developer may test the market for a new development before filing the offering plan and before construction is completed. The CPS1 statement includes rules on how the development may be advertised. All advertising must be approved by the Attorney General and during the CPS1 period or phase, the developer cannot declare a firm price. An alteration agreement describes the terms under which the cooperative gives permission to a shareholder before making any changes or improvements to the unit the shareholder occupies.

Conveyance of Real Property

66. B: An individual who makes a will is called a testator if a man or a testatrix if a woman.

67. B: Avulsion is the loss of land when a sudden or violent change in a watercourse results in its washing away. The gradual building up of land in a watercourse over time by deposits of silt, sand, and gravel is called accretion. Land may also be lost through erosion, which is the wearing away of land by water, wind, or other processes of nature.

68. C: The right of redemption occurs when the borrower redeems his or her property before foreclosure. Eminent domain is the power of the government to take private property for public use

with just compensation to the owner. A tenant in common may bring legal action to have a property partitioned so that each tenant may have a specific and divided portion of the property exclusively. Adverse possession is a method of acquiring a title after compliance with certain statutory regulations over a minimum 10-year period in New York.

Real Property Management

69. A: Public liability insurance is coverage to protect against claims alleging that one's negligence or inappropriate action resulted in bodily injury or property damage. Errors and omissions insurance is a type of professional liability insurance that protects professionals and services-providing companies and individuals. Commercial crime bond insurance, also known as a fidelity policy, insures a company against loss by fraudulent acts by employees.

70. D: The property manager is required to understand building systems, supervise others, and handle landlord–tenant relations. Property managers may not draw contracts, as this constitutes the illegal practice of law in New York.

71. B: In the property management business, the individual who oversees the day-to-day operation of the property or properties is known as the site manager. The asset manager focuses on maximizing property values for investment purposes. The portfolio manager analyzes decisions about investment purchases and mix and how to balance the decisions regarding the investment against the risk.

72. D: Some of the necessary steps in managing a property are to increase potential gross income, reduce operating expenses, and manage tenant selection to reduce vacancy and collection loss.

73. C: The cost of maintenance and repairs is a variable expense. Debt service, property taxes, and insurance are fixed expenses.

74. A: Amir offered a reduction in rent, a landlord concession on the lease, to induce the tenants to sign a two-year lease. A percentage lease has a base rent plus an additional monthly rent that is a percentage of the lessee's gross sales. An index lease is a method of determining rent on a long-term lease. The rent is tied to an index.

75. B: Lease escalation clauses call for increased costs to the tenant for different reasons at specified times during the lease term.

76. C: Modified gross rent refers to the apportionment of expenses between a landlord and tenant. For instance, the landlord pays the expenses of the common areas and the tenant might pay to paint the interior of the apartment. Lease escalation clauses call for increased costs to the tenant for different reasons at specified times during the lease term.

77. A: The property manager's fee is negotiated between the property owner and the manager. It commonly consists of a base fee and/or a percentage of the rents or effective gross income actually collected.

Taxes and Assessments

78. B: The amount that the municipality must raise by taxes on real property is called the tax levy. The stabilized budget is a forecast of income and expenses as may be reasonably projected over a short term, typically five years. A special assessment is a specific lien for an improvement to a property or properties that do not affect the entire taxing unit. The assessment roll lists all real property in the taxing jurisdiction, including information about each parcel and its assessed value and exempt status.

79. C: If a taxpayer is delinquent in paying property taxes, the taxing jurisdiction initiates a tax lien against the property. A mechanic's lien is a claim by someone who has performed work on a property and has not been paid. Taxpayers who disagree with their assessment may file a complaint called a grievance. A homestead misclassification occurs if the parcel has been designated in the wrong class on the assessment roll, or the allocation of the parcel's total assessed value between the homestead and the nonhomestead section is incorrect.

80. C: In order to encourage economic development, industrial or commercial properties are sometimes exempted from property taxes. To take advantage of the exemption offered by government to Industrial Development Agencies (IDAs), title to an economic development project such as a building or business location is often transferred from the private owner to the IDA for the duration of the project. In these cases, the exemption may be offset by payments in lieu of taxes (PILOTs) made by the original private owner. At the end of the project, title reverts to the original owner, who then pays taxes in a normal manner on the property. With a deed in lieu of foreclosure, a borrower in default conveys title to the lender to avoid foreclosure proceeding. A real estate investment trust (REIT) is a form of business trust owned by shareholders making mortgage loans.

Advanced Fair Housing and Fair Lending

81. A: Disparate impact is a legal doctrine under the Fair Housing Act that states that a policy may be considered discriminatory if it has a disproportionate "adverse impact" against any group based on race, national origin, color, religion, sex, familial status, or disability when there is no legitimate, nondiscriminatory reason. Redlining, steering, and blockbusting, illegal activities under the Fair Housing Act, also have disparate impacts.

82. D: Institutionalized discrimination refers to the unjust and discriminatory mistreatment of an individual or group of individuals by society and its institutions as a whole, through unequal selection or bias, intentional or unintentional—as opposed to individuals making a conscious choice to discriminate. Steering is a violation of the Federal Fair Housing Act and is illegally practiced by real estate brokers who encourage culturally diverse people toward or away from certain areas. Blockbusting, another illegal action, occurs when real estate salespeople tell homeowners that a member of a protected class is moving into their neighborhood, causing them to panic and place their homes for sale.

83. D: Laws that address fair lending include the Equal Credit Opportunity Act, the Fair Lending Law, and the Fair Housing Act.

84. D: Studies conclude that the extent to which property values are lowered depends on a variety of factors including design and management of affordable housing, compatibility between affordable housing and the host neighborhood, and concentration of affordable housing.

85. D: The NYS Human Rights law is broader in scope than the federal Fair Housing Act in that it covers, among other items: age as a protected class, discrimination in credit transactions, and employment.

86. A: A locally protected class in NYC, and possibly other municipalities in New York, that is not included in the NYS Human Rights Law is alienage or citizenship status. Sexual orientation (including same-sex marriage), marital, and military status are included as protected classes in the NYS Human Rights law.

87. D: In New York, to comply with fair housing laws, the real estate office should offer fair housing training and education, report fair housing misconduct, and comply with fair housing advertising regulations.

88. D: Lucinda and Marco are protected under the NYC Human Rights Commission laws as they are in the protected classes of lawful occupation and citizenship status. And they are protected under the federal Fair Housing Act, and the NYC and NYS human rights laws, as to race and family status.

Achieving Agreements through Transaction Analysis

89. D: A real estate agent, negotiating a transactional agreement, cannot draw up a contract of sale. Only attorneys can draw up a contract. In New York, in certain upstate areas, sales agents can use a fill-in-the-blanks contract of sale but cannot draw up the original document. An agent can assist a seller in deciding what price to ask for a property, assist a seller-client in gathering documents needed for a closing, and assist a buyer to prepare an offer to purchase.

90. D: Obligations that an agent must offer to a client are competency, skill, care, and the full range of other fiduciary duties under agency law.

91. D: Factors that an agent must consider in forming a transactional agreement include seller concessions, contract contingencies, and multiple offers.

92. A: The process of transaction analysis does not always culminate in a successful transactional agreement. The agent must always adhere to the laws of agency when negotiating the agreement. One who has good negotiation skills is more apt to negotiate a successful agreement. The motivation of the parties is an important consideration transaction analysis and in the formation of a transactional agreement.

93. C: A successful transactional agreement can be negotiated if the dual objectives of both parties are prudently addressed by their broker or brokers. The broker must always negotiate in the best interests of her client. The agency relationship between a broker and her client is confidential.

94. D: In transaction analysis, some of the duties that an agent must perform at the outset include estimating a range of value for the property, deciding how the financial climate can contribute to the success of the transaction, and inquiring into the financial limitations of the parties to the transaction.

95. D: Michael is violating the fiduciary duties of obedience, loyalty, and care. In addition, the primary objective of the broker should be to achieve a transactional agreement without sacrificing the interests of the client simply to achieve the agreement.

96. B: A transactional agreement should be mutually beneficial to both parties. The broker should always serve the best interests of the client. In this scenario, it appears that a meeting of the minds has not yet been achieved.

97. D: It seems that Howie is violating the fiduciary duties of competency, skill, and care, and is not able to manage a transactional analysis or reach a transactional agreement on his own. He should obtain the assistance of another agent in the firm with more experience or the principal broker. He might have to have another agent or the primary broker handle the transaction.

98. D: The principles of transaction analysis apply to the purchase, sale, and lease of real property.

99. A: In his role as the agent for the seller, Joshua is doing his job to negotiate with the broker for the buyer and is not violating any laws. Illegal self-dealing can occur when a broker has an undisclosed interest in the property under negotiation, which is not the case in this situation.

100. B: Donna must present all offers to the client but she can and should assist the client in analyzing the price and other terms of the offer. This activity falls under the fiduciary duty of care, skill, and diligence. Ultimately, the client chooses which offer to accept.